ART BEYOND ITSELF

Art beyond Itself

Anthropology for a Society without a Story Line

NÉSTOR GARCÍA CANCLINI

Translated by David Frye

DUKE UNIVERSITY PRESS

DURHAM AND LONDON   2014

Typeset in Whitman by Copperline Book Services, Inc.

Library of Congress Cataloging-in-Publication Data
García Canclini, Néstor.
[Sociedad sin relato. English]
Art beyond itself : anthropology for a society without a story
line / Néstor García Canclini ; translated by David Frye.
pages cm
Includes index and references.
ISBN 978-0-8223-5609-7 (cloth : alk. paper)
ISBN 978-0-8223-5623-3 (pbk. : alk. paper)
1. Art and society.
2. Art and anthropology.
3. Postmodernism.
4. Aesthetics, Modern—21st century.
I. Frye, David L. II. Title.
N72.S6G37213 2014
701ʹ.03—dc23   2013042792

Originally published as *La sociedad sin relato: Antropología
y estética de la inminencia,* copyright 2010, Néstor García
Canclini. Spanish edition published by Katz Editores,
Buenos Aires and Madrid, 2010.

Duke University Press gratefully acknowledges the support
of the Globalization and the Artist Project of the Duke University
Center for International Studies, which provided funds
toward the production of this book.

FOR MAGALI

CONTENTS

>

ILLUSTRATIONS

>

>

ART BEYOND ITSELF

What's happening with art, whose death has been so frequently pronounced? What in the past few decades has turned it into an alternative for disappointed investors, a laboratory for thought experiments in sociology, anthropology, philosophy, and psychoanalysis, and a resource for fashion, design, and other tactics for drawing distinctions? It's even being asked to take the place once filled by politics by providing collective spaces to deal with intercultural relations.

Since early in the twentieth century, sociology has showed that artistic movements can be understood only in connection with social processes. We can see this "external" entanglement of art more easily today because so many artworks are increasing in economic and media worth. To explain this phenomenon, it's no longer sufficient to make the sort of hypotheses that were once generated about religion, such as suggesting that art offers us imaginary scenes to compensate for our real frustrations, whether by escapism leading to resignation or by creating utopias that revive our hopes, turning art into "a kind of alternative religion for atheists," in the words of Sarah Thornton (2008: xiv).

Nor is it enough to argue, as critical sociology does, that aesthetic choices form a place of symbolic distinction. The ability to comprehend highbrow art and the surprises of the avant-garde, taken to be a gift, as Pierre Bourdieu said, euphemizes inequality and dignifies privilege. How can the role of art be reworked when there are so many other resources of taste, from clothing and design artifacts to vacation spots, for attaining aesthetic distinction, and when minority innovation is popularized by the media? Mass attendance at museums of contemporary art has thrown the distinction effect for cultural elites into doubt: in 2005–6, MoMA in New York had 2.67 million visitors, the Pompidou in Paris had 2.5 million, and the Tate Modern, London's most popular attraction, had 4 million. Worldwide Internet distribution now allows people in many countries to become familiar in real time with works of art, art criticism, and polemics about art, and so has reduced the secrecy and exclusivity of these sanctuaries.

Examples abound of the persisting social uses of art—as compensation for frustrations, as a symbolic way to draw social distinctions—but we have to look at the new roles of art that extend its activity beyond what has been organized as the art field. Other explanations, linked to the successes and failures of globalization, are possible: the arts dramatize the death throes of liberating utopias, and they renew our shared sensory experiences in a world that is as interconnected as it is divided, as well as our desire to live these experiences in nondisaster pacts with fiction.

Economics, which claimed to be the hardest social science, has now revealed that the evidence it is based on (statistics, the relations between costs and gains, between debts and productivity) are mirages. Neoliberalism, proclaimed the only form of thought capable of putting exchanges in order and keeping inflation from running out of control, has now subordinated the hard economy—the one that produces tangible goods—to money-based manias. Instead of organizing society through scientific laws, economists use metaphors to name its disorders: they put the blame on the "bubble" that inflated speculation in the benefits of digital technology, then on the real-estate bubble, then on the bubble in unbacked securities. Scientists who work with concepts and numbers have to turn to slippery images, as if they have nothing firm to hold on to in an era of labor without contracts and profits that soar and crash in a matter of hours.

Politics has also become an unconvincing display. For some time it has been unrecognizable as the place where people struggle over ways to truly control institutions, administer wealth, or guarantee welfare. We head out to vote every few years, trying our best to discern some politician who isn't corrupt, some promise that is credible. Skepticism prevails even in nations that have regained the right to elect their rulers after a dictatorship has fallen: there are high abstention rates in countries where the vote isn't mandatory, and where it is, we find voter nullification and cynical parodies of the game of politics on television and the Internet. A theater of suspicious simulations.

Art, in contrast, plays with images and their movements by constructing explicitly imaginary situations, with effects that we can enjoy or else cut short if they disturb us—we just leave the exhibit. Most of its interventions in society are confined to museums, galleries, or biennales. People invest in the art market for generally enduring tastes, for obtaining symbolic distinction, or for more stable returns on investment than can be found in the manufacturing or finance economy.

Trends in art do tend to be fleeting, but a broad segment of society has grown used to the idea that these fluctuations are part of the game. We can find pleasure in innovation or can adhere to particular trends and feel that a preference for Picasso, Bacon, or Bill Viola works for us. Jumping on the latest wave, or the one before it, or on earlier waves, which sometimes come back into fashion, presents fewer risks for social exclusion or personal collapse than investing in your own country's currency, U.S. dollars, or shares in some transnational corporation.

Does the success of art reside in its being "harmless" or ineffective? Let's explore it through a different hypothesis: art is the place of imminence—the place where we catch sight of things that are just at the point of occurring. Art gains its attraction in part from the fact that it proclaims something that could happen, promising meaning or modifying meaning through insinuations. It makes no unbreakable commitment to hard facts. It leaves what it says hanging. Dora García's exhibit in Santiago de Compostela in late 2009, titled *Where Do Characters Go When the Novel Ends?*, offers this reader's guide to her works: "A good question should at all costs avoid getting an answer."

I don't want to backslide into the discourse about the immateriality of artistic representation (the rain depicted in a painting doesn't get anything wet, an explosion on the screen doesn't hurt us). Or into the argument that the art field is insular, so that relations among the actors in that field follow a different logic than those in the rest of society. By saying that art is situated in imminence, I am postulating a possible relationship with "the real" that is as oblique or indirect as that in music or abstract paintings. Works of art do not merely "suspend" reality; they situate themselves in a prior moment, when the real is possible, when it has not yet broken down. They treat facts as events that are about to come into being.

This hypothesis must be tested not only against what's happening in museums; we can look for it too in the art spreading beyond its own field and becoming blurred as it mixes with urban development and the design and tourism industries. We can see how the predominance of form over function, which once defined the art scene, now characterizes the way things are done in politics and economics. The programs that differentiate between reality and fiction, truth and simulacrum, fall apart. Long after the era when culture was reduced to ideology and ideology to manipulation by the dominant, simulations appear daily in every section of the newspaper.

Dozens of Greenpeace activists climb to the top of buildings owned by Expal, a Spanish corporation that sells cluster bombs. On the fifth floor, they ask whether the workers have weapons in their offices, hand out a video of Cambodian children mutilated by bombs, cover the ground with silhouettes of bomb victims, and distribute amputated legs.

Guerrilla performances by people dressed up as police officers or soldiers used to take place only in a handful of countries that were rocked by "subversion." Now newspapers and television reporters in every city where there are active drug trafficking and kidnapping rings document gun battles between groups dressed in identical uniforms, whether because one side is wearing disguises or because they all belong to an organization that has been infiltrated. In Mexico authorities have known for years about "leaks" from oil and gasoline pipelines, but investigations into drug networks revealed in 2009 that some 30 percent of the 557 illegal taps into the pipeline system were made by the Zetas, the armed branch of the Gulf cartel, with the help of Pemex employees who supplied them with official vehicles and uniforms to carry out the operations.

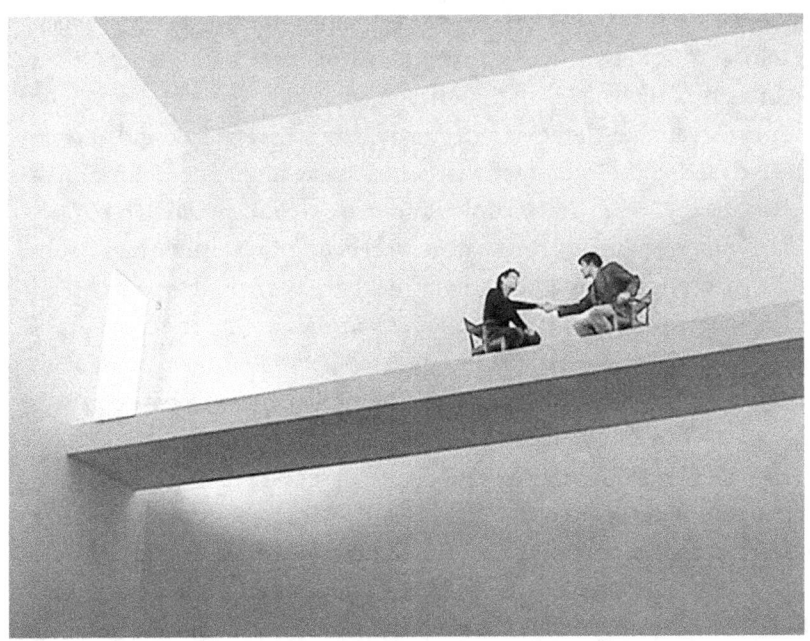

FIGURE PREFACE.1 Still from Dora García, *¿Dónde van los personajes cuando termina la novela?* (Where Do Characters Go When the Novel Ends?), two 14-minute videos, color, stereo, in Spanish with English subtitles. Produced by CGAC (Galician Contemporary Arts Center, Santiago de Compostela, Spain) y FRAC Bourgogne (Regional Contemporary Art Funds, Dijon, France), 2009.

What's the right section for these news reports: politics, police blotter, economics, or entertainment? If these zones are hard to differentiate, can artists still stake out a space of their own? The spread of simulacra creates a landscape in which some of the pretensions of art—surprise, the ironic transgression of order—become diluted. The various indefinitions separating fiction from reality grow confused due to the decline of totalizing visions that could assign stable positions to identities.

It isn't only art that loses its autonomy when it is imitated by disguised social movements. The murky mingling of the illusory and the real also harms the art market, as we will see in ethnographic descriptions of art auctions, where billionaires hide their unexplained profits by speculating on artworks. The secrecy surrounding buyers and collectors, the boom in art prices and their cyclical declines (as in 1990 and 2008)

Art beyond Itself

<

make one suspect that there are more complex intersections between art and society, between creativity, industriousness, and finances, than the ones that fueled the clash between economic value and symbolic value in classical aesthetics. There are more processes inside and outside the field, and in their interactions, contributing to the "de-definition of art" than there were when Harold Rosenberg (1972) coined that phrase.

The interweaving of art practices with everything else throws doubt on the theoretical tools and methods that have been used to understand art in modern sociology and postmodern aesthetics. Are the concepts of the "art world" (Becker 1982) and the art "field" (Bourdieu 1996) at all useful when there are plenty of signs of interdependence between museums, auctions, and artists, and the major actors in economics, politics, and the media? Do Bourriaud's (2002) analyses on relational aesthetics help, or are Rancière's (2010) critical suggestions about distinguishing between the aesthetics of consensus and those of dissent more productive? What roles do artists such as Antoni Muntadas, León Ferrari, and Carlos Amorales play when they reconsider these same ties of interdependence in their works and stagings?

From Transgression to Postautonomy

Artists, who have fought hard for their autonomy since the nineteenth century, hardly ever got along well with borders. But the meaning of borders has changed. From the days of Marcel Duchamp to the close of the twentieth century, one constant in artists' practice was transgression. The ways they did it tended to reinforce difference. The contemporary history of art is a paradoxical combination of behaviors devoted to securing independence for one's own field and behaviors committed to doing away with the limits that separate that field.

In utopian moments, the border that separated creators from the everyday world was breached, and the notion of being an artist was extended to everyone, the notion of art to every ordinary object—whether by engaging the audience in the artwork, by insisting on everyday ways of creating things, or by playing up the appeal of trivial objects (from Pop art to political art). In deconstructive moments, content was drained (monochrome painting from Kazimir Malevich to Yves Klein) or the container was dissolved (paintings escaping from their frames: Jackson

Pollock, Frank Stella, Luis Felipe Noé). To break down the borders of taste, Piero Manzoni exhibited ninety cans of *Artist's Shit*, selling them by the gram based on the daily price of gold. Other artists urinated or self-mutilated before an audience (the Viennese Actionists) or burst into museums and biennales with the carcasses of dead animals and bed sheets covered with the blood of drug-trafficking victims (Teresa Margolles).

Introducing "vile" objects or actions into artistic spaces generally ends up reinforcing the singularity of those spaces and of the artists. Two tactics have been used in an effort to escape this closed, self-referential circle, which can be understood only by those who share the secrets of the avant-garde.

One tactic has been to relocate ostensibly artistic experiences in profane places. In the economics section of *Le Monde*, Fred Forest and Hervé Fischer of the Sociological Art Collective offered investments in "the Artistic M^2," plots of one square meter each on the border between France and Switzerland, promising to give each purchaser the honorary title of "citizen" of this territory and the right to participate in public gardens, spaces for reflection, and protests. The other tactic was adopted in 1989 by Bernard Bazile when he had one of Manzoni's cans of *Artist's Shit* opened and demonstrated "not only the disconnect between the reality of its contents (exhibiting a bundle of fibers), the imaginary of the container (the most impure fragment of the artist's body), and the symbolism of the two together (one of the purest moments of transgression on the borders of art)" but also the added value that was thereby achieved and finally the increased value of the Manzoni can opened by Bazile, which was sold by Galerie Roger Pailhas in Marseille for twice the price of the original can (Heinich 1998: 92).

Is the art field doomed to be eternally absorbed in the repeated desire to pierce its borders and, as in these last two examples, rush through via simple second-rate transgressions that change nothing? Neither bringing the world into the museum, nor going out of the museum, nor emptying out the museum and the artwork, nor dematerializing the work, nor leaving the artist's name off the work, nor trying to shock and provoke censure can overcome the queasiness caused by this vacillation between the desire for autonomy and the inability to transcend it.

Perhaps the answers to this question will come not from the field of art but from what's happening when it intersects with other fields and becomes *postautonomous*. By this I mean the process that has taken place over the past few decades in which art practices based on *objects* have increasingly been displaced in favor of practices based on *contexts*, to the point that works are now being *inserted in the media, urban spaces, digital networks, and forms of social participation where aesthetic differences seem to dissolve*. Many works are still exhibited in museums and biennales, are still signed by artists, and are sometimes awarded art prizes, but art prizes, museums, and biennales share their roles of spreading information and anointing works as art with popular magazines and television. The signature, the notion of authorship, is subsumed by commercial advertising, the media, and collectives that do not belong to the art world. It is not so much the efforts of artists and critics to break through the shell as it is the new locations that have been given to what we call art that is pulling it out of its paradoxical experience of encapsulated transgression.

Acts of transgression presupposed the existence of oppressive structures and of narratives that justify them. Being stuck in a desire to end such an order, while insistently cultivating separation and transgression, implies that these structures and narratives remain in full force. What happens when they start to run out of steam?

Walls and Social Narratives Come Tumbling Down

We reached the end of the twentieth century with no paradigms of development and no explanation for society: it was said that all we had left were multiple narratives. We have begun the twenty-first century with scattered, fragmentary stories. Some are believed by Islamists, others by Christian fundamentalists, and the rest by followers of some strongman or other. These stories often lose their followers, allow dissent to undermine their efficacy, or crumble into self-parody.

The next-to-the-last great (Western) narrative, promoted by the fall of the Berlin Wall in 1989, imagined that there would be a single world with a single center—the United States—and that its style of capitalist modernization, in the formulation of Francis Fukuyama, would become homogeneous across the planet. This Grand Story lasted until the next Great Fall, that of the Twin Towers, turned our gaze to the arguments of

Samuel Huntington about the persistence of civilizations in conflict, the division of power between English and other languages, and economic and cultural multipolarity. Both formulations found echoes in artistic representations and in the social imaginaries about the globalization of symbolic markets—going from the perception of New York as the world's only metropolis to a recognition of multifocality and multi-culturalism. The profusion of biennales on every continent, which has led to interaction among distinct forms of modernizing, of globalizing, and of portraying these processes, cancels out globalized abstractions. When I speak of society without a story, I do not mean that there is a lack of stories, as in the postmodernist criticism of metanarratives; I am referring to the historical condition in which no one story organizes diversity in a world whose interdependence makes many people wish that a single narrative did exist.

In November 2009 books, magazines, television programs, and exhibits celebrated the twentieth anniversary of the fall of the Berlin Wall. In the Deutsches Historisches Museum of Berlin, the exhibit *1989–2009, the Berlin Wall: Artists for Freedom* recited an official reading of what took place on November 9, 1989: the fall of the Wall as a liberator of unstoppable flows of human beings. Nevertheless we now have our doubts about who benefited. What can be said about the walls that have gone up or that have grown taller since that time? The website of the *Artists for Freedom* exhibit remains mired in too many clichés: German reunification, a new structure for Europe, the end of the bipolar world order. Strictly speaking, the world order had long since ceased to be bipolar: China and Japan were growing, Arab capital was flooding into the West. A geopolitical reordering was moving forward that cannot be condensed into the fall of the Wall. The most productive celebrations are those that problematize the meaning of what they commemorate.

If we look at it from Latin America, contemporary democracies have more to do with other dates: the end of the dictatorships in the Southern Cone and in Central America in the mid-1980s; the economic crises of 1994 and 1995; the abandonment of national projects such as Mexico's after 1982, a change that was consolidated after 1994 in the North American Free Trade Agreement. These are events that increased inequality and the breakdown of capitalism in this region.

The twenty-first century had two beginnings. The al Qaeda attacks on New York and Washington on September 11, 2001, forced onto the political and media scene the displacement that some studies had already been talking about: we went from multiculturalism, understood as a recognition of the differences within each nation, to intercultural conflicts in a global geopolitics where all societies are interdependent. Cultural criticism and artistic practice, which had already been addressing these globalized tensions in their interethnic investigations, as well as discussions on borders and migrations, devoted books, artworks, whole issues of journals, and websites to elaborating the new situation.

This political and cultural agenda was shaken but not cut short when the century began a second time on September 15, 2008, the day when the Lehman Brothers bankruptcy dramatically brought to a head the neoliberal disorder on several continents. Millions of people lost their jobs, their investments, and their savings in a matter of weeks; consumer demand contracted; cascading bankruptcies spread through stores, factories, and other banks. Many foundations suspended their support to museums, cultural projects, and scientific research. Philippe Vergne, director of Dia Art Foundation, wondered aloud during a lecture he gave in St. Louis in mid-2009 about the meaning of the fact that September 15, 2008, was also the day when Damien Hirst "earned 198 million dollars by staging his own personal art auction at Sotheby's," bypassing the usual galleries. "It's a provocative coincidence," according to Anthony Huberman (2009: 109): on the same day that "the market dramatically proved itself to be imperfect and unpredictable—'subject to extraordinary delusions and the madness of crowds,' as Krugman says—an artist's strategic maneuver" to escape "the euphoric follies of the art market" for his own purposes had the refreshing and cynical effect of redrawing the rules of the art business.

Obviously only Hirst and the ten or twenty other top-selling artists could get away with such a gesture of autonomy from the market. That aspiration could not extend to the collective projects and art institutions that saw their financing collapse. The hesitant moves of first-rate museums after the 2008 crisis demonstrate instead their dependence on the market and their uncertainty about how to avoid being swept away by the economic chaos. Should they concentrate on star exhibits with lots of marketing, like the Tate Modern and other British venues? Sell franchises, putting up replicas in Abu-Dhabi that have been spectacularized by famous architects, as the Louvre has tried to do in that United Arab Emirates city by contracting with Jean Nouvel, and the Guggenheim with Frank Gehry?

The theoretical model of the *art field*—which, as we will see in Bourdieu, is associated with an era when it still made sense to analyze art movements as parts of national cultures—became less and less productive as we grew ever more globalized. The notion of nomadism, imagining a world without borders, is not very convincing either. Images flow transnationally at different speeds, depending on whether the countries they are coming from are economically powerful or impoverished. There are more barriers blocking the movement of people, including artists, than their works. Two grand abstractions—the universality of creativity and the autonomy of art—prove insubstantial whenever new walls go up, whenever more visas are demanded from workers than from the commodities they produce. Some producers of culture use their resistance to these forms of discrimination, or their insistence on their own difference, as material for their art. But these multidirectional interactions and obstacles no longer have a single organizing narrative. Although I will look at artists who use resistance and intercultural translation in their work, who critique the dominant narrative structures, detotalized narratives are what are growing now, fragments of a visuality without history, especially among young people. The period since the Soviet collapse, the period of recurring capitalist catastrophes, is an "end of history" in a different sense than Fukuyama had intended: a loss of historical experience. This "presentist" organization of meaning is made more acute, both in art and in daily life, by the obsolescence of technological innovations.

Art became postautonomous in a world that doesn't know what to do with the insignificance or contradictions of narratives. When we talk about this art, disseminated in a globalization that hasn't managed to articulate itself, we can no longer think of a directional history or of a transition state of a society unsure of which model for development to choose. We are long past the time when artists argued about what they should do to change life, or at least to represent its transitions by talking about what "the system" was concealing. They can hardly even act, like victims of a catastrophe who try to organize themselves, in the imminence of what might happen next, or in the barely explicable ruins of what globalization has destroyed. Art now works in the footsteps of the ungovernable.

On one hand, many art movements lost interest in autonomy, or they interacted with other areas of social life—design, fashion, the media, immediate political struggles. On the other hand, the paradigms that once constrained socioeconomic vicissitudes expired, and promises of revolution or comfort had the rug pulled out from under them. With art and society in analogous states of uncertainty, art cannot reestablish a place of its own, and perhaps its task is to see "what lies beyond the outer limits: the extra-artistic, the outside world, history as it is happening, other cultures," as Ticio Escobar (2004: 148) writes in an article that bears the same title as this introduction.

Art has left its autonomy behind in several ways. The best known of these has been its incorporation into a large-scale art market (more than $8 billion in sales in 2008), under heteronomous rules, sometimes like those that apply to the circulation of common goods. This market stretches from the centers of the Western establishment—New York, London, and Berlin—to China, Russia, and the Arab Emirates. It mingles with both capitalist and mixed markets, authoritarian and democratic regimes. The mysteries of art are transmuted into secrets of the auction, the prices of artworks are compared with those of stocks, bonds, and the Dow Jones Industrial Average (Artprice 2008).

Another place where we can judge the postautonomous situation of art is in the many ways that artists insert themselves into society. I will discuss one of the emblematic contemporary cases, that of Takashi Murakami, whose paintings resemble the clothing and handbags manufactured by Louis Vuitton, while his other artworks show continuities with manga and video games. But we should remember that earlier figures associated with transformational political forces, such as Frida Kahlo, were turned into symbols of feminism, subjects for commercial films, and cover images for magazines about politics and culture, tourism, and fashion. At an earlier time there were those who indignantly defended the proper uses of these symbols in the face of their degradation; later on one has to wonder whether there was something in the script of Kahlo's life that made it suitable for taking on so many jobs at once, and why manufacturers of clothing, tennis shoes, and watches have discovered in her a handy mechanism for giving transcendent meaning to their seasonal best-sellers.

Studies on the critical fortunes of artists, both during their lives (from Picasso to Hirst) and after their deaths (Van Gogh), with the intervention of people in the media, politics, the tourist industry, and the art market, reveal how aesthetic values are combined with other motives for admiration. Nathalie Heinich's book *The Glory of Van Gogh* (1996) showed that, far from being ignored or misunderstood during his lifetime, Van Gogh was celebrated by critics, and his tragic end cannot credibly be ascribed to any professional disillusionment. This finding has not stopped biographies and studies of his work from creating resonances with religious motifs drawn from the repertoire of saints' lives, building up a sense of collective indebtedness to the "great singular figure" sacrificed for his art, "while various forms of individual atonement are developed: through purchasing his works, through gazing upon them, through one's presence in the places where the painter lived, which have become cult places" (Heinich 2002: 58).

The job for sociological analysis, Heinich argues, is not to demythify beliefs nor to denounce illusions, but to understand the reasons why particular forms of singularization and regimes for creating symbolic value were formed in the modern era. As viewpoints multiply and the links between subjective experiences and globalization are deciphered, a new understanding of the place of art in the restructuring of meaning can be opened up.

Multiplying our points of view: we are distancing ourselves from the sociological reductionism that naturally irritates artists and researchers attentive to the specific nature of aesthetics. We must try out a view of the art that has spread into so many areas of social life without forcing it to represent "strategies for creating distinctions," to exercise "symbolic violence," or to show the domination of "the lawful authorities" over everyone else. It's a matter of seeing whether exploring the diversified links between creativity and the market, between aesthetic dissatisfactions and political discontents, can illuminate the correspondences between an art that is having trouble redefining itself, societies in which the sense of having a choice between left and right has diminished, and the social sciences that are trying to study this landscape with different tools.

This book seeks an analytic framework for studying contemporary art that pays attention to the art itself as well as the cultural and social conditions under which its postautonomous condition has become possible. I pay attention to artworks, to artists' singular projects, and to attempts to sustain a certain independence from religion, politics, the media, and the markets. Between the inevitability of being inserted into society and the desire for autonomy, what is at play is the place for creative transgression, for critical dissent, and for that sense of imminence that makes the aesthetic something that doesn't just happen, doesn't attempt to turn itself into a codified profession nor into profitable merchandise.

ACKNOWLEDGMENTS

>

Many artists, critics, social scientists, and philosophers who stimulated my rethinking of contemporary society and art are recognized in these pages. The sections that I devote to Francis Alÿs, Carlos Amorales, León Ferrari, Antoni Muntadas, and Gabriel Orozco are based on pieces that I was invited to write for catalogues or books about their works and on lengthy visits to their studios and exhibits.

To support theoretical arguments in a transnational ethnographic understanding of what is happening in the arts and cultures today, one must spend a lot of time in workshops, galleries, museums, biennales, art fairs, and symposia in many countries, talking with viewers who enjoy or reject them. When we have the chance to think in company, sometimes in the company of the same people in different cities and at institutions with differing strategies, and to continue conversations and debates over email, our chances improve of correcting a first impression or an intellectual habit that otherwise might persist in our thinking when the world has already moved on to other things. For this reason I owe a debt of gratitude to, among others, Rita Eder, Andrea Giunta, Manuel Gutiérrez Estévez, Nelly Richard, Graciela Speranza, and George Yúdice.

The Universidad Autónoma Metropolitana in Mexico City gave me the research time I needed and made it possible for me to take on these intellectual arguments in a graduate seminar in 2009. One of the students, Paz Sastre, helped search for information on the Internet and gave me suggestions for improving the text. Gabriela Alarcón, Rosario Mata, and Cecilia Meira also helped me as able research assistants. Four chapters were based on a seminar in January 2010 at the University of Barcelona, directed by Anna María Guasch and Joaquín Barriendos Rodríguez. Marcelo Cohen, Andrea Giunta, Alejandro Grimson, Jesús Martín-Barbero, Fiamma Montezemolo, Graciela Speranza, and Juan Villoro also read key parts of the book and helped me to understand what I was doing in them.

Sharing with Magali Lara the delight of her paintings and her view of my texts, seeing a few hundred exhibits with her in Argentina, Brazil, Colombia, China, Spain, the United States, Italy, Japan, and Mexico, being jointly surprised by the rituals, enjoying the work and the play of understanding art, its creators, and its audiences—all this had us crossing many more borders than those that separate states or aesthetic trends.

CHAPTER ONE

>

AESTHETICS AND SOCIAL SCIENCES

Converging Doubts

The arts have been acquiring more economic, social, and political functions than ever before in modern times, while also stimulating the renewal of the social sciences and philosophy, yet artists themselves continue to harbor doubts about their existence and their place in society. It seems paradoxical: while artists leave the museums and insert themselves into social networks (sociological art, ethnographic art, postpolitical actions), actors in other fields live and breathe thanks to art and are committed to its contributions. (Philosophers, sociologists, and anthropologists rely on artistic innovations and curating exhibitions to think about their fields; political actors and social movements use performance in social spaces.)

These movements rarely meet, and it is not even clear how they could. Artists throw a ball of modeling clay into the street (Gabriel Orozco) or create "collectors," toys made from tin cans, industrial discards, and magnets (Francis Alÿs), to pick up the loose scraps of urban life. Alÿs walked his collectors through the streets like dogs on a leash, gathering nails, pieces of wire, metal debris; on his strolls he was compiling a random record of the city. What stuck to the collectors ceased to be trash and became a document in his research into what is used and discarded.

Similarly his photographic series *Ambulantes* records the many kinds of carts that used to transport all sorts of merchandise through the historic center of Mexico City, identifying the peddlers and travelers who form fragments of the narratives about daily foot traffic there. Not just a creator of unique works, Alÿs conceives of his task as an artist as that of an observer of everyday characters, a discoverer of the "seven levels of trash," someone who tries to compile simple reports about the way dogs make their own use of one part of the street or about the way a block of ice melts as it is dragged through the downtown streets of Mexico's capital for nine hours. What place in the ranks of occupations can you assign to someone who defines himself as a spectator devoted to "waiting for an accident" to happen? He might let his sweater unravel as he walks, letting the thread get lost and the garment become completely undone along the way, as if his job were, in the words of Cuauhtémoc Medina, to lose "the 'thread' of the narrative" (Alÿs and Medina 2006: 34).

Meanwhile institutions and markets speak from the viewpoint of structures and programs, though we know that these social forms do not have the same coherence or certainty they had in other eras. How can we imagine, in this world without a center and without paradigms, among the wreckage of globalization, a conversation between the artists who turn trash into documents and the professionals disillusioned by structures and their modes of representation?

It is no small problem to speak of the situation of the arts—inconceivable if we don't view it on a global scale—when we lack universally valid theories of both art and globalization. Let us quickly review what has been happening in theories of art that have tried constructing a universally valid way of knowing.

Philosophical aesthetics sought to universalize its reflections, but it was associated with the development of European modernity, the rational Enlightenment, or Romanticism. Aesthetic thought became the interpreter of the autonomization of art when capitalism and secularization generated specific public institutions designed to connect with art, which they assessed using criteria different from those once used by religious or political powers. The predominant feature of modern

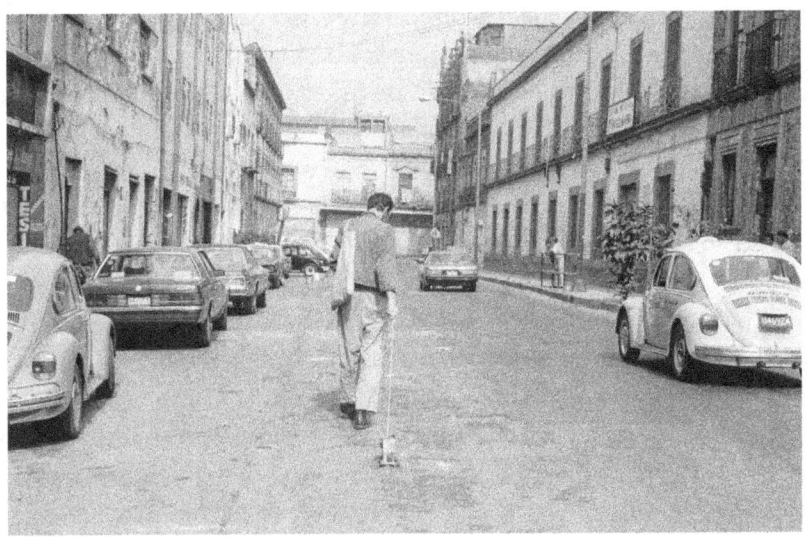

Still from Francis Alÿs, *El Colector* (The Collector), in collaboration with
Felipe Sanabria. Mexico City, 1991–92.

aesthetics was what Kant termed objects constructed in the pursuit of
finality without an end, in the words of Umberto Eco, experiences in
which forms prevail over function.

Sociology showed that the autonomy of art and literature was not
just a movement of mentalities. Beginning in the eighteenth century,
the members of the bourgeoisie—who had become the artists' clients—
together with the newly created museums, galleries, and literary salons,
autonomized their practices by establishing strictly aesthetic authorities
for evaluating art and literature. Bourdieu wasn't the first to note that
one of the features of the modern age was the creation of autonomous
fields in which art creators were linked with those who dealt specifically with their works, but he constructed the most sophisticated and
rigorous theory in sociology about the ways art separated itself from its
external determinants.

Together with sociological studies of art and literature, we could understand how other autonomous fields came to be formed in the modern
age: science carried out in universities and laboratories independently
of anything beyond the rules of empirical research and rational argu-

mentation; the political field as a secular struggle for power in a social order that did not spring from divine mandates.

In both the sciences and the arts, Bourdieu's "field" concept put an end to the romantic, individualistic notion of the genius who discovers unexpected forms of knowledge or creates exceptional works. All this without falling into social determinism either. By sticking to the internal structure of each field and its specific rules for producing art, literature, or science, sociological research surpassed all other attempts to explain creativity and knowledge on the basis of such macrosocial constraints as mode of production or class. Artists' works and practices are determined, but not by the social totality, rather by the set of relations in which the agents and institutions that specialize in producing art, exhibiting it, selling it, assessing it, and appropriating it interact. Thanks to Bourdieu we overcame the unbridgeable and abstract opposition between the creative individual and capitalist society and are able to understand the tensions between artistic projects and their concrete determinants in the form of galleries, museums, critics, collectors, and audiences.

Howard S. Becker, writing from a more anthropological, or rather ethnographic point of view, emphasized that making art is a cooperative activity; being a musician as well as an anthropologist, it was obvious to him that a concert calls for group effort—the combined labor of the band, the composer, the technicians, the schools where each of them learned their crafts, the advertisers, and the instrument makers. Studying art, and knowing when art is present, means understanding the work in the context of its production, circulation, and appropriation. But what is that context today? Bourdieu spoke of "fields" and Becker of "art worlds." Both considered that the definition, evaluation, and comprehension of art took place within *autonomous* spaces and circuits. This independence and self-containment of artistic practices, which once delimited who had the legitimacy to say what was art, has vanished.

Is it possible to extend this notion of art to nonmodern, non-Western societies? Anthropology has shown, for example in the works of Clifford Geertz (1983, 1988) and Sally Price (1989), that other peoples have been concerned with the forms of objects and the modes of working the senses, but that these cannot be understood via the Eurocentric aesthetic criteria of beauty or the priority of form over function.

Even in the West, avant-garde artists have cultivated distinct types of beauty, and also of ugliness, the abject, the sinister, and other disturbances of experience and the senses. It has been suggested that we should give the name "theories of art" rather than aesthetics to the conceptual propositions that guide the various artistic practices. But speaking of them in the plural, which has the advantage of allowing for many ways of making art, raises doubts when we award them the name of "theories." Can we really call them "theories," a term applied to scientific concepts that are internally coherent, proceed from a logical chain of propositions, and aspire to universality?

When twentieth-century avant-garde movements relativized aesthetic values and the foundations of taste, they accepted the existence of multiple *poetics*. When they placed *experimentation* above *representation* in the modes of representing or alluding to the real, they disturbed the classical order, and the museum as temple for consecrating it and exhibiting it. They ended up deconstructing the autonomous sense of art and the story, which had organized their ties with politics, the market, and the media.

A Conversation between the Sociologist and the Artist: Bourdieu and Haacke

The first difficulty in understanding the breakdown of the modern order is, as I have noted, a reluctance to recognize that it has never really prevailed outside the West and that it is unsustainable in an era of global interactions. The second problem is epistemological: seeking explanations only in terms of actors and processes to which modern theory attributed tasks that they did not actually perform.

In a conversation in 1991 between Pierre Bourdieu and Hans Haacke — the former speaking from his work in the sociology of intellectual and political practices, the latter from his experiences as an artist—they tried to reason out their disappointments: intellectuals had switched from critical thinking to management; governments were giving less and less money while trying to impose more and more control; Europe was yielding to the U.S. model of putting the survival of museums, radio, television, schools, hospitals, and laboratories in the hands of private sponsors. Simple observation of the very actors among whom the programs of the Enlightenment and the nation-state had distributed responsibilities confirms the impossibility: we cannot expect that patronage by private corporations will promote independent actions in the public interest or critical of their voracity; everything will go downhill if the state shirks its job and thinks about things only through the logic of profitability and earnings.

Bourdieu and Haacke are sufficiently clearheaded to recognize that the cultural and scientific actions of the state are no guarantee that the public interest will always win out, that research and art will be of quality, that the best books will be published or only qualified artists promoted. Nevertheless "a comparison of the contemporary acquisitions of the Museum of Modern Art in New York (which depends, as a private institution, mostly on donations) with those of the Centre Pompidou" in Paris leads Haacke to conclude that state-financed civil servants can "allow themselves to put together, with public funds, a more impressive collection of 'risky' works (daring in terms of the market, 'morality,' and ideology)" (Bourdieu and Haacke 1995: 75).

This statement is debatable, at least if we distinguish between the public and private (fluctuating) trends in the United States and France. We should also be concerned about the way Bourdieu interprets the disintegration of public systems and citizen voter approval: "A public system leaves a very large margin of freedom, but one must still make use of it" (Bourdieu and Haacke 1995: 75). And again: "Unfortunately, citizens and intellectuals are not prepared for this freedom in relation to the state, doubtless because they expect too much from it, in personal terms: careers, commissions, decorations" (73). This critique, trapped inside its own logic, begins with structural accusations against the state and corporations and ends by casting moral suspicion on individuals.

At one point in the conversation, Bourdieu returns to an epistemological principle that he had insisted on since his earliest books, most famously in *The Craft of Sociology:* "A truly critical form of thought should begin with a critique of the more or less unconscious economic and social bases of critical thought itself" (Bourdieu and Haacke 1995: 74). Indeed. This means questioning whether the state, corporations, and citizens are the only actors, or whether the only modality in which they exist is that which classical social science, art history, or the history of avant-garde movements has studied. Or whether, perhaps, other ways of doing research (under public-private agreements), of managing and communicating culture (where the audiovisual industries and digital networks play key roles) are remodeling the production, circulation, and reception of art, science, and culture into different circuits.

Bourdieu coins a good phrase to characterize the ineffectiveness of intellectuals, unions, and political parties under the current conditions of power struggle: "They are three or four symbolic wars behind" (Bourdieu and Haacke 1995: 20). He is referring to their use of "archaic techniques of action and protest to use against corporations and their very sophisticated forms of public relations" (20). He therefore values the ability of artists to shock, surprise, and disconcert.

That was just what Hans Haacke did in 1991, when he responded to an invitation to produce artworks using photographic documentation of the history of the building that once housed Nazi headquarters in Munich and to exhibit them on the site itself. Using as his title the first line from a Nazi anthem about raising the flag, Haacke arranged pennants with a list of German corporations that had sold war matériel to Iraq, including Daimler-Benz, Ruhrgas, and Siemens. The journalist from *Der Spiegel* who had written the article that Haacke had used as the source for this information was surprised when companies that hadn't reacted to his written text had then sued the artist. "The problem," Haacke notes, "is not only to say something, to take a position, but also to create a productive provocation" (Bourdieu and Haacke 1995: 21).

One of the differences between Bourdieu and Haacke lies in the fact that, while the sociologist analyzes structures and sees their failures as structural flaws or traps, the artist deploys a strategy of gaps: "It is always assumed that censorship and self-censorship exist wherever one turns—and, of course, they do. However, if one tests the limits, sometimes one discovers that there are holes in the wall, that one can get through" (Bourdieu and Haacke 1995: 77). We would be mistaken if we thought the artist is a more astute observer than the sociologist. In the course of the dialogue, Haacke demonstrates that, like the artists he mentions (Duchamp, Tatlin, Rodchenko), his skill at creating scandals derives from a careful consideration of the concepts and the slippages in meaning that happen when forms are made to perform unaccustomed functions.

> HH: I believe the public for what we call art is rarely homogeneous. There is always tension between people who are, above all, interested in *what* is "told" and those who focus primarily on the *how*. Neither of them can fully comprehend and appreciate a work of art. "Form" speaks, and "content" is inscribed in "form." The whole is inevitably imbued with ideological significations. That's also true for my work. There are those who are attracted by the subject and the information . . .
>
> PB: The message.
>
> HH: . . . explicit or implicit. They may find themselves reinforced in their opinions, recognizing that they are not alone in thinking what they think. It is pleasurable to come across things that help us better articulate vague notions we have and to give them a more precise form. Therefore, preaching to the converted, as one says, is not a total waste of time. A good deal of advertising and all political candidates do it, for good reason. Opposed to the sympathizers are, of course, the people who disagree. Some of them disagree to the point of trying to suppress my works—there have been several spectacular examples. The attempts to censor demonstrate, if nothing else, that the censors think an exhibition of my works could have consequences. Between these two extremes exists a sizable audience that is curious and without fixed opinions. It is in this group that one finds people who are prepared to reexamine the provisional positions they hold. Generally speaking, they match the target group of marketing and public relations experts whose job it is to expand the market for a product or for certain opinions. That's also where a good part of the press is situated. (Bourdieu and Haacke 1995: 85, 88)

The work of the artist does not appear in this dialogue as the priority of form over function or as the demythification of the hidden logic of each field. Haacke, like other conceptual and performance artists, understands the structure of political parties, churches, advertising, and audiences, and based on that understanding he moves objects and messages away from their accustomed places. His practice evades the autonomy of each field, counters it:

HH: It strikes me that insisting on the "form" or the "message" constitutes a sort of separatism. Both are politically charged. Speaking of the propaganda aspect of all art, I would like to add that the meaning and impact of a given object are not fixed for all eternity. They depend on the context in which one sees them. Fortunately, the majority of people are not particularly concerned about the presumed purity of art. . . .

One can learn a lot from advertising. Among the mercenaries of the advertising world are very smart people, real experts in communication. It makes practical sense to learn techniques and strategies of communication. Without knowing them, it is impossible to subvert them.

PB: To undertake forms of action which are at the same time symbolically effective and politically complex and rigorous, without concessions, wouldn't it be necessary to form teams composed of researchers, artists, theater people, communication specialists (publicists, graphic artists, journalists, etc.) and thus mobilize a force equivalent to the symbolic forces that must be confronted?

HH: I believe it is very important that it be fun. It has to be enjoyable. It must be a pleasure for the public to get involved. (Bourdieu and Haacke 1995: 89, 107–8)

In Search of the Cross-Disciplinary Object

In its confrontation with society, and with what the social sciences reveal about society, aesthetics lives on not as a normative field but as an open environment in which we search for *forms* not radically separated from any sort of function; *representations* more interested in knowledge—including knowledge of things that do not exist—than in truth; *experiences* unconcerned with any sort of transcendence and interested instead in opening up possibilities in a world without preestablished norms. Instead of aesthetics as a discipline, we find *the aesthetic* as a widespread reflection that works on practices that are still called artistic and explores the desire or the "will to form" (Richard 2004: 11). This emphasis on form appears in other settings: in the workplace and consumption sites, science and technology, the organization and rethinking of urban space, the messages and countermessages that circulate in the mass media.

We can better fathom the difference between philosophical aesthetics and social science–based theories of art by looking at their objects of study. Asking what art is isn't the same thing as asking what we are talking about when we talk about art or asking what are we doing when we say we're doing art. Those who still seek the essence or a universal definition of art are aiming at philosophical aesthetics. Others deem that discourses are what define the artistic: the impact of semiotics and of visual and cultural studies led them to overestimate the structuring of social practices through story or processes of signifying; the meaning of art had to be verified by deconstructing or interpreting the modes in which it was named. According to the third perspective, that of anthropology, to know what art is we must observe the behaviors of artists and listen to how they present them.

Philosophical aesthetics: What is art? Semiotics: What does art say and what are we talking about when we talk about art? Anthropology: What do the people called artists do?

According to writers such as Anthony Downey (2009), James Clifford (1988), and Hal Foster (1996), the third trend has prevailed in recent years. An "ethnographic turn" has taken place in the study of art and in the practice of artists themselves: faced with the difficulty of coming up with universalizable answers, we observe what the people who say they do art actually do, how they organize themselves, what operations they use to valorize it and differentiate it from other activities. This means simplifying the question to some degree, by moving from ontology to an analysis of what the people called artists in different cultures do, using their own rules and objects.

As we analyze over the next few pages the behavior of those who make art, exhibit it, sell it, criticize it, or form the audience for it, we will notice that something more than a linguistic or a sociological or an anthropological turn is going on with art. We are in the midst of a *cross-disciplinary, intermedia, and globalized turn* that is leading us to redefine what we understand by art not only in the modern West but also in the preglobal East. At the same time, the arts are also participating in the redefinition of the social sciences, which also have doubts about their identity and are discovering in art not a solution, not a way out, but, as Maurice Merleau-Ponty (1964: 12) said about Marxism, a place "where one goes . . . to learn to think."

Uncertainty is what draws artists and social scientists together: just as the collapse of metaphysics and the anthropological critique of Eurocentrism discredited the question "What is art?" and suggested replacing it with the question "When does art exist?," the breakdown and transitions of capitalism and globalization have abruptly left economics, anthropology, and sociology with no certainty about defining their objects of study or working out the scales of analysis and criteria for research.

Art suddenly became "unframed" because, as we will see, the attempts to organize it in terms of aesthetic prescriptions or a theory about the autonomy of fields (Bourdieu) or of worlds (Becker) hardly work. Nor do philosophers or social scientists have epistemologically convincing concepts of universalizable categories of analysis to provide to artists, politicians, or social movements.

Why is one painting better than another? Why are certain works preserved and exhibited in museums? Is it possible to extend the notion of art to non-Western and nonmodern societies? Do the notions of art and aesthetics still have any meaning, even in the West? The separate search for answers in historical, anthropological, and aesthetic studies is now being reformulated as we rethink the situation of the arts as well as the equally unresolved situation of heritage, handicrafts, the media, the organization of cities, and tourism. The arts are being reshaped interdependently with these social processes, as part of a globalized cultural geopolitics.

Can we talk about genuine cultural heritages? Is it desirable that they remain intact but unused? Does it make sense today to keep drawing a contrast between a cultural heritage or handicrafts as the field of that which should be preserved, and art as a set of movements of creativity and inventiveness?

As we discard questions formulated by disciplines in distinct territories—history and archaeology separate from the sociology of art, anthropology in departments disconnected from sociologists and other specialists in modernity and globalization—we discover that the questions replacing them are transdisciplinary. Many investigations on a global scale are creating the conditions for the training attained in each social science to be remade in projects that are sensitive to the cross-disciplinary complexity of the processes they study (Appadurai 1996; Escobar and Ribeiro 2006; Hannerz 1996; R. Ortiz 2004; Ribeiro 2003; Sennett 2006). Something similar is happening among artists and practitioners of the media, or the intermedia: they are interconnecting creative and communicational strategies. In the United States, China, Japan, Spain, and Argentina, since the close of the twentieth century those who direct museums, curate exhibits, and act as artists have been taking courses in anthropology, communications, and economics in order to develop cultural marketing strategies. They likewise read books and journals, both print and electronic, follow blogs, and cultivate social networks that transcend the art world.

A world ends not only when the answers have to be archived but also when the questions that gave rise to them lose their meaning.

For decades we've been trying to find the right question to ask instead of the one about what art is. It is a hard question to get rid of, given that the funeral that buried art didn't stop it from continuing to exist and renew itself or stop critics from arguing about works being exhibited in museums, galleries, city streets, and deserts. What words can we find to replace it? After so many "*neos* and *posts*" and uncentered discourses, Hal Foster (1996: 1) has written, there remains a melancholy that has distanced itself from its lost object. Or should we recognize that the objects of study are different now?

Now that idealist aesthetics declaring beautiful objects artistic and calling for the disinterested contemplation of art works have fallen into disrepute, what sort of objects would justify the existence of aesthetics, art as a differentiated practice, and the institutions that place objects on exhibit and determine their value? Many museum directors have decided that objects aren't very important anymore and are redesigning exhibit halls or displacing the aesthetic experience to intersubjective relations untied to commercial manipulation (Bourriaud). They are discovering that their new audiences visit museums not to see exceptional works of art or to learn a lesson about African natives or Afro-Brazilian rituals that they are unfamiliar with, but out of curiosity inspired by seeing a television program, because they are concerned about deforestation in the Amazon, or perhaps they're visiting the Louvre for the first time because they've read *The Da Vinci Code*.

Anthropologists are unsure whether their object of study should be called "culture." Museum professionals never quite succeed in exhibiting that "object" that has accumulated as many hundreds of definition as "art." And every year the "heritage" specialists begin again on the task of justifying its defense and preservation. The principle according to which the notion of heritage has grouped together "cultural works of outstanding value," as the documents from UNESCO put it, is no longer tenable. The attempts by UNESCO to rescue its World Heritage program from this dead end have all foundered on the problem of drawing meaningful distinctions between art, heritage, tourism, and the media.

Some sociologists reject the idea that their main task is to establish what society is or what a social fact is, arguing that there is no such thing as a stable and homogeneous structure of relationships or state of affairs. According to Bruno Latour, they are no longer trying to discover macrosocial models or describe large groups, but to understand how social actors join together, what the processes are by which they form networks, unmake them, and put them together again in a different way, and how they articulate a variety of connections to attain their goals. Latour has redefined the meaning of the social by proposing to read scientific and political groupings, social movements, and the structurings and destructurings of urban spaces as constantly changing strategies by actor networks. He would say that this new view of the social is more eloquently manifest in studies of young people describing the flexible combination of formal and informal resources they use to get work, turning to nonlegal institutions and networks, getting clothes, music, and videos in both cinemas and brand-name stores and in pirate markets, buying and selling the same products or imitations that become confused with the "genuine articles" (Reguillo 2007; Hopenhayn 2008) If the actors don't generalize from a solitary example of behavior, what right does a social researcher have to construct megastructural explanations that encompass a full range of practices? We need other tools than those once used to comprehend order and classification systems.

We find concerns similar to those of postmetaphysical aesthetics among those who have stopped asking what an economic fact or a political fact is. After consolidating the position according to which it makes no sense to seek the essence of art, of culture, or of society because what we call by those terms is constructed in different ways in each country and era, our task becomes to formulate analytic frameworks that allow us to understand why and how they are constructed in those ways and how they work or fail to work. And how, among these processes, unexpected interactions take place.

One methodological hypothesis of this book is that, in order to produce nonmetaphysical questions, the research carried out in each field must articulate with the questions posed in other fields. Thus when philosophers and sociologists such as Goodman (1977) and Edelman and Heinich (2002) replace the question of what art is with the question of when is there art, they are referring us immediately to the set of social relationships among artists, institutions, curators, critics, audiences, and even advertising companies and campaigns, which together construct a recognition of certain objects as artistic. This change in the question that aesthetics asks must at the same time also take into account the way questioning about the social is being transformed.

Ever since the artist was redefined as a producer (Benjamin and the Constructivists), artists have worked with the production-circulation-consumption process in mind. Recently changes in economic thinking have led to a nonsubstantialist conception according to which the material and the symbolic value of the economic cycle are equally important. Contributing to this new view are those who define the artist as an ethnographer or anthropologist, and also the relocation of art in the debate about identity, alterity, multiculturality, and interculturality. Research on these processes has changed the agenda of anthropology and other social sciences: it is now accepted that socioeconomic conditions cannot be understood without culture, nor the other way around; we have moved on from the study of local and national cultures to processes of transnational interculturality.

As an expression of the closer relations between disciplines in the arts and the social sciences, there are more books than ever being co-written by sociologists of art and philosophers or by anthropologists and artists, while they also cite each other more frequently and collaborate on exhibits. Foucault thought through Borges and Velásquez. Deleuze wrote about Proust, Kafka, and Bacon. Derrida took off from Artaud, Bataille, and Blanchot. Bourdieu is devoted to Flaubert and Haacke. These convergences are not always amicable. The transdisciplinary turn in art, in anthropology, and in sociology has formed a situation of knowledge in which the analysis of aesthetic processes as done in these disciplines conflicts with the experimentation of artists and the inter-cultural situations of circulation and reception. There are also changes in the ways works of art and artistic experiences are reinterpreted or disciplined by the institutions that exhibit them.

The projects and works of the artists covered in this book go beyond confirming the old idea that art is a pathway to understanding. I empha-size these works and their processes of resignifying, but I don't lose sight of their partly autonomous meaning, analyzing them in the context of social process, while at the same time I show that this meaning is not limited to what the materiality of the works says. I also pay attention to what these efforts, more than the works themselves, have to say about certain problems of the contemporary world. León Ferrari proposes a "theory" of the complicity between religion and the politics of terror by associating the Christian idea of hell with concentration camps. Antoni Muntadas and Santiago Sierra, coming from different directions, stage critiques of translation and intercultural approaches. Carlos Amorales uses interruptions to represent the social. Why put them all in one book? Because these are all ways of thinking through the paradoxes that disconcert us when one world has ended and another has barely begun.

These artists—some of them habitual readers of the social sciences—raise provocative sociological or anthropological questions. But perhaps their greatest interest resides in the fact that what understanding is to be found in their works demands that we modify our notion of science and the methods we use to learn about things. We are far removed from art as a path to knowledge that is the opposite of scientific rationality or as an illustration of political or philosophic ideas. These artists are researchers and thinkers who use their works to challenge the anthropological and philosophical consensus about social orders, about communication networks and the ties between individuals and the ways they form groups.

At the same time that I endeavor to confine myself to an internal understanding of these works, I argue that they are epistemological experiences that renew our forms of thinking, translating, and working with the incomprehensible and the surprising. The fact that none of these artists offers doctrinaire answers or programs can help us concentrate on the dilemmas of asking questions. They are freer than social scientists to use *metaphors* to express condensations and uncertain meanings that we cannot formulate as *concepts*; this freedom leads us to reconsider the articulations between these two ways of covering that which escapes our grasp at present.

Art among the Media

It isn't enough to talk about the transdisciplinary turn in art or to restructure artistic projects in connection with the social sciences. We know that the practice of art today, its formats and the ways it is communicated are being transformed as artists interact with audiovisual and digital technologies. Though film and television have been stimulating a reworking of the practice of art since the mid-twentieth century, the tremendous spread of video, computer animation, video games, and the multimedia uses of mobile phones has shattered earlier limits on the visual arts. Both new artists and artists who have devoted decades to painting can now use a diversity of materials and techniques in a single work: installations and videos can combine still photographs, drawings, and actions. Graphic novels, comics, and animations have changed the way films are made (*Watchmen, Waltz with Bashir*). Just as text can be read on paper or on a screen and music can be listened to live, on radio or TV or on an iPod, so visual creations have been resignified in many institutions, settings, and communication networks, such as YouTube.

The most recent stage is represented by Web 2.0, where so many "creations" by artists and users are in circulation, things that creators start and others modify, that the borders between art and nonart are blurred. The intentions of art from every period are subordinated to the trend of broadening participation. Networks are said to be better the more users they include, allowing videos, photographs, and blogs to multiply endlessly. Instead of works, we find dialogues, expressions of desire, exchanges, sales, information about what others said or bought. Instead of works and viewers, we find flows circulating via objects, people, and images. The content providers are not only professionals. Innovation is being democratized; we are entering an era of open, multidirectional innovation. The exuberant use of foggy ideas such as "multitude" doesn't help us define the character of the actors nor their interactions online, nor have we yet discovered the appropriate sociological or aesthetic concepts for judging what is creative and innovative about this communications ecology. Do a greater opening and more access mean more participation? Have YouTube, MySpace, or Facebook improved creativity and quality, or made any contribution to rethinking the aesthetic criteria that art and the audiovisual media have inherited?

The new habits generated among Internet users and the mixture of formats and alliances between visual, text, and software content producers are having an impact on art spaces, from museums to biennales, fairs, and specialized Internet sites. This process is altering the links between creation, spectacle, entertainment, and participation; between what up to a few years ago was sorted into the categories of highbrow, popular, and mass culture; between the local, the translocal, and the global; between authorship, reproduction, and access; between symbolic elaboration and the intensity of direct stimulation of the senses. The relocation of the arts that Walter Benjamin had begun to foresee with regard to "mechanical reproduction" has grown complex and expanded in a time of electronic intertextuality. One of the ways experience has been restructured is the displacement beyond art of an exclusively perceptual register. Going to exhibits means reading lots of texts, listening to long speeches on videos, walking through installations, and being exposed to sounds. The walls between genres, between art and advertisement, between play and reflection, are falling.

This intermedia experience widens when surfing the web. What do the websites tell us? Even if sites are dominated by information from their hosts (which tend to be groups, not individuals), they provide not only lists of galleries, museums, and biennales from all over the world but also debates and dialogues, photos, videos, interviews, heterogeneous texts, paid ads and noncommercial announcements, emotional analyses (www.wefeelfine.org), information for activists (www.critical -art.net, www.yomango.net), calendars of fairs, festivals, biennales, and articles about these events (www.artfairsinternational.com), how and where to buy works, and how to download current and out-of-print materials (www.ubu.com). And hundreds and hundreds more, such as the networks where cybercollectors from many continents exchange information and opinions about which artists are good and who is up-and-coming, or they gather various reflections to evaluate their collections and put them in order, each collector setting his or her own profile's confidentiality level, as on Facebook (www.independent-collectors.com). Between the last site, meant to facilitate interconnections exclusively among collectors, and those that allow unrestricted access the incredibly diverse uses of the web are reconfiguring the circulation of the visual arts, but not in only one direction.

The most radical reflection on these processes comes from the school of historians and art theorists who have reformulated the field of art as "visual culture," an interdisciplinary field that is the object of the quasi-discipline that they call "visual studies" (Bal 2002; Barriendos 2006; Brea 2005; Guasch 2003; Mitchell 2003; Moxey 2005; and others). Some of these writers argue that painting, sculpture, and graphic arts are finished as distinct practices (as is the history of art as the disciplinary organization of their study), having given way to a history of images, within which what we once called art has lost any specificity. Or is it more a matter of resituating, within the totality of media and visual languages, artistic practices in which various aesthetic questions— experiences that touch the imagination and the senses, placing value on formal properties—change their meanings? Whether we opt for one position or the other, it is clear that the autonomy of art and aesthetics was called into question as soon as we entered a new regime that, to follow Jacques Rancière (2004: 10), reorganizes the modes of production of works or practices, the "forms of visibility" of those practices, and the "ways of thinking about their relationships" by reconfiguring common sensitivities and politics.

What do we gain and what do we lose when we declare the end of the disciplines, as some cultural and visual studies have? One risk is that we will turn our backs on pieces of knowledge and methodological strategies that remain useful. Another is that we will forget that the current crisis of knowledge is in part a consequence of research in sociology and anthropology, social sciences that were able to critique their own historical projects by transcending the norms established by their own founders.

Just as it isn't so simple to declare art history, aesthetics, or anthropology over and done with, we also cannot proclaim the definitive death of art and its autonomy just because much of what continues to be called art is found outside of what has been designated as its proper field. Some analysts of art and literature from different parts of the world are declaring that their areas of study have gone into a postautonomous stage in the early twenty-first century. In an article titled "Post-Autonomous Art," Victor Tupitsyn (2004: 274–76) presents his position, shared by other Russian artists and historians (Ilya Kabakov and Margarita Tupitsyn), that contemporary art should be analyzed as a "global spectacle for tourists" because "the local zone of the museum visitor has been completely de-intimized" and artists, along with those who run museums, auction houses, and the entertainment and souvenir industries, have become "international businessmen" who act as "the service personnel for millions of Japanese, Chinese, Australian and other visitors" who have turned the museum into a sort of "multicultural church where a person is allowed to enter regardless of aesthetic beliefs."

The Argentine literary critic Josefina Ludmer (2007) described a type of novel and text in which she found two operations that set this type apart from what literature had been understood to be. First, for these texts "reality (if it is thought of through the media, which constantly constitute it) is fiction and fiction is reality," as evidenced in the mixture of referential and verisimilitude-building relationships in "testimonial literature, autobiography, journalistic reporting, *crónicas*, personal diaries, and even ethnography." Second, "everything that is cultural (and literary) is economic, and everything that is economic is cultural (and literary)," as seen in the fact that the same transnational corporations produce books, newspapers, and television programs as if they were interchangeable. Her conclusion: we are living in a continuum that she calls *realidadficción,* "realityfiction," in which even works that look like literature can't be read through the literary categories of "author, work, style, writing, text, and meaning."

Maybe everything would have been easier if we had gone from the autonomy of art and literature to a period in which both melted into the generalized flow of images and texts. Adopting the position of anthropology, which is to describe and understand processes through the words and actions of the actors themselves, doesn't allow us to draw conclusions quite as emphatic as those of some aesthetic theorists. Visits to artists' workshops and exhibits, museums, galleries, and biennales, while noting what the media and audiences say about them, reveal striking shifts in the *conditions* of the production, circulation, and reception of art. Some of these transformations in artistic practices took place when artists left the specialized institutions; the notion of an autonomous field therefore lost power just as the contemporary moment began. But this set of observations shows that works are made and reproduced under variable conditions, that artists, critics, and curators act both *within and outside* the art world. Research cannot force them into the restrictions of a field that they no longer accept as a walled compound, nor its melting into a social whole in which different languages and communication practices are no longer cultivated. It is legitimate to speak of a postautonomous *condition* in contrast to the independence attained by art in the modern era, but not of a *stage* that will replace this modern period as something radically different and contrasting.

In reworking aesthetic theory and critical analysis, we must pay attention to the multiple allegiances and mobile locations of actors who exhibit their art in museums, the media, cyberspace, and on the street, all at once, and who maintain a certain free will about form both in their "own" spaces and in other areas where images are made visible and texts readable under a heteronomous normativity. Our task is not to deny the difference of certain "creators" and "works" but to perceive how these creators come into conflict and negotiate the meaning of their works in their exchanges with the cultural industries or in the midst of their social pragmatism. These days there are more reasons for doubting the possibility of art than there were when Mallarmé wondered about the book or the Constructivists asked how they could get involved in graphic design or designing everyday objects. Since then, there have been a few new failures in seeking space for poetry among the prose of the world, but in observing and listening to artists today, it seems that for many, their aesthetic aspiration is not to achieve some happy integration but to keep alive their questions about their contingency. There is no story that can dissipate this tension. More than that: art seems to exist insofar as this tension remains unresolved.

What the Art Field Does Not Explain about Art

One criticism leveled at Bourdieu is that he has stretched the notion of the field too far, postulating the existence of entirely autonomous logics in the way health, housing, fashion, sports, and other areas of social life are managed. We can credit him, however, with showing how important it is that each human activity in modern life is organized according to the peculiar dynamics of its own jobs, not in obedience to religious prescripts or political orders. Art, literature, medicine, and other disciplines can develop only by paying close attention to the logic proper to their own subjects: painting, writing novels, discovering the origins of diseases and curing them.

A second, more recent criticism of Bourdieu's work questions whether art and literature function today as autonomously structured fields. Do writers decide how to write their works only in relation to editorial criteria and according with what their readers expect, or do writers and readers both depend instead on those who invest their surplus profits from oil or financial corporations in publishing? Is the success or failure of a novel or a performance the result of an aesthetic relationship between writer or artist and the public, mediated by specialized institutions, or is it the result of advertising, prizes that seem to line up with marketing surveys, or maybe the novel's potential for being made into a screenplay? The sociology of contemporary art and literature investigates, beyond the internal articulation of those artistic fields, their ties with markets and fashions whose objectives have nothing to do with the logic proper to the creations. Parenthetically it's worth noting Nathalie Heinich's (2007) observation that, although Bourdieu didn't reformulate his theory of the autonomy of fields, being occupied with the uproar caused by "illegitimate" cultural productions, the journal *Actes de la recherche* that he directed and in which he published his famous text on the field of high fashion and high culture included many articles on other domains of taste, such as sports, the body, and advertising.

A third criticism of Bourdieu's sociology of art and literature regards its limits in dealing with innovation. Sociologists describe the social organization of artists who have already created paintings or performances, or writers who have already written and been published. They show us, a posteriori, how a canon came about, as well as the community of specialists who structured it and defend it, or their opponents who would renovate it. But how can we deal with the creative role of individuals? Marxism, as Sartre wrote in his *Critique of Dialectical Reason* (1976), can explain why Valéry was a petit bourgeois writer, but not why all other petit bourgeois intellectuals were not Valéry. Sociology can help us to understand how cooperation and competition among many actors mold an era's art and literature, including the logic of the rebellious avant-gardes. Nevertheless there is something about this phenomenon that each era calls "art" that can't be captured by the sociological gaze; aesthetic facts are not limited to the positions taken by artists or to buyers' and viewers' strategies for drawing distinctions.

A brief example will document that the material for this revised view of the intermediality of art and the joint participation of artists, members of the art field, and other social and media agents takes decades. We will look at how the increasing value assigned to Frida Kahlo was managed in exhibits associated with multimedia operations in 2007, the hundredth anniversary of her birth.

The main reevaluation of Kahlo's work took place in the exhibit that was held from June to August 2007 in the Palacio de Bellas Artes in Mexico City, with 354 pieces, including paintings, photographs, letters, and documents. Over the course of two months, some 440,000 visitors came to see the exhibit, which later traveled to the Philadelphia Museum of Art, the San Francisco Museum of Modern Art, and museums in Japan and Spain.

Kahlo's works, like those of other artists, have to be placed in context. The curators decided to display her paintings, letters, and images of public performances next to documents dealing with lovers, friends, and people who appear in her paintings or who promoted her exhibits: Diego Rivera, Trotsky, Henry Ford, Nelson Rockefeller, and André Breton.

The media recalled her indigenous clothes and her adoption by top-line fashion designers, as well as the fact that her painting *Raíces* (*Roots*) was purchased by telephone at a Sotheby's auction in New York in May 2006 for $5.6 million, the highest price ever paid for a Latin American work of art. How can we demarcate the reinterpretations of her work in a Tate Modern exhibition from displays of her images in the shop windows of London clothing stores, or the research-based books about her from the film that won Salma Hayek an Oscar nomination in 2002 for her portrayal of Kahlo?

Does it help or harm Kahlo's work to recall her membership in the Communist Party, the disturbing relationship she drew between pain and pleasure, the mass reproduction of her image in issues of *Elle*, *Harper's*, and other magazines that devoted articles to her to create the "Frida look," or her feminism, adopted in distinct versions by Mexican, Chicana, and European women? It is not easy to mark the border dividing the tequilas, glasses, perfumes, Converse sneakers, and Italian corsets bearing her name from her paintings, when her own works include the corset on which she painted the hammer and sickle.

Sociologists dismissed the notions of exceptional creativity and artistic genius. Modern aesthetics asked us to focus on the works themselves. But now there were stories appearing in the mass media that hailed creators for their exceptionality, which they tied to the biographies of these suffering or downtrodden figures. Magazines and television programs used interviews with the artists and inventions about their personal lives or the "anguishing" work they undertook before painting a new piece to keep up the romantic image of the solitary, misunderstood creator and the spiritually uplifting work of art, in contrast to the general materialism of society. The idealist aesthetic discourse, which no longer serves to represent the creative process, is recycled as a complementary resource intended to "guarantee" the verisimilitude of the artistic experience at the moment of consumption.

If, as studies of museum visitors have shown (García Canclini 2007a, 2007b), the figure of Kahlo as an artist is imbricated for the public with postrevolutionary discourse, feminist discourse, and the sacrificial sense of some of the avant-garde, if she herself elaborated her character to be the intersection between these twentieth-century narratives (for example, by changing the year of her birth from 1907 to 1910 so that it would coincide with the beginning of the Mexican Revolution), it seems unreasonable to omit these contexts if we are trying to understand the cultural significance of her work and gain access to it.

Nevertheless, her biographical narrative and the conditions of its production and sociocultural involvement do not, by themselves, tell us why she painted the way she did or what we can read in her works. There were other women close to Diego Rivera (Lupe Marín), other women who were both artists and beautiful (Nahui Ollin), who painted their bodies in tragic poses and were lovers of famous male artists (María Izquierdo, with Rufino Tamayo), but none of them produced Kahlo's works.

It is no waste of time to learn the context of a work and the ways an artist constructed her place socially. But the question remains: Why was it Kahlo who painted *Mi nana y yo*, *La venadita*, and *Raíces*? Answers that center on her accidents and illnesses, the narcissism of her insistent self-portraits, her loves and politics are insufficient. This is the point where explanations based on historical conditions and the cultural industrialization of images grind to a halt; to move forward, we must confront the enigmatic labor that for the time being we still call art. This is the point when we turn from the sociology of art back to aesthetics.

Clearly our first difficulty will be to establish which notion of art or aesthetic experience we will choose and to decide why we should select it from among the hundreds that exist. Given the proliferation of definitions and dissents, isn't the only possible conclusion to dismiss all universal theories and resign ourselves, with anthropological relativism, to bestow the name of art on the things made by people called (or calling themselves) artists?

The Power of Imminence

Do they call themselves artists, or do others call them that? We'd typically answer this question by examining socially established conventions and the negotiations between institutional programs and creative projects. In this game of back-and-forth, how can we tell whether or not something has satisfied the requirements for being considered art? We're stuck in a closed circle between things that proclaim themselves art and a sociology that reveals each response as an echo of prior conditioning.

There may be a way out that does not consist of giving in to aesthetic arguments or sociological explanations. I'm thinking of artists and writers who think their job consists of doing something they can't really describe. Let's explore whether we can draw a tidbit of knowledge from their befuddled statements about what it means to make science about art (or about any social object) and what it means to make society.

One of the best writers at clearly expressing the experience of what cannot be captured was Jorge Luis Borges. In "The Wall and the Books" he wondered about the coincidence that "the man who ordered the building of the almost infinite Chinese Wall" was the same one who "decreed the burning of all the books that had been written before his time" (1964: 3). Borges argued that the two decisions were not a mystery at all for historians: Emperor Shih Huang Ti, who brought the six kingdoms under his control and "put an end to the feudal system," built the wall as a defense and "burned the books because his opponents were invoking them to praise the emperors who had preceded him" (3). Borges proposed to read not only the deeds but the metaphors. He was struck by the fact that the same emperor who built the wall and burned the books also "forbade the mention of death and searched for the elixir of immortality" and finally "became a recluse in a figurative palace, which had as many rooms as the number of days in the year. Those facts," Borges concludes, "suggest that the wall in space and the fire in time were magic barriers to halt death. . . . Perhaps the Emperor and his magicians believed that immortality was intrinsic and that decay could not enter a closed sphere" (4). He also noted that "anyone who concealed books was branded with a hot iron and condemned to work on the mammoth wall until the day of his death. . . . Perhaps," Borges thought, "the wall was a metaphor; perhaps Shih Huang Ti condemned those who adored the past to a work as vast as the past, as stupid and useless" (5). One set of forms refers to another, and the least important thing is the "content" they contain on any particular occasion.

What does this correspondence among forms speak to? Since their content is not decisive, Borges (1964: 5) concludes, what is important is what they insinuate without ever quite naming it: "Music, states of happiness, mythology, faces molded by time, certain twilights and certain places—all these are trying to tell us something, or have told us something we should not have missed, or are about to tell us something; that imminence of a revelation that is not yet produced is, perhaps, the aesthetic reality."

Being a writer or an artist, then, doesn't mean learning a codified profession, fulfilling requirements that have been set by a canon, and thus becoming a member of a field in which you achieve effects that justify themselves. Nor does it mean making deals between this field and other practices—politics, advertising, institutional arrangements—that can lend greater repercussions to aesthetic play. Literature and art give more resonance to voices that come from diverse places in society, listening to those voices in ways that others don't, turning them into something that political, sociological, or religious discourses can't. What do they have to do to turn them into literature or art? Nobody can say beforehand. As Ricardo Piglia (2001: 11) says, "A writer writes to learn what literature is."

Perhaps this way of saying things without pronouncing them fully, this imminence of an impending revelation, is the key to the nature of art. I find an antecedent to this position in a phrase by Walter Benjamin (1968: 222) from 1935, fifteen years before Borges's story, that defines the "aura" of art as "the unique phenomenon of a distance."

Two clarifications are necessary: speaking from the place of imminence does not make the artist an exceptional being, nor does it make a work singular. The word that sticks out today in Benjamin's beautiful phrase is "unique," alluding to the singular meaning of each artistic work—an aspect that began to evaporate when works could be mechanically reproduced, as with photographs and film. In the early 1990s José Luis Brea was still finding the aura in contemporary art, and he said that, instead of watching it disappear, we are witnessing its cooling down. In a more recent study, Juan Antonio Ramírez documented the enduring search for the mystery of the aura through other means, not only in the aesthetics of museums or of ideological restorations, but also in innovative explorations of images, from Beuys to Pistoletto, from Mariko Mori to Francesc Torres and Ana Mendieta. The work of art reignites its aura in "the era of the multiplied original" (Ramírez 2009: 190).

Maurice Merleau-Ponty, who was better able than most at relating linguistics to the wisdom of artists, said that the only thing artists do is specialize in the "creative use" of language, but by sharing its inter-dependence with "empirical use," as we all do every day. The empirical form of language is "the opportune recollection of a pre-established sign" or, "as Mallarmé said, the worn coin placed silently in my hand" when I need to communicate (Merleau-Ponty 1964: 44). Painters and writers also use the conventional structures of language, "the stock of accepted relations between signs and familiar significations without which" the reader could never understand the writer (Merleau-Ponty 1969: 13). But like anyone who wants that "spoken language" to become a "speaking language," they must first raise it to a point of creativity. The writer who seeks to address the reader directly "transfigures" the cus-tomary order of signs "so that in the end a new signification is secreted" (13). He doesn't establish a radically different, consolidated meaning but rather "the imminence of a world's creation" (Merleau-Ponty 1964: 45).

The book or the painting, as finished objects, give this search the ap-pearance of an exceptional and emphatic discovery. But Merleau-Ponty recalls the slow-motion camera that once recorded Matisse at work: "That same brush which, seen with the naked eye, leaped from one act to another, was seen to meditate . . . to try ten possible movements, dance in front of the canvas, brush it lightly several times, and crash down finally . . . upon the one line necessary." What did this film reveal? That the painter wasn't "like the God of Leibniz," a "demiurge" resolv-ing an immense problem of minima and maxima, nor was he simply someone going "to look for a hammer to drive in a nail." Matisse's hand hesitated in front of the "twenty conditions" that he saw "scattered out over the painting," much as the writer hesitates in front of the word be-fore pronouncing it, in front of "the background of silence which does not cease to surround it and without which it would say nothing. Or to put the matter another way, we must uncover the threads of silence that speech is mixed together with" (1964: 45–46). In this way, the artist "adds a new dimension to this world too sure of itself by making contin-gency vibrate within it" (50).

Imminence, contingency, the phenomenon of a distance: along with this aesthetic line, we observe in what those who call themselves artists do and say they do that some value is still placed on form over function. Sometimes these two tendencies join forces, as when a formal work with no pragmatic efficacy presents artistic deeds as the imminence of something that hasn't happened. In other cases, we see that art *does things*, has a function, albeit of a different order than ordinary social acts. It's a way of getting something to remain unresolved.

There have been several attempts to exorcise this ambivalence of knowledge between the rigor of science and the intuitions of artists, between concepts and metaphors. Epistemology, from positivism to constructivism, sought to circumscribe the realm of science in order to differentiate it from other territories. Thus logically supportable speech, put forth in an academic format, is set apart from essays that make use of the multivocal potential of metaphors. Interdisciplinary and intercultural works place us in a more fertile era for reexamining what we mean by knowledge: how to join the rigor of concepts together with other modes of explanation, comprehension, and expression. The undisciplined pages of this book are attempting, in part, to transcend the walls of academia and the frames of artworks by discussing the attainments and mistakes of Bourdieu, Heinich, and Rancière as aesthetic theorists (insofar as their philosophical, sociological, and anthropological exercises have aesthetic underpinnings), or those of Borges, Alÿs, Antoni Muntadas, León Ferrari, and Carlos Amorales, not only for their artistic creativity but for the philosophy or anthropology that they imply: Gabriel Orozco conceptualizes his workshop-studies, located in various countries, as mobile "platforms for thinking."

That is why each chapter in this book draws together research and debates from social scientists and philosophers on the destabilized borders of their disciplines and, at the same time, the works of artists, their reception, and the ways they incorporate social, cultural, and even epistemological connections. Artworks are presented not as illustrations for ideas but as ways to observe their conceptual and formal mechanisms, which change the way questions can be made visible. In these theoretical statements and research results, we experience not propositions or conclusions, but the pathways and enigmas of knowledge.

>

CHAPTER TWO

VISUAL CULTURES

Between Art and Heritage

When Benjamin, Borges, and Merleau-Ponty wrote about the boundaries of art and literature, they were dealing only with museums and not with the nearly two hundred biennales and art fairs we have today, and the art and literary markets were not interwoven with tourism, the media, urban expansion and decay, global migrations, and the Internet. Back then it was easier to value artists' actions, as Merleau-Ponty did, and describe them as unlike and unrelated to museums and other institutions, which according to him transformed "efforts into 'works'" (Merleau-Ponty 1964: 62).

The sociological demarcations of the place of the arts in the modern world were also overwhelmed by recent trends. Bourdieu carried out innovative studies of the literature and art fields, museums, and their publics; he held a handful of dialogues with cutting-edge artists (for example, Hans Haacke) and resisted the industrialization of culture, as is clear in his lectures about television.

Benjamin and Borges are said to have anticipated the effects of technology on art, the slippages between reality and virtual representations, uncentered intertextuality, and the play between originals and copies. In Merleau-Ponty's writings about Cezanne and Matisse, "Indirect Language and the

Voices of Silence" (1964), and in his final books, *L'Œil et l'esprit* and *The Prose of the World* (1969), he expressed aesthetic reflections that still stand up, but he postulated an irresolvable enmity between the creativity of acts and the institutionalization of museums. Though he recognized that "all culture prolongs the past" (1964: 79) and that the invention of meaning in any work of art would be impossible without what had been constituted before it in social and personal history, in overvaluing the event with respect to structure, he concluded that "the Museum kills the vehemence of painting" (63); "the Museum converts this secret, modest, non-deliberated, involuntary, and, in short, living historicity into official and pompous history" (62).

Aesthetic theorists devoted to justifying the existence of works of art aren't the only ones concerned with discussing the originality and singularity of certain cultural items. As we all know, every class, ethnic group, and period tends to overrate its own works. We see much the same thing, though in a different guise, among organizations and doctrines trying to overcome ethnocentrism that have come up with supposedly universal criteria for ranking art. One such organization is the World Heritage Sites program created by UNESCO in 1972. This program interests me as an effort to organize differences, classify objects and places, and improve their dissemination and interpretation. Moreover it gives us material for seeing at a glance what scientific knowledge and artistic reflection—working with concepts and working with metaphors—are able to do about the tensions between cultural consolidation and innovation.

One way of understanding philosophy and the sciences as disciplines devoted to concepts seeks to define and settle what the world means. By contrast, when the arts and literature work with metaphors they destabilize meaning; they are trying to say something about what is empirical and observable in relation to what is figurative and imagined. For much of the modern period, scientific language pursued univocality and exactitude; artists and writers meanwhile seemed to be in charge of ambiguity. Though we've grown accustomed to finding metaphors in science and philosophy books, while on the other hand a number of art trends are characterized by concepts and intellectual representations of the real, the divisions between the two positions persist.

Recent "scientific" criticisms of postmodernism and cultural and visual studies—for example, Alan Sokal and Jean Bricmont's (1998) critique of Jacques Lacan, Julia Kristeva, and Bruno Latour—have reinfused our debates about epistemology and aesthetics with the question of what we gain or lose when we use concepts and metaphors. To begin with, we ought to question whether the job of concepts can be reduced to setting limits, and that of metaphors to working with displacements of meaning and moving back and forth between zones of the real.

To get into this topic, I analyze the uncomfortable assumptions made by the UNESCO World Heritage program. Then I compare that program with the ways institutions and the media use the idea of world heritage, and also with contemporary artworks that alter the meaning and value of heritage items and symbols.

Globalization of the Local

The notion of "cultural heritage," according to the UNESCO convention that governs these matters, covers things as varied as monuments, groups of buildings, sculptures, paintings, inscriptions, caves, and sites that have "outstanding universal value" because of their historical, aesthetic, archaeological, scientific, ethnological, or anthropological character. To this disparate set of material items, UNESCO added manifestations of what it termed "intangible cultural heritage": oral creations, specialized knowledge, ritual celebrations, and handicraft techniques.

Given this definition of cultural heritage in terms of the outstanding and universalizable value of certain objects, studying those items is reminiscent of the idealist aesthetics that valued artworks as singular objects whose originality made them uniquely representative of their creators' "genius." Few contemporary theorists would still support such an idealization of artistic objects. What justifies clinging to this conception in the case of cultural heritage?

The information kit on this program that UNESCO published asks "How can a World Heritage site in Egypt 'belong' equally to Egyptians and to the peoples of Indonesia or Argentina?" Instead of providing a definition, it launches straight into a pragmatic institutional explanation: "The answer is to be found in the 1972 *Convention concerning the Protection of the World Cultural and Natural Heritage*, by which countries recognize that the sites located on their national territory, and which have been inscribed on the World Heritage List, without prejudice to national sovereignty or ownership, constitute a world heritage 'for whose protection it is the duty of the international community as a whole to cooperate'" (UNESCO 2008: 5).

The difficulties involved in selecting sites that deserve recognition while rejecting others can be seen with every type of heritage, but they are less disquieting when the ones chosen are historical items with long pedigrees. The criteria become less sure when modern cities and neighborhoods are given the nod, such as Brasilia, University City in Caracas, or the National Autonomous University of Mexico enclave in Mexico City, each of which has been added to the World Heritage list.

The mounting number of inconsistencies led the committee in charge of deciding these things to use "changing parameters" and finally, in 2005, to form a commission of philosophers, anthropologists, sociologists, and semiologists to debate the concepts of "world heritage" and works of "outstanding universal value." The call for applications to this commission itself recognized that, during its first decades, the convention on world heritage had privileged aesthetic value or "authenticity," that it had later criticized Eurocentrism, and that it was now seeking to make "the plurality of cultures" visible. The shaky trajectory of UNESCO makes one think that, as we have seen with regard to art, the most pertinent question is not "What is heritage?" but "When is there heritage?" Taking off from this reformulation, does it make sense to talk about a "world" heritage? Perhaps it would be easiest to attribute the quality of world heritage to UNESCO, or to other global organizations such as the United Nations or the World Bank, given their aspiration to deal with what everyone has in common. But why pick the Casbah of Algiers, the city of Ouro Preto, or the Thracian tomb of Kazanlak, each of which is rooted in its own particular culture? The idea that they each should be raised to global status is hard to accept.

The UNESCO list of World Heritage Sites includes places that not only condense meanings central to their local history but are so significant that they've become objects of wonder for other societies: the Bauhaus sites in Weimar y Dessau, Tiwanaku in Bolivia, the Great Wall of China, the city of Cartagena in Colombia, the cave of Altamira in Spain, the Acropolis of Athens, the Taj Mahal in India, and the historical centers of Mexico City, Prague, and San Gimignano and Siena in Italy. Why are some more significant than others? To what degree, and for whom, have they become "universal"? Strictly speaking, their universalization is partial and relative to various processes of selection and exclusion, of spreading awareness and lingering ignorance. If millions of people on several continents know the significance of the twelve examples just cited, that is because certain religions, aesthetic trends, and urban models have spread widely and because of the dominant trends in tourism and media communications. On the other hand, it would be easy to name dozens of UNESCO World Heritage Sites in Albania, El Salvador, Kazakhstan, Senegal, Sri Lanka, Surinam, and Venezuela that are scarcely visible in our unequal information and geocultural distributions of value. Is this because they are less exceptional heritage-wise, or because tourist, media, and religious publicity hasn't budged their fame?

Studies of changing aesthetic and cultural values by Bourdieu ([1979] 1984), Martín-Barbero (2005), and Smith (1988), among others, show that the multifactorial constitution of value has largely been guided by nation-states and academic communities. State politics can make it seem that such-and-such a pyramid or historical city center is the shared heritage of all the members of a nation, but in strict point of fact a cultural heritage expresses a series of agreements by certain groups about how the things and practices that identify them should be valued. These sites therefore tend to be places of social concern. The activities aimed at defining them, preserving them, and spreading news about them, with the help of the historical and symbolic prestige of certain cultural items, almost always involve a simulation: they pretend that society isn't divided into classes, genders, ethnic groups, and regions, or they suggest that such divisions are trivial in comparison with the greatness and respect possessed by the things that have been named a cultural heritage. They ignore everything we should have learned from hundreds of studies about the place of indigenous people, women, and the urban poor: the diversity of national memories, the discrimination that subalterns face, and the way they have been devastated by war and dictatorships (Martín-Barbero 2005; Richard 2004).

The cultural items that each society singles out as historical do not *really* belong to everyone, even if they *formally* seem to be everyone's and to be available to anyone who wants to use them. When we study how each society transmits knowledge through schools and museums, we see that groups appropriate their cultural heritage in different and unequal ways. Research on museum visitors show that, as we go down the social and educational scale, each group's ability to appropriate the cultural capital transmitted by these institutions diminishes (Bourdieu, Darbel, and Schnapper [1960] 1991; Cimet et al. 1987; Eder et al. 1977).

Though cultural heritage may sometimes serve to unify a nation, the inequalities in its formation and appropriation make it essential for us to study it also as a space of material and symbolic conflict between the sectors that form the nation. Neighborhoods, objects, and forms of knowledge generated by the hegemonic groups are deemed superior because these groups have the information and the education needed to understand and appreciate them, and therefore to better control them. Cultural historians, archaeologists, and politicians decide which items are superior and deserve to be preserved. In this way they reproduce the privileges that people with economic and intellectual means have held in every era, people with the work time and free time at their disposal to give such items the stamp of higher quality.

In the popular classes, we sometimes find refined ways of using manual dexterity to find technical solutions that fit a working-class lifestyle and that also play imaginatively with the available resources. But what they come up with can hardly compete against the works of people who have a historically accumulated store of knowledge at their fingertips, employ architects and engineers, have economic power, and are able to match their designs to the latest international advances.

Many international exhibits since the 1980s, including *Primitivism in Twentieth-Century Art* at MoMA in New York and *Magicians of the Earth* at the Centre Pompidou in Paris, have recognized that "the primitive" and "the popular" in peripheral societies have created objects of sufficient aesthetic value to be included in the programs of globally recognized institutions. But in the early twenty-first century both UNESCO's list of World Heritage Sites and the agendas of museums and biennales make it clear that, given the geopolitics of culture, the odds are against popular classes and peripheral societies doing what they'd need to accomplish to make their cultural items part of a globalized heritage: (a) accumulating them historically, especially when these groups are suffering from poverty or repression; (b) turning them into an objectified knowledge base that is relatively independent of individuals and simple oral transmission; and (c) expanding them through institutional education and perfecting the practices of peripheral groups through research and systematic experimentation.

The ambition to constitute a heritage for all humankind merely amplifies these inequalities and contradictions, no matter how altruistic the declared aims of UNESCO might be. When we look at the map of World Heritage Sites published in 2009, we are struck by its Eurocentrism. Of the 878 sites recognized as of that year, 435 were located in Europe and North America (especially Western Europe: 43 in Italy, 40 in Spain, and 33 in Germany), as compared with 182 in Asia and the Pacific, 120 in Latin America and the Caribbean, and 76 in Africa. That is, in the whole world outside of Europe and North America, there were only 443 outstanding sites. At the same time, on every continent the UNESCO list reveals an indirect Eurocentrism, because the choices demonstrate a preference for former European colonies such as India, Algeria, and Mexico. We also see a large number of European urban models (Vienna, Bruges, Toledo, Salamanca, Cáceres, Paris, Florence) and of their reproductions in Latin America: the list of sites includes the historical centers of Havana, Mexico City, Oaxaca, Puebla, Morelia, Zacatecas, Lima, Santo Domingo, and Colonia del Sacramento.

Even taking into account the map's incomplete and slanted nature, the surprising thing is just how common being exceptional is: some 878 sites were declared to belong to "world heritage" because of their "outstanding value." Outstanding, compared to what? And how can they be made valuable to all cultures, Western and Eastern, elite and popular, in rich nations (with more resources and personnel qualified to construct and preserve their buildings) and in poor nations (without the institutions for protecting their past or that have been pillaged by war)? The studies carried out by UNESCO experts themselves prove that successive corrections to the program haven't protected the weakest and less recognized from discrimination on the part of global authorities with control over economic wealth, interpretive power, and both analog and digital media dissemination.

These inconsistencies accentuate doubts about the program's theoretical principles and selection processes. It is impossible to select a set of "authentic" sites, objects, and rituals in isolation from the social ways that have molded them historically, such as urban development, the communication industries, their insertion into commercial networks, and media representations.

Heritages Destined for Reinterpretation

Let me spend some time on two ways in which heritage is used: in urban development and by the media. These are the two processes with perhaps the greatest influence today on how people learn about and value many cultural items. Urban transformations modify monuments and pieces of historical evidence by changing their scale in relation to huge new buildings and spectacular advertising. Meanwhile the mass media can get millions of people who've never been to a museum to see the works that they have on exhibit from inside their own homes, on television or over the Internet. The role of the media is interesting not only because they broadcast information but because of the work they do at reconceptualization and metaphorization in other fields of social life.

An eloquent example of resignifying heritage in urban, commercial, media, and popular uses occurs when crowds gather around a monument during political protests or sports celebrations and change its original meaning. Two of the most familiar monuments in Mexico City, the Monument to the Revolution and the Ángel de la Independencia, are constantly reappropriated by political events for a variety of causes. The results are sometimes unforeseeable, as has been the case with the statue of Columbus in Mexico City. In a study of protest rituals in urban demonstrations, Francisco Cruces observed that this monument, which becomes an object of (official) celebration and (indigenous) scorn every October 12, was reutilized on May 1, 1995, by the union of university workers who made it join their protest march: Columbus, now just one more protester, was made to carry the union flag. The "imaginative actions of the protesters resignifies in an ephemeral form the symbolically marked characters and places of the city center" (Cruces 1998: 43).

We know that this phenomenon is international. Recall the student protesters of 1968 who changed or defaced monuments in Paris, Berlin,

Prague, and Mexico City. Today it should perhaps be easy to recognize that the memory of 1968 has become part of the heritage of protest movements. That is not the case when it comes to seeing the sociocultural value of modern and supposedly less noble rituals such as those surrounding sports. Soccer, as a source of socialization and an organizing point for identity, generates festive rituals and theatricalizes social interactions and divisions. Its heritage is largely intangible: chants, costumes, and ephemeral celebrations. There are lasting buildings such as stadiums, and then there is another set of appropriations that belongs more to the field of intangible heritage, such as the fleeting occupation of urban space by marches and celebrations, as well as the mass media programs that instantly broadcast the spectacles.

The Spanish anthropologist Carmen Ortiz García documented a phenomenon in Madrid that has been reproduced in many cities: the use of historical and symbolic urban monuments to ratify a sports celebration. The Cibeles fountain, one of Madrid's most iconic monuments, has been used many times since 1986 for celebrations by fans of the Real Madrid soccer team. In May 2001, when Real Madrid beat Valladolid and won the national championship three days before the finals were to end, the fans were able to stage their Cibeles celebration right in the stadium. This is how the sports columnist for *El País* described it:

> A public that could enjoy the goddess Cibeles without leaving the stadium of Santiago Bernabéu. A montage via video special effects created the illusion that a helicopter was carrying out the titanic task of dismantling the statue and bringing it to the Madrid team's field. In the middle of the field a reproduction of the goddess's chariot appeared—still without the goddess herself riding in it—on top of a huge sheet of canvas marked with Madrid's shield. Then Cibeles arrived, descended, and occupied her throne as the players and fans went wild. The footballers in white [Real Madrid's home colors] were able to climb all over the statue without fear of being reprimanded by the mayor. (quoted in Ortiz García 2004: 199–200)

Carmen Ortiz García has analyzed the arguments among the various actors involved. The "public guardians" of the city's monuments tend to assert their value and protect their historical form as untouchable. On the other hand, "critical political movements" and "sports demonstrations," in the name of a different kind of legitimacy that has nothing to do with the hegemonic sense of "correct behavior," reappropriate these imposed symbols in order to give them a popular significance. The "mass media," which live from the colonization of hegemonic and popular symbolic repertoires, subordinate both kinds to their own logic of commercial profit and creating spectacles. In these cases, the monuments are a heritage being disputed among distinct actors. A perspective that values popular protests can interpret the ways that they appropriate a monument to support their social demands, or to celebrate the present, as bringing its significance up to date.

In other cases, reappropriation on the part of an actor from the media or the government tends to legitimate politicians who want to look like heirs of the founding fathers or of the nation's foundational events. Tourist industry practices bring a hegemonic modality with a different meaning. In either case, criticism usually focuses on the "distortion" of the monument's original meaning, as if every building or object in the nation's heritage were destined to remain forever unchanged—as if erecting a statue to commemorate a founding father or adapting a historic building to be repurposed as a bank or as government offices wasn't already a contingent interpretation of its social meaning.

Emptiness as Heritage

One very special example of what I've been talking about is the case of empty heritage spaces. I'm thinking of Tiananmen Square and the Zócalo, the huge central city squares of Beijing and Mexico City. Power is manifested not only in the monumental buildings that surround them but also in the creation of enormous empty spaces. These squares may function on occasion as the settings for large crowds of people acclaiming their leaders, serving them as a mirror. But most of the time they are vacant: there's nobody celebrating, no objects representing power. They're empty, spreading out in monotonous rows of paving stones, testimony to the fact that no one will change the people in charge of this country.

Protest movements sometimes try to conclude their marches in these gigantic plazas, which is why harsh acts of repression have taken place in them. Attempting to give new meaning to these flat, gray, grandiosely stripped-down areas, where the powerful represent absence and silence, is as serious a matter as trying to assail the halls of government themselves.

The great change posed by video culture and the industrialized massification of leisure can be seen the first time you go to Tiananmen Square: the crowds that fill the square in lookalike clothes, some in yellow caps and others in red, carrying flags that they wave every minute or two, evoke for me the political demonstrations in the Zócalo of Mexico City. In Tiananmen those crowds were composed of tens of thousands of tourists; the flags were being waved by guides leading the crowds so that they could circulate in an orderly fashion through the square and then, after paying the entrance fee, enter the Imperial Palace. From disputes over public space to its firmly guided use, from activism to tourism. It has been decades since a government was last housed in either Beijing's Imperial Palace or Mexico's National Palace. Through the mechanics of tourism, the crowds go from their occupation of the empty squares to the halls and corridors of the palaces, or rather to the vast and empty patios where power is no longer exercised. The rulers can be seen on television or in newspaper photos. These temporary, tedious occupations of the square, these visits to phantom seats of power, are for some people a way to evoke the storming of these buildings by revolutions that are no longer revolutionary; for others, they are a living reminder of a historical process that benefits them; and for many more, they mean glimpsing through windowpanes the ballrooms and furniture that still fill their national history with pride, the last remnants of empire or of revolution.

The Great Wall, stretching for 5,500 miles through valleys and soaring mountains, whose construction and reconstructions took more than two thousand years, is another way of monumentalizing power. Why did it become so important that its construction went on for so long, overcoming the obstacles of snow-bound peaks and sacrificing a fifth of China's population of about five million people, possibly almost half of its working-age men? The Wall, we are told, defended China from possible invasions, especially by the Mongols, and from commercial trade. It also served as an elevated highway, enabling people, merchandise, and the army to travel more freely through the mountains.

Who was it defending? It's usually said that it defended the dynasties that ruled China from the seventh century B.C. to the seventeenth century, and not the common people who lived there, who were more likely to perish during and even because of its construction. Its aim of endless protection, of forcing unlimited labor, has analogies with the boundless empty plazas. But in the case of the Wall, the space spreading as far as the eye can see has the function of delimiting an inside and an outside. Considering all the things that couldn't be done on the inside because the empire's men, time, and wealth were being used to mark the border with the diversity of the world left outside, one gets the feeling that the Wall was not only excluding the outside; it was also locking up the people who remained inside.

In 1987 a China opening up to international trade and foreign investment had UNESCO put the Great Wall on the list of World Heritage Sites. Can a wall built to separate, to distance China from the rest of humanity, be considered part of everyone's heritage? In April 2009, when I visited the Wall, the sober four-by-six-foot plaque marking its UNESCO designation contrasted with the gigantic billboard, dated 2008 and displayed higher, atop one of the mountains that the Wall crosses, which bore the slogan for the Olympic games that had been held in China that year: "One world, one dream." Why must we have only one dream? Don't borders erected and guarded by walls, soldiers, and thousands of surveillance cameras (which the Great Wall also has) add up to a paradoxical way of saying there's only one valid dream? The obsessive wall and the Olympic billboard exclude everyone else's dreams, turning their backs on diversity.

Great empty spaces and walls devoted to the infinite were once devices for exercising or signifying despotic powers. They continue to have that function in authoritarian regimes and in democracies that discriminate against foreigners, against their neighbors, and thus they mark emphatic distances. But nowadays there are other motives for creating such huge, empty areas. Dean MacCannell (1992: 2) relates them to a historical moment when "the human community . . . can no longer contain everything that it does contain, at least not in the framework of older ground rules." He has looked at this sort of experience in relation to the growth of tourism, migration, and the numbers of refugees. And also to the privatization of large territories, even whole countries, and their aggression against the dispossessed. "The earth, the ground, only appears to provide reference points for the sedentary" (4).

In a broader sense, like the sense in which this book links artistic practices and visual cultures to contemporary discontents, we can read the growth of empty spaces and confining walls in the key of the loss of a social narrative. The difficulty of constructing global cultural and political legislation—the absence of worldwide forms of governance— makes unifying narratives like those of the World Heritage program a little hard to swallow. Although the UNESCO policy has its valuable aspects, from the perspective of preserving cultural phenomena it doesn't resolve intercultural conflicts, nor can it support a narrative of worldwide integration.

We shouldn't end with the regressive or authoritarian meaning of empty spaces and the loss of a social narrative as its only significance or function. In later chapters I will try alternate focuses, such as looking at alien status as uprootedness and lacking something or as liberation and an impetus to creativity. Now I'd like to bring in the experience of a group of artists, known collectively as Campement Urbain, who came together in the Paris suburbs where rebellions against interethnic discrimination burst out in the fall of 2005. The project turned on its head the dominant discourse, which explained these violent acts as the result of the loss of social ties. Under the title "I and Us," Campement Urbain "mobilized some of the people to create a seemingly paradoxical space, a 'totally useless, fragile, and unproductive' space that was open to everyone and under everyone's protection, but that could only be occupied by one person at a time for solitary contemplation or meditation" (Rancière 2008: 70). A collective struggle for a solitary place? "The ability to be alone only seemed like a social experience made impossible by the conditions of life in the *banlieues*," the poor neighborhoods where foreigners and the children of immigrants lived. This empty place presupposes a community of people who are able to be by themselves, to enunciate a self within "an aesthetic or dissensual community." In a video that Sylvie Blocher made about this action, we see people from the neighborhood wearing T-shirts emblazoned with phrases that each chose as their own aesthetic mottos; one veiled woman wrote on hers, "I want an empty word that I could fill" (70).

The Global Distribution of Symbolic Power (Gabriel Orozco)

The notions of national and world heritage were always problematic, but they seem even more mistaken in this globalizing age, when news of cultural items and events spreads through every continent, sparking clashes between hostile heritages and among public, private, and social, local, national, and transnational actors.

I've said that, historically, a nation's heritage (national museums, great walls) reaffirms something about itself, valuing it more highly than comparable heritages of others, and by the same token dividing people. If it makes any sense to call it part of world heritage, it's not so much because we can all be proud of hundreds of faraway sites that we'll never get to know, but because, due to intercontinental tourism or to the fact that the sites were filmed or associated with some world event such as the Olympics, knowledge of a few of them has been spread as part of a globalized imaginary.

The many factors that must combine in order to turn a cultural item or work of art into a bit of world heritage call for a more flexible theory than the polarized concepts that have been used to organize the distribution and concentration of power: colonizer/colonized, North/South, East/West. The first studies of globalization, such as those by Ulrich Beck and Roland Robertson, emphasized how much interdependence among nations there is in the globalizing process. With time, we see that this isn't a matter of unlimited interdependence or of the constant interdependence of everyone with everyone else, but an asymmetric and selective interdependence in which we participate unequally. This is something more complex than a fluid circulation of people, capital, goods, and messages among all societies.

The notions of East and West, for example, lost coherence, as Renato Ortiz has shown in his book on Japan and "Modernity-World." In it, he analyzes several examples of how the national origins of material and symbolic products can be diluted: McDonald's enjoys a higher growth rate in Asia than in the United States; many cartoons originally made in the United States are now produced in Asian countries, but manga, karaoke, and certain video games that seem a part of Japan's cultural heritage are gaining fan bases in plenty of countries far from their place of origin. "Madonna is no longer North American, in the same way that Doraemon is no longer Japanese" (Ortiz 2000: 173). With regard to items of food and clothing and sports such as sumo wrestling, "Westernness and Japaneseness act as signic references, but at no point do they constitute forces that can structure the market in symbolic goods and lifestyles" (148).

From a non-ethnocentric geopolitical perspective, "every place has its own west, and everywhere is a west for somewhere else," as David Morley notes, quoting Naoki Sakai's citation of an earlier observation by Gramsci. If the continent of Europe assigned itself the position of The West, that's because its modern domination of the planet gave it the power to make the maps. In the late twentieth century this privileged position, having moved to the United States, led Sakai to write that the West could be defined as "the group of countries whose governments [at any given moment] have declared . . . their military and political affiliation with the USA" (Sakai 2001: 82, quoted in Morley 2006: 178). There's no religion, no specific form of economic life, democratic politics, or artistic or architectural styles that would agree to be an index of "Westernness" unless it first forgot how widespread it was in other lands or how partially it represented what was happening in the vast heterogeneity that is Euro-America.

In South and East Asia the most persuasive models of modernity do not come from the United States but from several Asian capitals. In Vietnam, among other places, the symbols and products of popular culture that "symbolise the desirable forms of urban cosmopolitanism and 'cool' for many young Vietnamese people" are "Taiwanese soap operas, Hong Kong videos, Cantopop and Japanese computer games and 'Manga'— rather than those of America" (Morley 2006: 184). There are many modernities, and their centers are mobile.

The opposition of inside and outside vanishes in more places than China or Japan. Everywhere you look, the notions of importing and exporting, traveling abroad or returning home, are insufficient to describe what's going on. There are plenty of reasons to think that certain countries, accustomed for centuries to conceive of themselves as empires, may want to expand as nations and subordinate others. But even this has to be imagined in a different way than in the past. The mutually engaged economies of China and the United States (due, for example, to Chinese investments in the dollar), the parallel positions that the two countries take at intergovernmental meetings, and the similar analyses of those meetings in the Western and Chinese press demonstrate interdependence more than they do distinct projects or one country's fear of being dominated by the other.

This interdependence is asymmetrical and unequal. It obliges us to change our research methods and the way we are present on the strategic stage. Domination versus submission? This polarized, vertical concept, discredited by political and economic analysts, is also unhelpful for understanding an unstable globalized cultural system whose logic is changing in multidirectional ways and in which the positions of "the dominant" and "the dominated" do not describe compact groups. The bookstores of Beijing, Shanghai, and Tokyo carry plenty of works by Western authors translated into Chinese and Japanese, a few magazines and newspapers in English, only a handful in French or German, and rarely any at all in Spanish. The large Instituto Cervantes building in Beijing and the rapid growth of Spanish as a third or fourth language in some Chinese universities has no correlate in the publications that are for sale or the media that comes in from the West. Unlike what is happening in several Latin American countries where the cultural activities of the Spanish state are matched by those of Spanish corporations (the newspaper El País, publishing houses based in Madrid and Barcelona, corporate foundations such as Telefónica's), in China and Japan even those Spanish companies that are quite active in business display little cultural eloquence.

One Western corporation that stands out in China is Iberia, with its well-appointed building for exhibiting and selling bilingual Spanish-Chinese books, located at The Factory. This is a neighborhood of Beijing, also known as 798 Art Zone, where aging electronics factories have been converted into artists' workshops and galleries, some of them from "the West," as well as cafés and small cutting-edge cultural centers—something like New York's SoHo and certain East Berlin neighborhoods a few years ago: aging neighborhoods taken over and renovated by artists, gallery owners, and independent cultural initiatives. In Beijing corporations are engaged in precarious activities: the most cosmopolitan art, reviving traditional materials and craft techniques, together with works that reread national or revolutionary iconography in a parodic way. Especially noteworthy is the Cynical Realism movement, which has received international media and market attention. Yue Minjun, for example, creates gigantic sculptures evocative of monumental Buddhist or Maoist figures in exaggerated laughing poses that, according to the artist, express "a sense of loss, of meaninglessness in the world" (Barboza 2008); they sell for as much as $600,000.

The relaxed character of the streets and exhibits in The Factory, the diversity of things people seek there, and the way visitors look, all suggest similarities between the art movement in China and the aesthetic trends and the economic and cultural crisis and rethinking in the West. The international boom in Chinese creativity, which is assuming a leading role in the major international biennales, fairs, auctions, and art magazines, has meant that there are now five Chinese artists listed among the ten best-selling artists in the world, when in the first year of the twenty-first century only one, Cai Guo-Qiang, had landed on the list of the top one hundred (Chen 2009). Also active in this context are those who sell art over the Internet without ever meeting the buyers (the websites are in Chinese, Japanese, and English), those who try unsuccessfully to scale this summit, and critics such as Zhu Qi who are alarmed by the dizzying pace of the market, which is more about pleasing Western buyers and new Chinese collectors ("seventy percent of all collectors have entered the art world in the past two years") than it is about asking whether they have "something to say" (Chen 2009).

We've also seen that this is a *selective* globalization. More African, Asian, and Latin American artists are being exhibited than ever before in the flagship museums of New York, London, Madrid, Beijing, and Tokyo. A few critics and curators from "third-world" regions, such as Okwui Enwezor from Nigeria, director of *Documenta XI* in 2002, Cuauhtémoc Medina from Mexico, curator of Latin American Art Collections at the Tate Modern from 2002 to 2008, and Gerardo Mosquera from Cuba, adjunct curator at the New Museum of Contemporary Art in New York, have been recognized as expert interlocutors in the major metropolitan centers, but there aren't more than twenty of them. The encyclopedia of trends, artists, and tastes in contemporary art is opening up, more ways of knowing and of creating are being considered, and there is interaction among the widest range of scenes. But has the hierarchical structure changed? For whom?

In some international relationships it is appropriate to speak of post-coloniality; in others colonial or imperialist ties persist. Perhaps the most comprehensive notions are those of the international division of labor and the global redistribution of cultural power. In a sense analogous to the classical division of labor between raw-material-exporting countries and industrialized countries, in the realm of cultural production we find a division between countries that concentrate on technological access to advanced resources, with consumption spread beyond the elites, and on the other hand, countries that have little industrial development of symbolic goods and an uncompetitive position for participating in the art, music, film, television, and digital markets.

In film production, digital technologies have helped separate the production, editing, audience research, marketing, and distribution stages. Studying recent changes in Hollywood, Toby Miller concludes that film studios no longer have to manage all these moments in film-making from Los Angeles but can instead subcontract with companies large and small, or with individuals, in other countries to carry out specific activities: the Hollywood economy is thus now said to be based on a model of "decentralized accumulation" (Wayne 2003: 84, quoted in Miller 2005: 116). In this globally scaled regime of audiovisual production, Hollywood "coproduces" films transnationally, buying cheap the labor of screenwriters, actors, technicians, even landscapes, and distribution in other countries, all of which is subordinated to the strategies of multinational corporations. They achieve this with the support of the protectionist policies and tax privileges that the U.S. government offers its film industry, as well as through international pressure on other countries to favor the expansion of its cinema.

There are similarities between the audiovisual industry and what's been happening in heritage governance and the visual arts. In analyzing how historical and natural heritage sites are chosen and established as such, we've just seen that the unequal recognition received by African, Asian, and Latin American countries derives from the fact that, to put it briefly, these regions provide a large portion of our landscapes and memory, while the metropolitan centers supply the aesthetic criteria and the cultural evaluation. Some contribute local forms of knowledge and images; others, the arrangements for financing, organization, interpretation, and the ability to market the "products" to the whole world.

In managing the visual arts and running biennales and international fairs, Europe and the United States are still ahead, but Asian countries are becoming more active participants, with their new museums, collectors, and foundations supported by their own endowments, transnational funds, and strong support from public funding. They are also more actively involved in producing cultural and critical discourses about art; though the great majority of art books and magazines, especially in the Northern Hemisphere, are written in English, a more diverse map of universities, museums, and fairs rebalances the international production and evaluation between North and South, East and West. To take one of the main European examples: from *Documenta I* through *Documenta X* there were thirteen Latin American artists, five African artists, and even fewer from Asia; in *Documenta XI*, curated by Okwui Enwezor, of the 116 participating artists, forty came from other continents, and of the five preparatory conceptual platforms or encounters, three were put on in New Delhi, Santa Lucia, and Lagos.

I'd like to point out, apropos of this chapter's theme, one of the common ways in which the interpretive power of critics forms divisions between metropolitan and peripheral art: while works created in the centers are looked at as aesthetic deeds, the works of African, Asian, and Latin American artists are typically read as part of their visual culture or cultural heritage. One of the most widely recognized Mexican artists worldwide, Gabriel Orozco, who has been given individual exhibits at biennales and top-notch museums in the United States and Europe, who has studios in Paris, New York, and Mexico City, is still being interpreted as a spokesman for Mexican culture.

In a collection of essays on Orozco, a number of metropolitan critics who on other occasions have shown a distrust of nationalism try to discover how this artist represents his home country. According to

Jean Fisher (2009: 20–22), the fact that "the sentient body remains a referent in Orozco's work," as well as his use of "salvage and recycling, of improvisation and taking advantage of immediate situations," derive from "lived experience in Latin American societies" and "spring from a sensibility and life-world not wholly appropriable to Euro-American categories." In Orozco's works Fisher finds an "intimate connection between sex and violence" that "points, in turn, to the trauma of Conquest" (22), or "confusion and chaotic energy" that correspond to "the constantly changing states of decay and renewal characteristic of daily life in Mexico City" (25). She confidently declares that in Mexico "cultural artifacts, from architecture and domestic furniture to pottery, traditionally possess a sturdy geometry that organizes form and space in relation to the demands of the human body rather than to an Ideal of pure form independent of any concrete reality so characteristic of the Euro-American tradition" (25). I don't really know what Fisher means when she speaks of a "sturdy geometry," but I feel dizzy when I watch her grouping together all of architecture, household furniture, and pottery, giving them all the job of adapting form and space to the demands of the body without bothering about formal ideals independent of concrete reality: is it possible to lump together pre-Columbian, colonial, and neocolonial architecture, that of Barragán and Norten, and the ceramics of Ocumicho, Jalisco, and Oaxaca in this way? I won't even mention the household furniture, because it would take a very abstract form that had little to do with reality to encompass such a heterogeneous mess.

Fisher (2009: 21) praises Orozco for having distanced himself from "Mexicanicity," understood as "a marketable and institutionalized national 'identity,' invented from a sentimentalized past." She also makes clear that she doesn't plan to fall into the temptation of ascribing the origin of Orozco's works "to the melancholy that inscribes the stereotype of the Mexican character," and to convince us she asserts that "there is a wit and sense of optimism in Orozco's chimeras" (24). Sometimes that's true; at other times it isn't. But instead of arguing about it, I'd rather look at what the point is of all this preoccupation with finding confusion, chaotic energy, and other homemade furniture in order to situate what she so often calls "opaque" and "enigmatic" in Orozco's attempts. What if, instead of looking for national causes, we tried looking at the enigma and its opacity?

Elsewhere in the book, in his extraordinary dialogues with Buchloh, Orozco talks about how Germans showed very little interest in his Schwalbe project (photographs of yellow East German scooters parked in pairs around the streets of Berlin), which was better understood in other countries. "Working for the context," Orozco concludes, "can be demagogic. I think it's a problem to try to say something to people in their own context" (Buchloh 2005: 103).

It is obvious and one-sided to link the skull that was Orozco's contribution at *Documenta X* with Mexican visual culture, as has been done. The skull also has forerunners in Cezanne and Picasso, and, as Orozco emphasizes, in New York, where he made the piece, it is linked with the world of rock and heavy metal. It is curious that in the field of art, where there is such a long tradition of dealing with polysemy and ambiguity, so many critics behave like immigration police. *Define yourself: Are you a Mexican or a world artist?* "Neither of these postures interests me," Orozco responds (Buchloh 2005: 108). Why this maniacal pursuit of national roots for an artist who uses bicycles from the Netherlands, an elevator from Chicago, a French billiard ball, German and Italian scooters, and things he found in a cemetery in Mali? Maybe because it would be hard to bear the trauma of finding that national origin has become relative. I recall something Hal Foster said, to the effect that the deconstruction of the subject and of national orders, which was experienced in the late twentieth century as liberation, is now felt as trauma. Let's not be so satisfied about the death of art and the disappearance of the nation.

This is where Orozco's reflections on how he works inside and outside of the studio come in. "I took the word 'studio' literally," he explains in his interview with Hans Ulrich Obrist, "not as a space of production but as a time of knowledge. That time of knowledge can be generated in different places: outdoors or indoors" (Obrist 2003: 646). Later he compares the models of artists' studios, such as Warhol's factory, Richard Serra's workshops located all over the world, and Beuys's notion that his work is like that of a teacher, so that his studio comes to resemble a school. "I can use all of these models. But my favorites are the street,

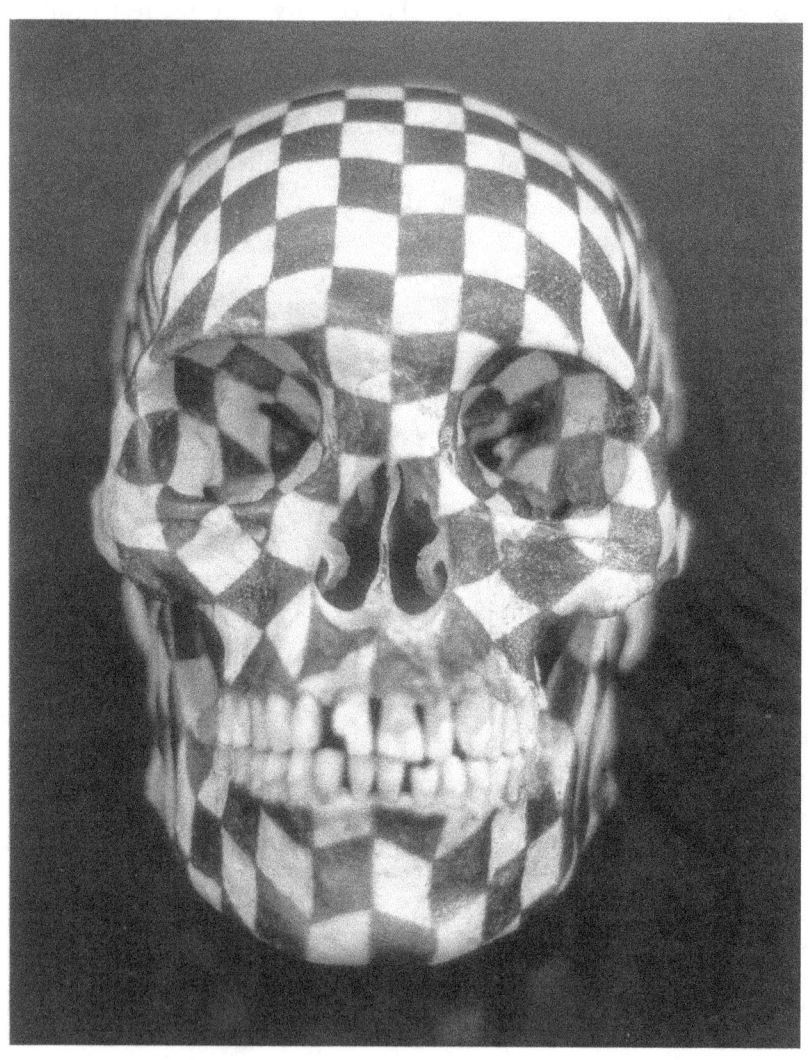

FIGURE 2.1 Gabriel Orozco, *Papalotes negros* (Black Kites), 1997. Graphite on skull, 21.6 × 12.7 × 15.9 cm.

kitchen, and table. And, most important of all, light. All of these supports, on a temporary basis, are important to my work, but where there is good light, there is my time to work" (647).

Thus his studio houses are not so much production spaces as what he calls "platforms for thinking" (Obrist 2003: 648). When he talks about how he has organized his houses, he maintains that "architecture should be a receiving space, a yielding space, not an imposing space" (650). It receives what happens outside, and it yields to what can't happen inside a workshop—what bursts into a cemetery in Timbuktu, a Cachoeira market in Brazil, or a Mexican beach.

At this point it makes no sense to demand that Orozco's work be affiliated with a particular country. But that doesn't make him a nomad, indifferent to the places where experiences happen. I don't see him devoted to merely wandering about through cities and countries but rather to turning his "open houses" into "intimate places" that are receptive, private, and experimental. "I don't like walls. I don't like dark rooms, and I don't like vitrines. I always try to generate the notion of landscape, maybe a forest, maybe a desert" (Obrist 2003: 652).

How can we define this search for home in the midst of global dispersion, this interaction between what stays put and what can be seen on the other side? Orozco says that he's "not interested in the horizon very much. I believe in the possibility of several vanishing points or gravitational points. That's why I mix up sculptures and images, and I like the tension and possible translation between the vanishing point and the gravitational point" (Obrist 2003: 653). I like this as a definition of imminence. Faced with critics from the metropolitan centers who want to reduce his work to a national or cultural heritage, the artist speaks of light as support, of unresolved tensions.

Here I find an attractive concept of what art could be today. And of something more: the way we, as artists or as plain citizens, can find meaning and intensity in experience beyond passports or the frivolous pretence of ignoring them. This tension between not living as if national markers were all that mattered and at the same time living in a world where passports remain important is what makes us feel the trauma and the drama. The question left hanging is how to transcend the too-cool conceptualism that reigns over the contemporary art scene in order to

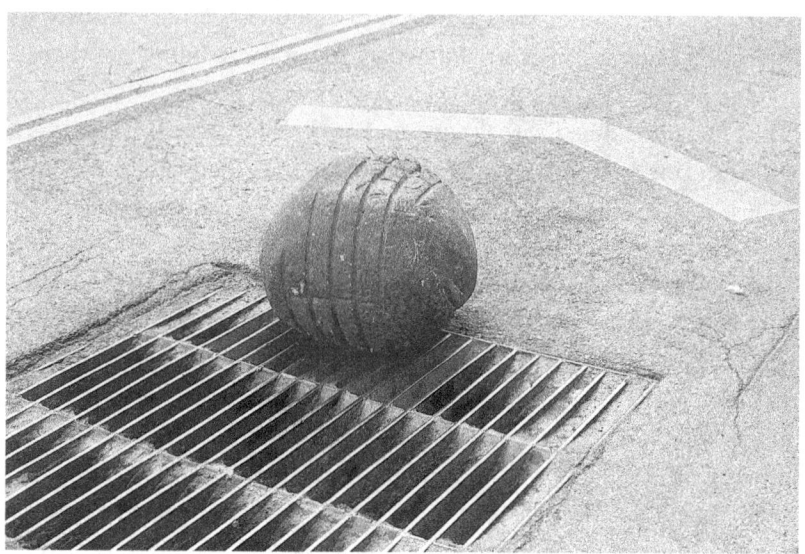

make room for the dramatic sense of belonging to lots of places, or of being a migrant and not fully having a place, or of being able, like Orozco's ball of modeling clay roaming the streets, to count only on indecisive markers of identity.

I don't want to suggest a predominant trend: neither the disastrous ascendancy of the hegemonic countries nor the correction of inequalities through increased participation by *all* the marginalized or excluded. Neither the wide range of biennales nor the fragile trends in the art markets authorize a linear view or a landscape structured as rigid blocks. What do the reports in Artprice over the past few years reveal? The "bulimia" of shoppers in the 1980s came to a halt in 1991. Since 2000 the market has become active again, in part because of the emergence of new collectors from Asia, Russia, and the Middle East. The breakdown of the global economy and the plunge in U.S. and European stock market values in the second half of 2008 led to a fall in sales (down 7.5 percent in the first trimester of 2008 compared with the preceding trimester) and then generated volatility that endured to the end of 2009. After

2008 New York lost its leadership position, giving up first place in sales to London. China came to occupy third place in the world, and the growing presence of artists and collectors from China, as well as from Indian and some Arab countries, changed global preferences: prices and sales of contemporary artists, those born after 1945, went up, while the percentages of art from the nineteenth century and the first half of the twentieth century were down (Artprice 2008). Of the ten top-selling painters born after 1945, seven were Chinese.

If we look at the ten artists from all periods who had the highest earnings in 2009, third place, right after Picasso and Warhol at the top of the list, went to Qi Baishi. As a portion of global sales, according to Artprice, the United States occupied the first spot with 27.9 percent; the United Kingdom had 21.3 percent; and China bumped France from third place by getting 17.4 percent (Serra 2010).

We'd be making a mistake if, ignoring the instability of the past few years, we concluded that the art world is moving from New York to London and a couple of large Asian cities. On the current map of this division of cultural labor, there are *national* conditions at work (unequal access to economic, technological, and educational development) and also *regional* policies that can expand national cultures or isolate them. We find countries associated with cultural and communications programs that foster the development of their arts and cultural industries (the European Union), countries that favor the transnational expansion of their industries and of cultural commerce (United States, China, Japan, Canada), and other countries that routinely insist on a management policy that orients their artistic and cultural heritage inward (most of Latin America). The inequality in the production, distribution, and access to cultural goods cannot be explained as simple cultural imperialism or colonialism (though these behaviors do subsist) but rather as a result of a combination of expansive processes, exercises in domination and discrimination, cases of nationalist inertia, and cultural politics that cannot act in the new logic of exchange.

As we've seen, it's a matter of a map with lots of multidirectional actors and processes, where the globalization of some localities and the isolation of most others is shaped by interactions among states, private corporations, migrations, and cultural, media, and tourist movements.

This map calls not for a doctrine about world heritage, as impracticable as universalist aesthetics, but for another sort of debate on transnational disagreements about what constitutes value.

The contingent, variable nature of aesthetic and cultural values in relations between North and South, or between countries that are developed, peripheral, and emerging because of greater mobility for their actors, has been eloquently expressed in texts by artists, curators, and critics. As one curator, Cuauhtémoc Medina (2007), has declared, we no longer talk about "living" or "residing" in particular cities or countries, but of "being based" or "having your base" in a place temporarily. "To be based" in such-and-such a site suggests an ephemeral residence, one step in a career. Nevertheless, Medina notes, it would be wrong to consider the global system as a complete coming together of particularities. There are structures (and not just flows) that differentiate between at least two elements: "the (private) jet set" and "the proletariat jet set." The jet set in art is a partner in the transactions of the upper classes and leading institutions that inflate the prices of art investments and produce "the overheated global cultural market." The proletariat jet set is composed of the artists, curators, and critics who travel tourist class, occasionally form part of group exhibits, and sometimes try "to inject a measure of critical tension" into this global circuit.

Heritage and Art: The Conditions They Share

In the humanities, the social sciences, and the management of cultural goods, modern and contemporary art is usually held separate from cultural heritage. Historians and critics, museums and biennales deal with art, doing it as if they had solved the problem of defining their object and were able to set it neatly apart from other items of culture. Heritage is the business of archaeologists, anthropologists, and historians who have been educated in a different way from the ones who analyze art, as well as the museums and institutions that specialize in distant eras and peripheral societies.

In Mexico, for example, the administration of art and cultural heritage is divided between historically differentiated organizations: the National Institute of Anthropology and History is devoted to preserving, restoring, and administering pre-Columbian, colonial, and nineteenth-century monuments, museums, and artifacts; the National Institute of Fine Arts does the same for items from the twentieth and twenty-first centuries. In Europe, though a distinction is drawn between "ethnographic museums" and "art museums," specialists from both kinds agree that it is impossible to draw a line clearly demarcating them, and that the separation between the ethnographic and the artistic is decided "less in terms of the objects" than by the inertia of the institutions that possess or exhibit them (Mack 2007: 22).

Instead of taking a long time drawing distinctions between artifacts that are valued only for their historical significance and those that are appreciated for their aesthetic value, it is better to examine the uses of heritage, the points of agreement and conflict between eras and cultural productions inspired by different objectives. It seems more productive to compare the many responses that arise from the uses (economic, political, religious, media, touristic, and aesthetic) of what is being called heritage or art.

That would reformulate the study and administration of the national heritage, not only as the selection and conservation of pieces of extraordinary value, but as a way of participating in the cognitive, ethical, and sociopolitical dilemmas of interculturality. It would perhaps be simpler to carry out these tasks if we had some sort of world government capability that could arbitrate disputes as we try to live together. Neither the United Nations in the realms of economics and politics nor UNESCO in the education and cultural fields has the power to overcome its modest role as the stage on which political and intercultural disagreements are talked about, and many of them are silenced by the vetoes of the more powerful nations. Even the agreements adopted by majority vote, such as the Convention on Cultural Diversity, have little effect on international quarrels: they can't stop national heritages from being plundered during wars, or keep migrant cultures from being abused, or even regulate the trade of tangible and intangible goods to make access to them more equitable. So long as such a government does not exist, a nonethnocentric view, one that isn't simplistically culturalist or mercantile, must pay attention to the many forms in which human practices are given value and the ways they combine with each other and confront each other.

I'm not ignoring the importance and the necessity of preserving the artifacts that bear witness to developments or extraordinary moments in cultures. The action of the UNESCO World Heritage Committee has been useful in supporting awareness and positive valuations of some cultural and natural sites, in conserving and rehabilitating them, in educating specialists and giving strategic assistance in the processes of decay, destruction, catastrophes, and war. But this job will remain limited and erratic if it continues to depend on the abstract concept of humanity as conceived in the Enlightenment and cannot accept conceptual instability, variable meanings, in the ways the artifacts are used, and position itself to be effective in international disputes.

We've seen too many such international organizations fail not to perceive that, within the unequal division of labor and cultural power, the lack of governance has implied—for a long time—that the interdependence begun by globalization is going to be contradicted by the processes of deglobalization. We're witnessing national or regional entrenchment and invasions in which the preservation of historical and artistic heritages, as well as the democratization of access to those things, has been deeply harmed or simply abolished. This is one of the conclusions that can be drawn from such events as what happened in Iraq on April 14, 2003.

Robert Fisk, correspondent for the *Independent* in Baghdad—the "cultural capital of the Arabic world" for nearly a thousand years—watched as the Qur'anic Library and the National Archives went up in flames thirty meters high: "First came the looters, then came the arsonists." Fisk ran to the offices of the occupying troops, the U.S. Marines, "gave the map location, the precise name—in Arabic and English—of the buildings" that were on fire, and told them the smoke could be seen from five miles away. At the scene of the fire, the journalist found documents from the Ottoman caliphate and the Iraqi royal archives sailing through the air. The burning papers included accounts of camel thefts and attacks on pilgrims; he picked up off the floor a description of the Sublime Porte of Istanbul, descriptions of "the opening of the first telephone exchange in the Hejaz" and of "the theft of clothes from a camel train by Ali bin Kassem," letters from over the centuries on matters ranging from the history of Mecca to Lawrence of Arabia. "There was a time," he recalled, "when the Arabs said that their books were written in Cairo, printed in Beirut and read in Baghdad. Now they burned libraries in Baghdad." The U.S. officer who received the report, instead of mobilizing his troops, commented to a colleague, "This guy says some biblical library is on fire" (Fisk 2005: 1224–25).

>

CHAPTER THREE

REAPPROPRIATING OBJECTS

Art, Marketing, or Culture?

Let us look at some of the sticky points in the aesthetic treatment of heritage, reconsidering what is currently understood by the words *ours* and *theirs*, by art and artifact, in national politics, in the strategies of researchers and museums, and in the practice of some artists.

How to Build an Artistic-Heritage Brand

Writers such as James Clifford (1997) and Lourdes Méndez (2009) have observed similar museological, discursive, and aesthetic logics in ethnographic and contemporary art museums; they have in common the ways they value objects, their cosmopolitan vocation in spite of their devotion to local cultures, and their simultaneous hospitality to traditional and recent material. I turn first to the example I find most eloquent: the Quai Branly Museum in Paris. This institution, inaugurated in June 2006, is doubly interesting. First, it aims at renovating the criteria for selecting, exhibiting, and evaluating objects from non-European cultures; it aims to renovate the relations between architecture, cultural artifacts, and art; and it seeks to return France to the center of global exchange. Second, both before and after it opened, the Quai Branly Museum generated studies and debates among anthropologists, museologists, artists, architects, and cultural studies scholars from many countries, on a level perhaps never produced by any other museum, biennale, or artistic or cultural event.

The museum grew from a presidential project (on the part of Jacques Chirac) to combine the collections of the Musée National des Arts d'Afrique et d'Océanie and the ethnographic department of the Musée de l'Homme, the intellectual and political concepts of which had been criticized as anachronistic. One objective was to produce an outstanding, internationally recognized museum and so regain France's leading cultural position, which, according to Serge Guilbaut's (1983) well-known book, it had lost when New York "stole the idea of modern art" in the mid-twentieth century. The idea was to generate an event as major as the creation thirty years earlier of the Centre Pompidou, devoted to modern art.

Why doesn't the Quai Branly Museum sport a name that tells us anything about its contents? They tried to give it one: first the Museum of Arts and Civilizations, then the Museum of First Arts (a stilted effort to avoid saying "primitive arts"). In the end, it was given a name that alludes to the district of Paris where it is located—a result that contrasts sharply with its announced goals: "to do justice to non-European cultures" and "to recognize the place occupied by their artistic expressions in our cultural legacy, and also our debt to the societies that produced them." President Chirac's inaugural address promised to break "with a long history of disdain" and "to return all their dignity to humiliated peoples," and proclaimed a rejection of any sort of hierarchy, whether in the arts or among peoples.

Architecture and museology were tasked with "celebrating the universality of the human race." The Quai Branly building, designed by Jean Nouvel, with many of its walls made of glass to reflect the garden designed by Gilles Clément that surrounds it, "filters the natural light in order to give the gallery the atmosphere of being inside a grotto," according to the museum guidebook (Musée du Quai Branly 2006). Setting aside the works of "eight Australian aborigine artists" on the south façade and the ceilings, the most prominent nationality at the museum is that of its architect and landscape designer, both of them French aborigines. Then there is the fact that the museum looks out onto the Seine and is situated not far from the Grand Palais, near Les Invalides, and almost next door to that French contribution to world iconography, the Eiffel Tower.

The interior offers an enormous open space where more than 3,500 works from Africa, Asia, Oceania, and the Americas are on display. Several of the museum's brochures assert that the museum's lack of partition walls favors "communication" and "exchanges among civilizations." The visitor can experience this communicative fluidity by walking through the museum and viewing costumes, masks, weapons, canoes, and musical instruments arranged in glass cases without any obvious structure. All this is oriented by maps, still images, and animations, as well as music and multimedia set designs suggestive of multicultural contexts.

The route that visitors take through the museum was conceived by the architect and museologists as a series of passages through tunnels, caves, and dark gorges, in which the eye is attracted by the glass cases and the rest areas where the works are displayed. These provide the viewer with no contextualization, only texts introducing the halls and a few videos of rituals or everyday scenes from the societies represented. The lack of explanation and especially the darkness throughout the museum do nothing to communicate the meaning of the pieces and the historical misunderstandings or conflicts between peoples; instead it sets forth a uniform aestheticization. African, Asian, and American works, and works from distinct regions in each of these continents, are all "integrated" into a single discourse. Very few dates are given and almost no historical or social orientation. Everything—objects from different eras, videos of jungles and high-tech music—flows together into a single show that makes operative, in the words of Clifford (2007: 14), "Chirac's aesthetic universalism and Nouvel's mystical/natural environment."

The texts emphasize the "elegance," "inventive richness," stylization, and exceptionality of the pieces. But because these concepts are applied indiscriminately to diverse cultures, while the tension between monumentality and miniaturization is marked in every geographic area, and on top of this, changing museological conceptions fail to pick up on ways appropriate to each society for staging their works, it is easy to feel unsure about which continent we're in. Clifford (2007: 10) overheard the conversation of a visitor trying to find his companion by cell phone: "'So where are *you*? I think I'm in America.'"

The museum guidebook provides descriptions that contextualize each object. As in other museums, only a minority go around reading the printed guidebook or listening to the audio guides. The dim lighting makes it hard to read the few posted texts, and it discourages the idea of seeking information that the museum hasn't provided by its staging of exhibits. The guidebook states that the selected pieces "reflect the great French phases of collection" and "the objects collected on expeditions." The contemporary outlook of the Quai Branly Museum can be seen in the building and its inclusion of a multimedia center that holds 250,000 documents and three thousand journal titles, rooms for reading text and viewing film, lecture and symposia halls, reading rooms with children's sections, and areas for archive consultation—in short, multiple access to pieces of specialized knowledge. But the exhibition, its most visited area, presents an aestheticized reading with universalizing aims that have been conditioned by French colonial history, centering on the exhibition of what the museum judges to be "masterpieces." The guidebook pays attention to the history of the continents "but also to the history of the collectors" (Musée du Quai Branly 2006: 153) and to the preferences incorporated into the European gaze by artists like Picasso and Gauguin who were fascinated by African and American forms.

A visitor who reaches the multimedia center will find an exuberant collection of photographs, books, travelers' diaries, and reports from French and European ethnological missions that document the collection criteria in each country. A visitor might also get a glimpse of how the European gaze directed at "the others," with its mixture of curiosity and conquest, was slowly constructed. The guidebook offers a less ingenuous view than is customary in museums of ethnography and non-Western art, together with slips revealing its Eurocentric vision, as when it refers to the pieces representing the god Gon, from the republic of Benin, produced in the mid-nineteenth century, by saying that "they are surprisingly modern in execution and reminiscent of the formally audacious works of Picasso" (Musée du Quai Branly 2006: 298).

Here we see once more the problems with the notion of "world heritage." How can we construct a universally valid vision for interrelating

diverse cultures, allowing us to compare them and find a common de-
nominator between them without denying them their singularity? In the
American section, the museum calls on the debatable Lévi-Straussian
theory of the unity of thought among Amerindian populations, according to which a single myth can be found in a transformed fashion in
several different regions. In other cases the museum poses as a stage for
reconciliation, where works can dialogue.

The "hanging gallery" that rises like an island above the main con-
course through the museum is a space for temporary exhibits where
selected specialists try out other ways of dealing with intercultural complexity. When I visited the museum in January 2009, it was featuring a
special exhibit, *Planète Métisse: To Mix or Not to Mix*, curated by Serge
Gruzinski and Alessandra Russo. This display put forth a less unifying
reading than the permanent exhibit by asking whether the convergences
between objects and images from the fifteenth century to the present,
from the Bourbon Codex and an African sculpture of Queen Victoria to
U.S. westerns and the films of Wong Kar-wai, require a knowledge of
colonization, globalization, the clash of cultures, and *mestizaje* as a key
to interpretation. It also alluded to the place of recent migrants in Paris
(a "mestizo city") and informed visitors which parts of the French capital they should go to if they wanted to "savor Asian culinary traditions."

What is this "mix-mix"? Not classical, not primitive, not ethnic, not
folkloric. It alternates among these different positions. Although this
temporary exhibit, through Serge Gruzinski's research on mestizaje, offers a well thought-out view of intercultural slippages, the unsure aestheticization of the permanent museology largely keeps the museum's
vocation indeterminate—as does its name. Branding it after its location
in Paris was an attempt to "solve" its lack of conceptual definition. When
the magazine *Le Débat* asked the museum's director, Stéphane Martin,
why he had named it after the quay on the Seine where it is located,
he replied that he had defended the choice of a "conventional, non-
programmatic term, because it gives more freedom to the evolution of
the institution and allows it to adhere to society's expectations" (Martin 2007: 10). It's true that other museums, such as the Guggenheim,
have branded themselves. There are precedents in France such as the
Centre Pompidou, named after the president who promoted its creation

(though it is known locally as the Beaubourg, after the neighborhood where it is located), and the Musée d'Orsay, also named after the quay on which it was built. For the Quai Branly Museum, where names alluding to its contents (arts and civilizations, primitive arts) were rejected, the choice of an arbitrary brand should make us think about a couple of problems with the museum's declared mission: first, the fact that it cannot clearly name the exceptional character it is attributing to the pieces it has put on display; second, the fact that this is a museum that doesn't know what to call other people.

It's worth pointing out that, at a time when social networks, distribution among groups, and many cultural activities are associated with commercial brands or trademarks, France is an atypical case. It identifies its artistic possessions or products with the names of presidents or urban locations instead of participating in this international idiom of icons, in which we are invited to name ourselves after and identify ourselves with the stuff that is being sold to us. The French haven't avoided the prevailing currents of global capitalism—privileging the symbol over content and function, franchising their brands (as they have done with the Louvre)—but they are seeking to attract tourists and the media by using their presidents and Paris place names as their trademarks. Maybe this is because they haven't privatized the referents of their identities quite so much and because, even after two decades of neoliberalism, the French state still has a role as a social organizer.

From the "Authenticity" Canon to Intercultural Translation

Most critiques of the Quai Branly Museum center on its deficiencies as an institution that displays ethnographic material without proper contextualization. As Philippe Descola (2007) has argued, similar objections should be raised about art museums that don't ask about the historical and social background of the works they exhibit. They lean on post-Duchampian indefinition with regard to which objects are artistic and which are not, wavering between what tradition and the avant-garde decide is art, what the marketplace values, and what certain cultures hold in high esteem about themselves.

Many ethnographic and art museums feel that they have discovered a way to resolve the question of what is museum-worthy: by presenting multiple points of view. Both ethnographic and art museums tend to treat the perspectives of each local group, ethnicity, religious community, or gender as legitimate. Especially in the United States, Descola argues, though not there alone, museums appreciate these movements among actors as a reappropriation of their fate on the part of those who had been forgotten by history and as interesting manifestations of contemporary ethnogenesis. Community museums rarely problematize the scientific rigor of self-representation, its partiality, or the things it leaves out. Descola (2007: 144) jokingly suggests that the Quai Branly Museum could be defended as a sort of community museum, not because it displays the customs of the French—as the Museum of Arts and Popular Traditions does—but because "it is symptomatic of a certain universalist and encyclopedist view of world cultures characteristic of French tradition."

We thus find strong similarities between museums of art and museums of anthropology. For years both have been developing polyphonic museologies, multiple narratives in which objects "speak" with the meaning of those who made them, those who used them or saw them being used, those who collected or studied them. Expanding the range of audiovisual resources and settings helps to combine these kinds of knowledge and these gazes and to put them on display. Ethnographic objects and works of art can be seen in themselves and also by following their changing identities as they move from one context to another. The life of masks—which in some cultures are made not to last forever but to be used in a ritual and then discarded, as with Yup'ik masks in Alaska—is prolonged when they are later sold in a shop and perhaps discovered, as happened with this collection when André Breton and Robert Lebel found them in a New York boutique.

At the inaugural academic conference for the Quai Branly Museum, in which dozens of art historians, museologists, and anthropologists participated, John Mack synthesized one of their conclusions: "There are no ethnographic objects and no art objects. There are only objects regarded from ethnographic, aesthetic, or historic points of view, and it could be the same object seen from many different points of view" (Latour 2007: 371).

Descola analyzes the expressive qualities of some ancient objects that were not made with artistic intent but that inspire wonder today; he argues that beauty may have ways of renewing itself through different forms of ordering the contrasts between colors and balance. But we also know that the emotions these objects bring out in us are sometimes the result of misunderstandings and paradoxes. It is possible that particular secret correspondences between distant and current ways of identifying oneself, or of distinguishing oneself from one's neighbors, of reinforcing male domination, or of subjecting oneself to the unknown move today's occasional visitor to a museum or to a great wall. Our fascination can increase if we ask about their history and understand how they are recharged with meaning in different contexts and whether the museum (of anthropology or of art) offers understandings that are contained not in the object but rather in the trajectory of its appropriations.

Appropriations are movements of power. One antecedent of the Quai Branly Museum was the task that Chirac gave to his friend, the gallery owner Jacques Kerchache: to create a department of "first arts" in the Louvre. After examining the hundred "masterpieces" that Kerchache chose, Maurice Godelier found that eighty-three of them were linked to power—the power of African chiefs, of gods, of spirits. The beauty for which the gallery owner had chosen them was tied to this ethnographic dimension, which was "the sense of power, the bond between human beings and the invisible world, with the forces of nature." Godelier (2007: 27–28) concludes that "the borders between ethnography and art are blurry."

If what non-Western societies consider an aesthetic experience has to do with the relation between the things we keep under control and the things that escape us, between the visible and the invisible, between the forces of people and the forces of nature, then we see a family resemblance between these "first arts" and contemporary art. The specific nature of current art consists, as I said earlier, in working with the imminence of a revelation, in insinuating what cannot be said. This doesn't authorize us to ignore the different practices of the creators of the works and the ways they inscribed their works or performances in distinct social connections. The problem is how to interpret the continuities, coincidences, and discrepancies between what we value in ethnographic objects and in artworks for what they don't quite say.

It might be suggested that, just as art works with imminence, cultural heritage professionals deal with its opposite (*ex*-minence?). The artist stands in expectation of what hasn't yet happened; in contrast, people devoted to cultural heritage are attracted to items that are deteriorating or at risk of disappearing. Historians and archaeologists are fascinated by negative imminence. We find a remarkable family resemblance between Benjamin's (1968: 222, 255) definition of the artistic—that is, the aura—as "the unique phenomenon of a distance" and his assertion (though he was not speaking literally about cultural heritage) that we get to know the past when we "seize hold of a memory as it flashes up in a moment of danger."

What hasn't yet happened, what may disappear, the distant, the moment of danger: despite the uncertainty that these phrases suggest, don't forget how often they are related to power. Both museums (whether of art, anthropology, or history) and the media carry out exercises in power when they appropriate objects, select them, place them in more or less prominent locations, illuminate them, and edit them into narratives that freeze the virtual projection of attempts and reduce them to works. One way to deconstruct the partitions between the ethnographic and the artistic is to give an account of the historical operations through which these objects became beautiful and powerful. Another way is to question yourself and make explicit the acts by which museums and the media intervene in this course of resignifying.

Visual cultures, ordered as collections and trophies during the time of colonialism, arranged in hierarchical order by the authenticity of the objects at a certain stage of anthropology and national pride, might now be a site where communications and intercultural disagreements can test new ways of being translated. What can we understand about others, and how can we live with what we don't understand or don't accept? Some anthropologists are shifting toward this inquiry and away from the old questions about the extraordinary value of certain items; in the same way, some artists are less interested in the exceptionalism of their own works than in making visible and rethinking the unresolved dilemmas of interculturality.

Artists Who Refuse to Represent Brands

The list of world heritage items has so far been an anthology of responses given by different cultures. A new question then arises: What do societies do with things that they find no responses for in their culture, their politics, or their technology? For example, how should they manage globalization? How should they live with different people in a world of dense, globalized exchanges? I have in mind a few artist-thinkers who pose these problems while trying to avoid traditionalist celebration and commercialization, who instead assume that there will be inequalities in these exchanges and negotiations because of unequal access to information, unequal interculturality of migrants, and asymmetry between North and South in border crossing. Here are three examples.

First, *La mesa de negociación* (The Negotiating Table) by Antoni Muntadas. This was a large round table, divided into twelve sections "like pie slices," each of different heights, that were leveled by balancing the legs on piles of books whose spines bore titles on conflicts in the communications market. The surface of the table displayed a dozen back-lit maps representing the distribution of wealth among different countries. Exhibited at the Fundación Arte y Tecnología, located inside the Telefónica building in Madrid, during the very months when a dispute was intensifying between national and global corporations over rights to broadcast digital television in Spain, the piece evoked the imbalances, self-absorbed circularity, fragility, and lame accommodations that negotiation can show.

Second, *Muro cerrando un espacio* (Wall Enclosing a Space) by Santiago Sierra. This artist's work at the 2003 Venice Biennale consisted of closing the Spanish pavilion and allowing entrance only through the back door, over which armed guards kept watch, to those who could show a Spanish national identity card. Neither the critics nor even the judges for the Biennale were able to get in. On its surface, this action metaphorized the exclusion of undocumented aliens in Spain; it can also be read as being about the difficulty of putting a national culture on display.

Intercultural conflict was represented not only by the distance between the Spaniards who could get in and those who were excluded but

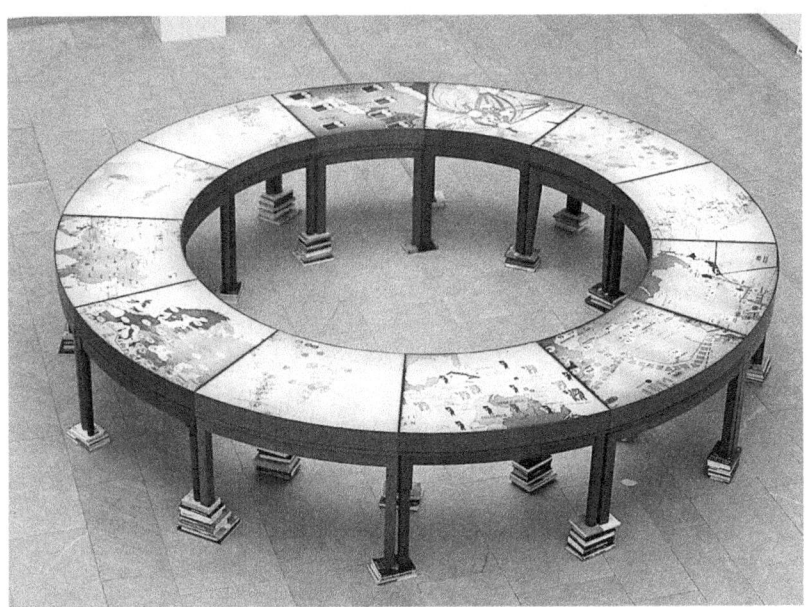

FIGURE 3.1 Antoni Muntadas, *Mesa de negociación* (The Negotiating Table), installation, Madrid, September–November 1998.

also by what was hidden from those of us who had to stay outside. Since I wasn't able to enter, I will transcribe the description written by the Spanish critic Juan Antonio Ramírez, who relates that on the inside one saw an abandoned building "with large, bare rooms, and the remains of the last exhibit, its texts still on one of the walls." The pavilion, this critic emphasized, was not empty but rather

> filled with the seemingly random residue of human labor: a bucket of paint, pieces of paper, footprints in the dust, cigarette packages, old stickers, and so on. The two uniformed guards have orders to prevent visitors from altering these remains or, for example, drawing graffiti on the walls. That is, if these traces must be treated with the respect afforded to "art works," it is because these residues *are* the creations that the pavilion holds. The part of the Venice pavilion reserved for Spanish visitors thus seems like a huge installation devoted to the residue of human labor. To give us some more clues about this, Santiago Sierra arranged to have his third project on

display there—*Mujer con capirote sentada de cara a la pared* [Hooded Woman Seated Facing the Wall]—staged on May 1, 2003, when Labor Day is celebrated in countries including Italy and Spain. In any case, the visual result is striking. In consequence of the restricted entrance, the exhibition rooms are almost always empty and silent; the walls, painted black—a tremendous "found color" from the previous exhibit—and lit from directly overhead, with no windows opening to the outside, create a space of rare solemnity, elegant and macabre, as if it revealed a grandness or a glorious past that had been irretrievably lost. . . . It seems to me no coincidence that the woman in his third piece at Venice was old; we see her only from the back in the catalogue, seated on a low stool, her legs stretched in front of her, and a pointed black hood on her head. We immediately think of the hats worn by those condemned by the Inquisition (the official catalogue reproduces a Goya painting on this subject) and of the Nazarenes in our Holy Week celebrations. But making someone sit in the corner was a very popular form of punishment in Franco-era schools. What we see in this case is a different form of occlusion, the erasing of the face, a way of imprisoning the person's identity. One could say that the secret Spain of this pavilion, the Spain of its natives, of "the walls of my native country," punishes the working woman with a dreaded hat and presents the blackness of her corner as a spectacle for meditation. Isn't this the true "dark night of the soul"? (Ramírez and Carrillo 2004: 295–99)

After such an installation, it wasn't easy to go back to using national pavilions. Muntadas took on the challenge at the next Biennale, when the Spanish government asked him to do the exhibit at their pavilion in Venice. The Catalan artist did not reconsider the meaning of his country's pavilion but the significance of the Biennale itself, as a place for intersection and competition among the thirty pavilions that represent as many nations (plus another twenty or thirty that had exhibits out in the Giardini), dramatizing every two years the latest top trends and artists. What kind of global legitimacy does this event have when more than a hundred nations recognized by the United Nations have no pavilion at all, not even a marginal presence? What can it mean in an era when it

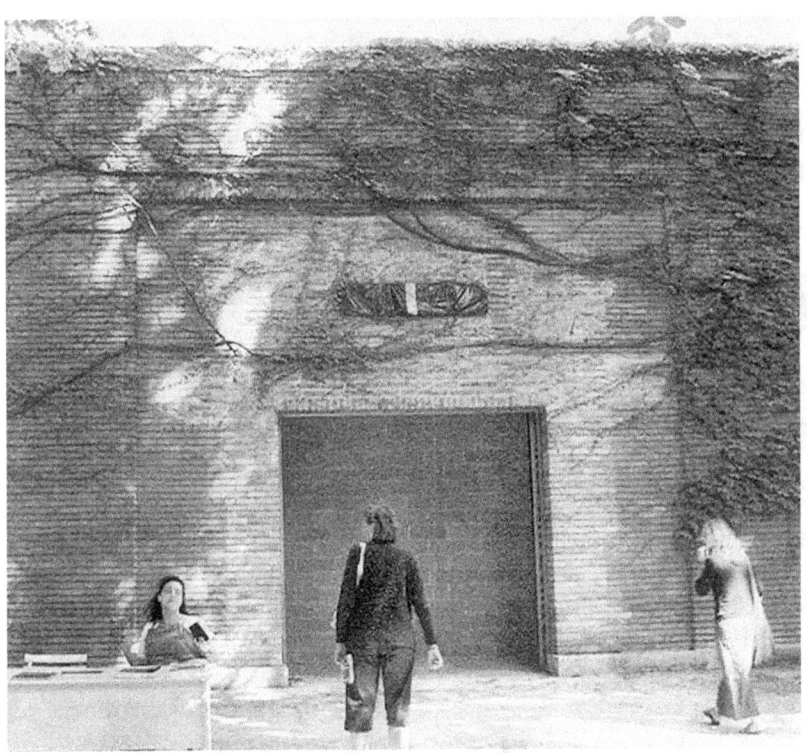

FIGURE 3.2 Santiago Sierra, *Palabra tapada* (Covered Word), Spanish pavilion at the Venice Biennale, 2004.

makes no sense to stroll from pavilion to pavilion, as people did in times past, to discover what the English, the Spanish, or the French are up to? Many artists feel so little commitment to representing a country, and many pavilions are so little inclined toward exhibiting their works as part of the national heritage, that over the past few years artists from one country are appearing in another country's pavilion, such as the Korean artist Nam June Paik in the German pavilion. In 2003 the Dutch pavilion was occupied by foreigners who lived in the Netherlands. Muntadas turned the Spanish building into an airport or information office waiting room, with rows of benches, monitors, illuminated signs, and a telephone set up like an audio guide to tell the history of the Biennale, as well as a kiosk with a list of the countries left out of the Biennale and

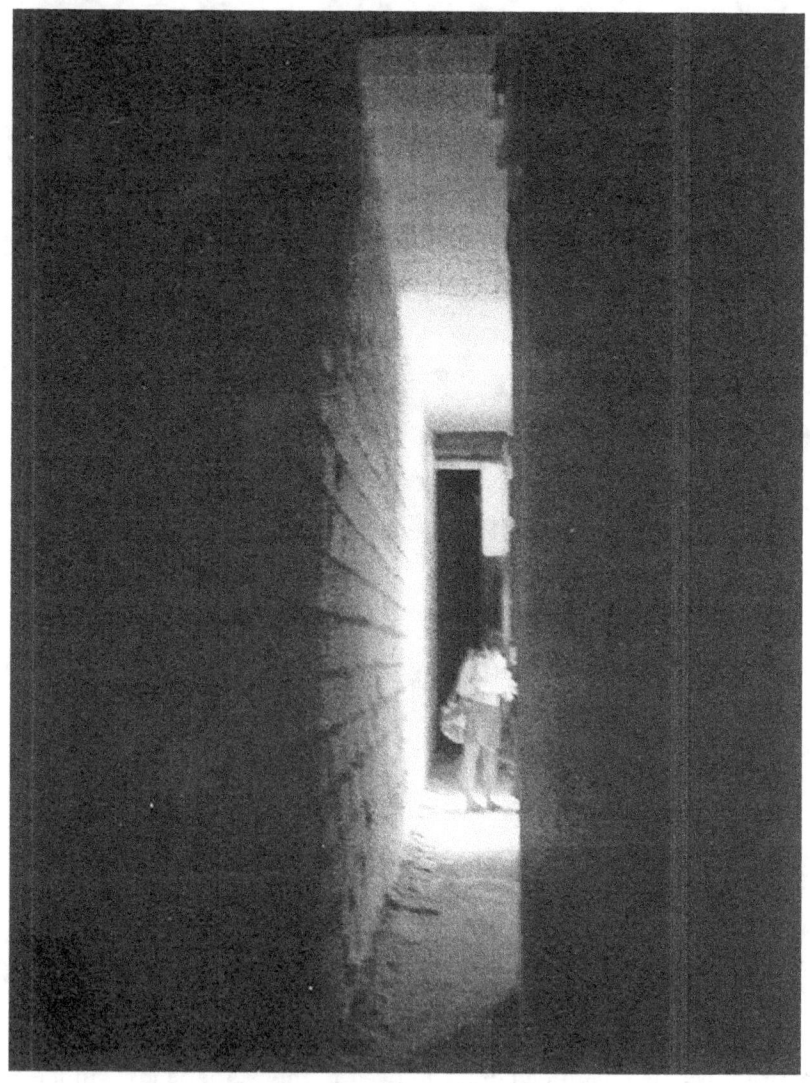

FIGURE 3.3 Santiago Sierra, *Muro cerrando un espacio* (Wall Enclosing a Space), passageway between the outer walls and the wall built by the artist at the Venice Biennale, 2003.

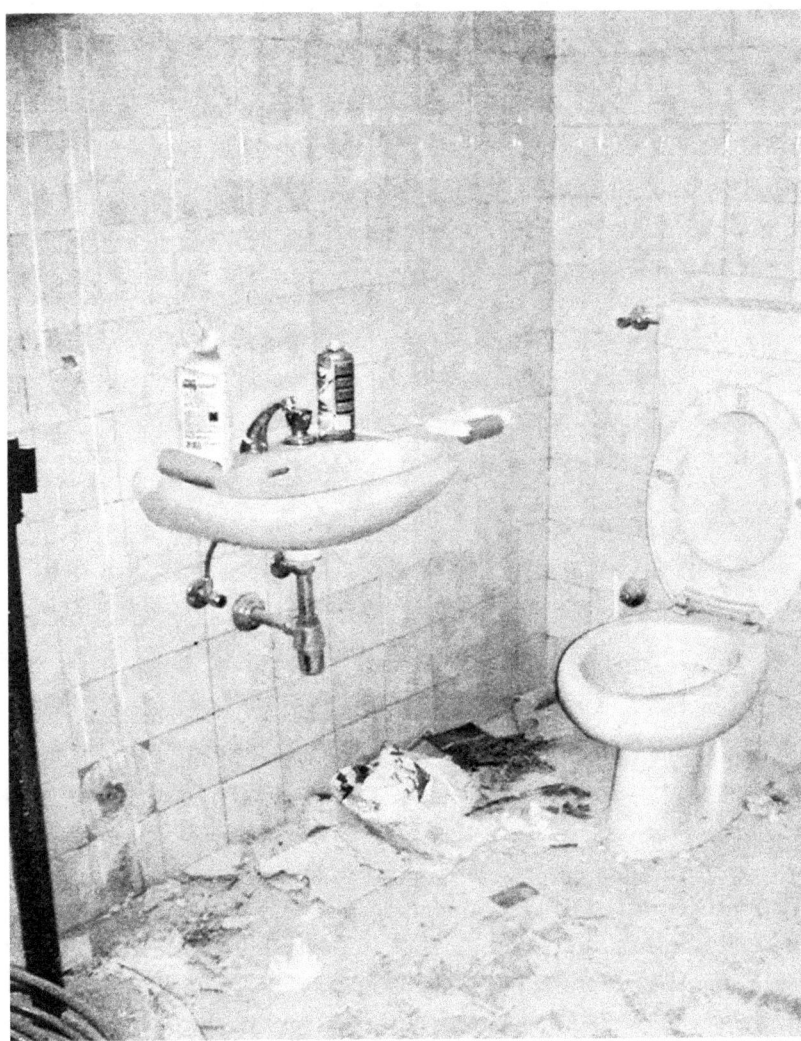

FIGURE 3.4 Santiago Sierra, *Cuarto de baño* (Bathroom), created in the Spanish pavilion at the Venice Biennale, 2003.

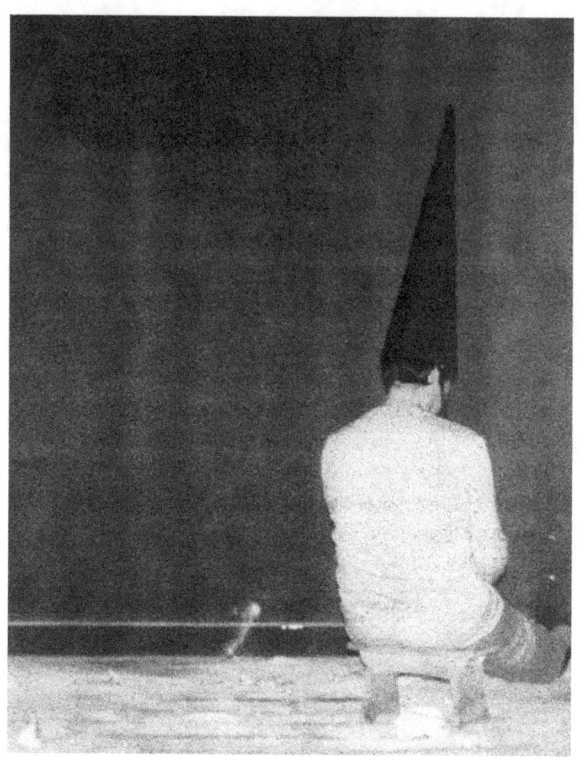

FIGURE 3.5 Santiago Sierra, *Mujer con capirote sentada de cara a la pared* (Hooded Woman Seated Facing the Wall), performance enacted in the Spanish pavilion at the Venice Biennale, May 1, 2003.

new versions of the works in his series *On Translation*, created in different countries, including *The Negotiating Table*. Confrontations among languages, countries, institutions, and cities: "You, for example, would never exactly be a representative of Spain," Mark Wigley tells him, "but you could be a Spanish translator" (Muntadas and Wigley 2005: 285).

Third, *Toy and Horse* by Marcos Ramírez ERRE. Here I build on my earlier analysis of this work (García Canclini 1999). On the border between Mexico and the United States, next to the guard booths that control the crossing from Tijuana to San Diego, in 1997, with funding from the public art program inSITE, this Mexican artist set up a thirty-three-foot-tall wooden horse with two heads, one looking toward the United

States, the other toward Mexico. He wanted to avoid the stereotype of the unidirectional penetration of the North into the South, and also the opposing illusions of those who say that migration from the South is bringing in, unnoticed, contraband that the people of the United States don't accept. The artist told me that this fragile, ephemeral "antimonument" is "see-through, because we already know all of their intentions toward us, and they know all of ours toward them." Amid the Mexican vendors circulating among the cars jammed in front of the guard booths, selling Aztec calendars, Mexican handicrafts, and "souvenirs" of Disneyland, Ramírez ERRE did not present a work that would be an affirmation of nationalism. He chose a universal symbol that had been transformed into a brand of intercultural infiltration, and he modified it ironically— by its looks and its placement—to indicate the multidirectionality of its messages and the ambiguity caused by its use in the media. He printed reproductions of the horse on T-shirts and postcards to be sold alongside the Aztec calendars and Disneyland symbols. He also set out four Trojan costumes so that those who wanted to get their photograph taken next to the "monument" could put them on, in an ironic reference to the tourist photographs taken next to brand markers of Mexicanness and of the "American way of life." He was making the conflict along the border explicit but not representing it with nationalist images or with an abstract symbol of interculturality. He was inviting people to reflect on a particular border.

When I presented this work at the meeting of the UNESCO commission of scientists and philosophers who were rethinking the notion of cultural heritage, the semiologist Paolo Fabbri asked me, "Who was inside the horse?" After a couple of minutes, he answered his own question: "I know—the translators."

Perhaps intercultural translation is a strategic function of art in times of continual global interactions. Instead of establishing a canon of works for all humanity, or national brands, the policies that deal with cultural heritage could assume the dynamic and experimental sense of the artistic gaze. The tasks of storing and protecting could be broadened to include translating, helping to form flexible publics that can value different sorts of works, representative of various cultures. The idea of cultural heritage would thus be reconceptualized: in addition to a canon of

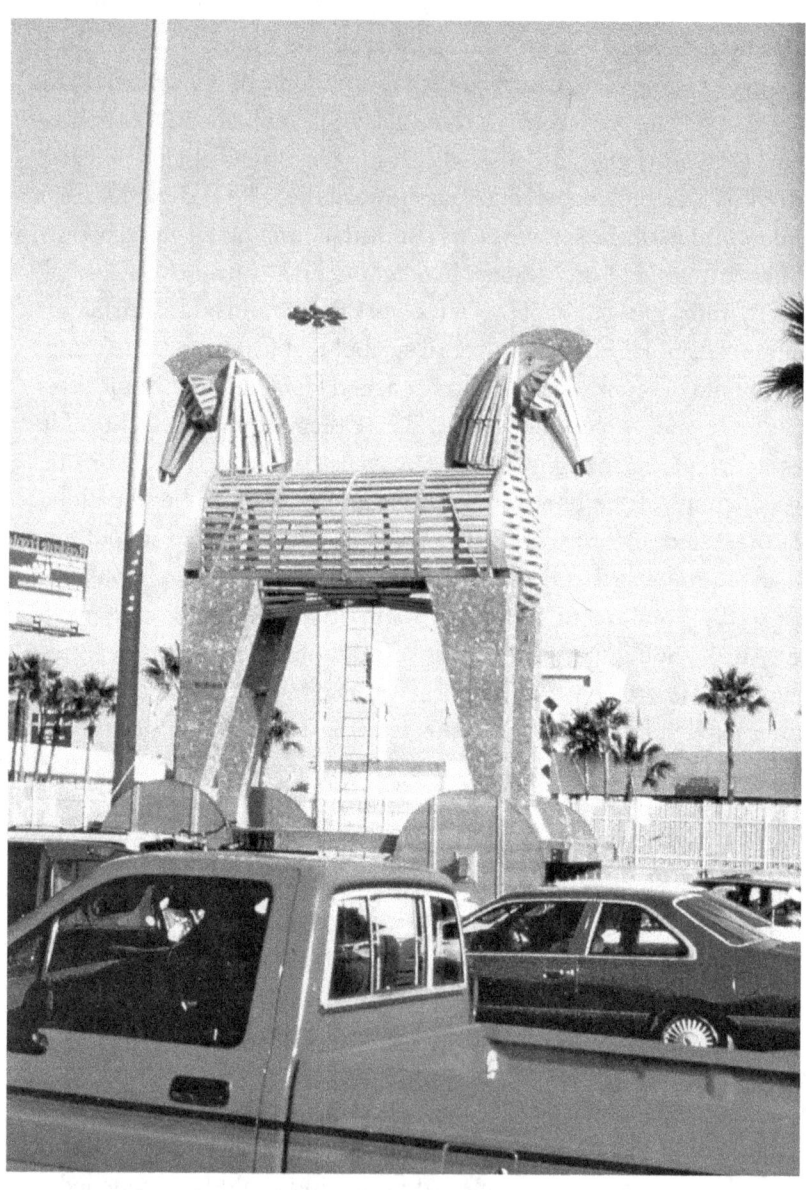

FIGURE 3.6 Marco Ramírez ERRE, *Toy and Horse*, inSITE, 1997. Border-crossing gateway from Tijuana to San Diego. Photograph: Jimmy Fluker.

items, it would also recognize canons of uses—adaptable performances that are not always mutually compatible.

The works of these three artists, by eschewing symbolic representations of a nation's culture, create unconventional ways of looking at intercultural crossroads, at the limitations on international cooperation and negotiation. Their value consists not in the eloquence or showmanship with which they exhibit the creativity of a people but rather in the way they generate dialogical spaces where new forms of understanding and interdependence open up. They aren't preoccupied with marking the borders of each culture but with elaborating what it is that links them to other cultures—even through the negative method of contrast and exclusion, as in Santiago Sierra's work. These experiences are found not in the canon of established works but in the invention of cognitive openings or networks.

Concepts versus Metaphors?

Reconsidering urban space, museums, and the media as spheres conditioning how art and cultural heritage are administered, we observe that *works* are defined in ways that vary depending on how their meaning is accessed and who has the right to participate in such decisions. By locating the problems of value in accordance with current theories of art and culture, not in the nature of the object or in an authenticity that derives from an arbitrary selection of a moment in the history of its use, we open up a space that brings to light various meanings and the struggles between them. Instead of settling into the limits set by restrictive conceptual operations, we put the translatability of meanings into play. I'm imagining a cultural action that would operate like the movement of metaphors—that is, by displacement and articulation between different meanings—rather than by the limiting straightforwardness of concepts.

There is no need to draw a sharp line between concepts and metaphors. We could, following a line of thought derived from hermeneutics, deal with what knits the two together. The idea is that interpretation, the act of conceptualizing, should not destroy the density and diversity of experiences described in metaphors. Moreover the dialogue between metaphors and the work of conceptualization makes metaphors more concrete, keeping us from getting lost in a luxuriant abundance of meanings. Paul Ricoeur (1976) argues that metaphor not only brings constructed language to life but spurs us to "think more," to understand what we can name as well as what poetry implies or announces.

Concepts, for their part, aren't merely objective and delimiting operations. They never settle the meaning of facts once and for all, for they are not settled themselves. We distrust sedentary views of concepts: "Every concept has a history," Gilles Deleuze and Félix Guattari (1994: 17) have shown; each concept is derived from other concepts, is a "point of coincidence, condensation, or accumulation of its own components" (21), since "concepts are centers of vibrations, each in itself and every one in relation to all the others" (23). No moment of condensation is definitive. According to Mieke Bal (2002: 22), "Concepts are the tools of intersubjectivity: they facilitate discussion on the basis of a common language." We ask concepts to be explicit, clear, and well-defined, but concepts travel—from science to science, between science and art, between heritage and uses. They are formed in contexts that depend on the moving focus they effect among changing objects. Concepts are not true representations for all time; their "adequacy is not realistic" but the result of approximations that seek "the effective organization of the phenomena" and also "that the new organization be compelling, and that it yield new and relevant information" (31–32).

Concepts "offer miniature theories" (Bal 2002: 22), useful so long as we are always ready to review their productivity and admit it when they're worn out. What differentiates them from grand theory is that they aren't constrained by rigid linkages between propositions. "Concepts are centers of vibrations, each in itself and every one in relation to all the others. This is why they all resonate rather than cohere or correspond with each other" (Deleuze and Guattari 1994: 23).

This itinerant character of concepts, which travel between disciplines, between historical eras, and between geographically dispersed academic communities, shouldn't get us down. Bal gives an example that I find particularly attractive, that of hybridity, because after I wrote a book to demonstrate its fertility in the analysis of learned, popular, and media arts, I had to write a new introduction to argue against some who objected to using this concept in the social sciences because its allusion to biological infertility made it irrelevant to the study of sociocultural transformations. How, Bal (2002: 24) wonders, did the concept of hybridity, which had "as its 'other' an authentic or pure specimen" and which was associated with sterility and "was current in imperialist discourse with its racist overtones, come to indicate an idealized state of postcolonial diversity?" How did it come to represent the creativity of encounters and fusions? "Because it travelled. Originating in nineteenth-century biology," it moved to Russia, where "it encountered the literary critic Mikhail Bakhtin" (24). It was then picked up by postcolonial critics in India and postfoundational thinkers in Latin America. Since "all of these forms of travel render concepts flexible," these migrations can be "an asset rather than a liability" (25).

Concepts aren't the only things that travel. The very notion of the concept has changed constantly, from classical philosophy—where concepts were deemed universal—to the social sciences, whose models of understanding recognize the intersection of conceptual labor, empirical evidence, and the diverse ways of naming and legitimizing knowledge in each culture. "The most shameful moment," according to Deleuze and Guattari (1994: 10), "came when computer science, marketing, design, and advertising, all the disciplines of communication, seized hold of the word *concept* itself" and set it to work naming innovations that sometimes amounted to nothing more than a new way of selling a product. When concepts are aimed at selling products—a dryer, a museum exhibition, the redesigned image of an artist or an intellectual—we have "replaced Critique with sales promotion" (10). The philosopher or scientist has been replaced by the product packager.

What changes is the link between concept and creation. Concepts always had to do with a creative movement: "The concept is not given, it is created; it is to be created. It is not formed but posits itself in itself— it is a self-positing." Like a work of art, it "enjoys a self-positing of itself, or an autopoetic characteristic by which it is recognized" (Deleuze and Guattari 1994: 11). Advertising promotes what it is selling not by letting it reveal its own worth but by plastering a simulacrum onto it: the woman who seems to come with the car; the transparent reflective-glass building that homogeneously aestheticizes all the artworks without allowing the tensions between the works and their contexts to speak. Simulacra are periodically renovated in order to cancel the metaphorical power of objects and the movements of conceptualization with which their emergent power would be named. Allied with the polysemy of metaphors, concepts gain metaphors' productivity. Turned into interchangeable simulacra, they presage only emptiness.

The concepts with which we try to define certain cultural ideas, such as "heritage," are ways of holding onto the answers that societies were giving themselves. The use of metaphors in art reminds us that there are multiple answers, that they are unstable, they travel, and sometimes they manage to tell us only what they haven't found. What's left is imminence. The politics surrounding heritage have offered a handful of human monuments the possibility of being preserved as memories; art says, over and over again, that this is a fragile exercise whose meaning depends less on the pride it calls forth in the heirs than on the power it finds in the agreements or arguments between different people.

I won't go on, for now, about the changes that are taking place as we free aesthetically valued objects from the limits art history has imposed on them and rethink them as part of cultural practices or as part of the production, circulation, and reception of images now studied by the field of visual studies. Instead of the cut-and-paste work done by heritage professionals, including archaeologists and art historians, to isolate a canon of major works using aesthetic criteria as arbitrary as those employed in creating lists of "world heritage" sites, repositioning the arts as integral to visual culture may help redraw the links between art, heritage, and culture. In a sense analogous but not identical to the interactions we have analyzed between heritage and media customs, the borders of art blur when the artists' works intersect with other audiovisual means and mediations.

What should we do with the intellectual, artistic, and institutional traditions that continue to differentiate between the artistic and the everyday? Though there are no reasons to maintain strict differences between objects, artworks, and artifacts, we do still have persistent forms of labor and appreciation that distinguish them. It's worth asking whether there's any productive way to use such distinctions. By which I don't mean essential differences between them, of course, but operative strategies of the sort that begin showing up when cultural research and policies are carried out. The best anthropological research isn't the kind that describes a tradition and assigns concepts to it ("national culture," "folklore," "popular art") but the kind that offers a map of the highway on which a landscape and its names begin to change. What we have agreed to call art has the ability to condense various moments in this trip into a metaphor.

The critical questions about heritage are these: Where is a socially shared meaning established and shored up, how does it continue to transform as it is being used, and does it run a risk of dissolution in the dispute among political, commercial, cultural, and tourist uses?

The question for artists is this: How do you begin anew, after a heritage has become established? How can you make art in Mexico, for example, after the great muralist movement? With the abstract geometrism of the 1960s and 1970s; the neo-Mexicanist Pop or the urban folklorism of the 1980s; the cosmopolitanism that elliptically took up some Mexican iconography once more in the works of Gabriel Orozco and Gerardo Suter; the performances, videos, and installations that work with the movements of urban meanings or contemporary culture in Francis Alÿs, Santiago Sierra, and Carlos Amorales?

The questions change when we change the context, for example, in Argentina: How can you make literature after Borges? With the cosmopolitan experimentation of Julio Cortázar's *Rayuela*, the rewriting of history in Ricardo Piglia's *Respiración artificial*, or the experimenting in many literary genres and publishing your works in different countries through different publishing houses with varying levels of distribution, as practiced by César Aira?

Muralism and Borges can be read as the cultural heritage of Mexico and Argentina. Artistic reinterpretations and transgressions, the acts that get meaning going again, sometimes allow for the experiences that were talked about in these "origins" to be revised, or even for new ones to be spoken. One significant difference is that, with heritage, we are still asking ourselves about *where*. Artists explore *how* to move on from the known and settled into the possible. Researching about space and limits remains in the realm of the reconceptualization of heritage. In art, we are looking into imminence and new beginnings.

Heritage sought to be, and succeeds less and less at being, the settling of certain verities. Art attempts to narrate, to translate indecisions and enigmas, to make visible the tension between rootedness and traveling.

>

CHAPTER FOUR

PUTTING A VALUE ON ART

Between the Market and Politics

It is possible to redefine what we mean by art in contemporary societies as we have done in previous chapters, according to the differences between art and heritage, ethnographic objects, and product brands, without giving any essential value to those traits. This exercise has revealed a series of interdependencies between artistic and other practices and the fact that on some occasions their institutionalization creates similar conditions for them, as seen in the quest for singularity in heritage objects and in works of art. We find only a slight difference between the two cultural practices or "fields" in the ways they each related to that which transcends the empirical, that which we do not control: art deals with imminence, while heritage deals with what is at risk of deteriorating or disappearing.

Artistic practice does not initiate meaning. It uses heritage to restart or reinvent things that have already been made, said, and organized into collections or discourses. We could go a step further and ask ourselves whether some particular type of labor and social relations might distinguish artists and their works, and whether those tasks, and the links they require, might perhaps compose something that could still be called the art field or art world.

One way to answer this question would be to observe which people, actors, and places art publications talk about and deal with. Who decides our tastes? In recent years the British journal *Art Review* has published lists of the hundred most influential people in the art world. There is an implicit "theory" behind this way of identifying decisions: power is attributed to individuals instead of structures and institutions. Nevertheless the fact that only 20 percent of those chosen for its 2005 list were artists (Damien Hirst being in first place) and that most slots were filled by gallery owners such as Larry Gagosian, collectors such as François Pinault, museum directors such as Nicholas Serota at the Tate, and architects such as Herzog and De Meuron, Renzo Piano, and Rem Koolhaas, points toward the complex transnational web of museums and architectural enclosures, journals, fairs and biennales, foundations, stores, Internet sites, and para-aesthetic activities. The transnational reach of these actors and institutions makes the circulation of visual arts akin to what we see in the industrialization of images—a connection already made by art historians such as Benjamin Buchloh (2000) in his book *Neo-Avantgarde and Culture Industry* on the period 1955–75, but one that we can now document not only in iconography and the spectacularization of images, as in Warhol and Coleman, but also in the ways artworks and actions are produced, inserted into social development, and given value.

In the 2009 issue of *Art Review* the list of the hundred most influential put the Swiss curator Hans Ulrich Obrist in first place and gave high positions to other curators, collectors, and institutions such as the Museum of Modern Art in New York and the Tate in London for their ability to adapt to the impact of the 2008 economic crisis on the art market. It also valued the role of digital networks such as e-flux in guiding investors and circulating information.

The Relations We Talk about When We Talk about Relational Aesthetics

"Maurizio Cattelan feeds rats on 'Bel paese' cheese and sells them as multiples, or exhibits recently robbed safes. In a Copenhagen square, Jes Brinch and Henrik Plenge Jacobsen install an upturned bus that causes a rival riot in the city. . . . Pierre Huyghe summons people to a casting session, makes a TV transmitter available to the public, and puts a photograph of labourers at work on view just a few yards from the building site" (Bourriaud 2002: 8). How can we elaborate, Nicolas Bourriaud asks, a definition and a body of knowledge for such varied practices, which may be set in the urban landscape, fun parks, or electronic media, and which take on such diverse forms of sociability? He proposes the notion of "relational art" to describe the forms that have as their "theoretical horizon the realm of human interactions and its social context, rather than the assertion of an independent and *private* symbolic space" (14). He argues that the historical conditions that once made it possible for modern art to seek independence and singularity have disappeared, yet "the spirit informing it" remains (11)—the spirit of acting in "the interstices" that "elude the capitalist economic context" (16), suggesting other possibilities for everyday interactions, instant communities generated by unconventional forms of participation.

Some of the examples Bourriaud (2002: 17) cites have a clear political meaning: "When Jens Haaning broadcasts funny stories in Turkish through a loudspeaker in a Copenhagen square (*Turkish Jokes*, 1994), he produces in that split second a micro-community, one made up of immigrants brought together by collective laughter"—turning their situation as exiles upside-down.

The artists' actions in these cases have no specific direction. They aim not to change society and make it more just or more suited to creativity but to move things from the existing state to a different one. In his book *Postproduction* Bourriaud (2005) collects dozens of experiences that use montage, subtitles, or sampling to generate situations that aren't radically new but that select readymade objects and remodel them or insert them into new contexts. The deejay and the programmer are the emblematic figures, Bourriaud says: "The artistic question is no longer: 'what can we make that is new?' but 'how can we make do with what we have?'" (17).

We can suppose that Bourriaud's (2005: 17) texts have been so influential because there is a need to conceptualize a stage in which artists are acting no longer in relation to museums or canons of what he calls "works that must be cited or 'surpassed'" but within a society that we think of as open. We've stopped drawing sharp distinctions between created and copied works. All that exists takes the form of "signals already emitted," "paths marked out by their predecessors," and "stockpiles of data to manipulate and present" (17). The borders between production and consumption have become blurred.

Bourriaud (2002: 107) writes in *Relational Aesthetics* that today "the word 'art' seems to be no more than a semantic leftover of this [art history] narrative, whose more accurate definition would read as follows: Art is an activity consisting in producing relationships with the world with the help of signs, forms, actions and objects." For an era that doesn't believe in originality and perceives the obsolescence of the familiar or its incessant reutilization, here's a theory of semi-innovative and de-institutionalizing practices: the visual arts, like people who channel-surf or who download from the Internet and use their downloads to compose other series, are interested not in the conclusion of the creative process but rather in whatever could be "a portal, a generator of activities" (Bourriaud 2005: 19).

He paints this theory with a counterhegemonic face: "Art challenges passive culture, composed of merchandise and consumers" (Bourriaud 2005: 20). In reality Bourriaud's view continues to place the highest value on originality and innovation; it just transfers them from the objects to the processes. As it does so, it maximizes the value placed on movement, rootlessness, and precariousness. Since objects and institutions don't matter anymore, there is nothing to stabilize meaning. Communities are temporary and require fragile compromises. On the one hand, Bourriaud promotes art as a way of inhabiting the world; on the other, he praises the trend of residing in no place.

As a theorist of the pathbreaking work of Rirkrit Tiravanija, Liam Gillick, Pierre Joseph, and installations and performance art in general, Bourriaud distances himself from the history of art and even from recent works that place value on objects. But he treasures everything that unsettles relations between subjects. "The subversive and critical function of contemporary art is now achieved," he declares, "in the invention of individual and collective vanishing lines, in those temporary and nomadic constructions whereby the artist models and disseminates disconcerting situations" (Bourriaud 2002: 31). This is a kind of neo-Dadaism or neo-anarchism, revitalized through the ephemeral tactics of performativity.

His aesthetics seem to avoid committing to any social theory. He has nevertheless staked a position in sociopolitical debates by concentrating on conjunctural relations and alliances, never structural ones, and by eschewing conflict. He would establish constructive or creative relations in microspaces that pretend to have nothing to do with the social structures that made them possible or with disputes over appropriating the works that circulate in them.

What we have to do, Claire Bishop objects, is examine the quality of the relations that relational art produces. As in 1968-era communitarian Romanticism and Situationism, any relation that facilitates nonhierarchical dialogue is taken to be democratically, ethically, and aesthetically valuable. The works by Tiravanija and the other artists promoted by Bourriaud tend not to be political, Bishop (2004: 68) argues, or are so only "in the loosest sense of advocating dialogue over monologue." As she emphasizes, Bourriaud notably omits from his canon artists who displace art from the work to the process, such as Thomas Hirschhorn and Santiago Sierra, whose performances and installations provoke disquiet and discomfort, putting on view the antagonism that is an inescapable component of works dealing with relations—as we saw in Sierra's action at the Venice Biennale. True, the way Sierra stages this fact in other works—as when he pays workers to display their oppression, or pays Tzotzil Indian women from Chiapas to chant the phrase "I'm being paid to say something whose meaning I don't understand"—calls for a finely nuanced discussion of his pieces. For the moment I would point out that not all performance and installation artists think of their impact on social relations in terms of the angelic experimentalism that Bourriaud (2002: 70) attributes to their art forms when he presupposes that they are simply a matter of inventing new ways of being together.

I want to contrast Bourriaud's slanted view of the social with that of a philosopher who proposes, within a postautonomous view of art, a different way of articulating aesthetics and politics based on a more consistent social theory: Jacques Rancière. Then I will measure how far I can go with relational aesthetics, taking into account an ethnographic description of the types of relations constructed between artists, gallery owners, curators, critics, collectors, and nonart actors, all of whom, as we will see, behave differently at auctions, art schools, fairs, and biennales and with respect to the great economic, political, and media powers.

Artists as Workers in Dissensus

Rancière has developed an aesthetics of disagreement. By relating his concept of social and political dissensus to a postautonomous notion of art, he uses critical radicalism to reopen philosophy to the possibility of thinking about culture in a way that is unlike modernism or Bourriaud-style postmodernism.

At times in the twentieth century, most famously in the 1970s, some sought to transcend the elitist isolation of art by taking artworks out of the museums and into the streets and by joining forces with transformative social and political movements. This avant-garde conception linked the critique of elite institutions and oppressive society with the utopia of a future sociability that the artist community was trying to anticipate. Occasionally aesthetic innovation was articulated with the political vanguard, though the creators preserved their autonomy with regard to the obedience that political activists demanded.

"On the one hand, the avant-garde movement aimed to transform the forms of art, and to make them identical with the forms for constructing a new world in which art would no longer exists as a separate reality. On the other, the avant-garde preserved the autonomy of the artistic sphere from forms of compromise with practices of power and political struggle, or with forms of the aestheticization of life in the capitalist world" (Rancière 2010: 199). Rancière proposes to link aesthetic and political practices in a different way. He argues that "aesthetics can be understood in a Kantian sense—re-examined perhaps by Foucault—as the system of *a priori* forms determining what presents itself to sense experience" (2004: 13). Political practices, like any other social practices, are based on ways of feeling, of forming experiences of the visible and the invisible. He defines this "distribution of the sensible" as "the system of self-evident facts of sense perception" that shows "the existence of something in common" (12). Nevertheless there also exists a distribution of spaces and times, possibilities of naming, abilities of seeing, and status for speaking. There are distributions of the sensible that are used to organize particular hierarchies of what is imagined as "common," but the seeming unity of the common is split between truly shared uses and other uses that are exclusive and that exclude.

Aesthetics is not art theory but "a specific regime for identifying and reflecting on the arts: a mode of articulation between ways of doing and making, their corresponding forms of visibility, and possible ways of thinking about their relationships" (Rancière 2004: 10). This seeming common ground is fractured by groups with distinct occupations, places that are separate—and that differ in quality—where discourses cover the ways they should be represented and the proper ways of behaving within them.

There are two ways to understand politics: as constructing a consensus or as working with disagreements. The version that seeks consensus is centered on shared sensible experiences and tends to ignore disagreements. Spurning this conciliatory view, Rancière comes to redefine politics. "Politics is not the exercise of power," he insists (2010: 27). "Politics is first of all a way of framing, among sensory data, a specific sphere of experience. It is a partition of the sensible, of the visible and the sayable, which allows (or does not allow) some specific data to appear; which allows or does not allow some specific subjects to designate them and speak about them" (152). In contrast to what Rancière calls the "police" adaptation of functions, places, and behaviors with which there will be no conflicts, he postulates a politics that will introduce new subjects and objects, make the hidden visible, and listen to the silenced.

Aesthetics and politics are linked when what is concealed is given visibility, reconfiguring the distribution of the sensible and making dissensus apparent. What is a dissensus? It "is not a conflict of interests, opinions, or values; it is a division inserted in 'common sense': a dispute over what is given and about the frame within which we see something as given" (Rancière 2010: 69).

As a result, he questions art and aesthetic reflection aimed solely at reestablishing or reinventing social ties. He gives two examples that show how things have changed in recent decades. During the Vietnam War, "Chris Burden created a work entitled the *Other Memorial*, dedicated to the dead on the other side, to the thousands of Vietnamese victims with neither name nor monument. On the bronze plates of his monument, Burden inscribed Vietnamese-sounding names of other anonymous people randomly copied from the phonebook to give names to these anonymous people" (Rancière 2010: 193).

Rancière compares this work with one made thirty years later by Christian Boltanski: his installation *Les Abonnés du téléphone*, which "consisted of two large sets of shelves containing phonebooks from around the world and two long tables at which visitors could sit down to consult them."

> And whereas yesterday's aim was simultaneously to give names and lives back to those who had been deprived of them by State power, today's anonymous masses are simply, as the artist says, 'specimens of humanity,' those with whom we are bound together in a large community. . . . Earlier, producing an encounter between heterogeneous elements would aim to underline the contradictions of a world stamped by exploitation and to question art's place and institutions within that world of conflict. Today, it is proclaimed that this same gathering is the positive operation of an art responsible for the functions of archiving and bearing witness to a common world. (Rancière 2010: 193–94)

Rancière concludes by rejecting the "programme of relational art," which is to "repair the cracks in the social bond" (193–94) and to construct mini-spaces of sociability, such as those official programs that tend to put art, culture, and social welfare on the same level. He proposes instead to reconfigure the division of the commonsense world over which consensus is simulated, to rebuild the divided public space, and to restore equality of standing.

One of his favorite examples is Krzysztof Wodiczko's visual projections displaying the ghostly bodies of the homeless on public monuments in the neighborhoods from which they were dislodged: "The homeless abandon their consensual identity as excluded in order to become the embodiment of the contradiction of public space: those who live materially in the public space of the street and who, by that very token, are excluded from public space understood as the space for symbolizing what is held in common and for participating in decisions on common affairs" (Rancière 2005: 63).

I'd like to cite a few examples, apart from the ones Rancière praises, that show constructive or playful and not merely indulgent facets. I'm thinking of artists whose aim is not to beseech or to transgress the institutions of art or politics but rather to explore conversations, forms of organization, or "experimental communities." First example: in the St. Pauli neighborhood of Hamburg, artists, architects, and neighbors jointly carried out a series of protests demanding to have a park built instead of conceding a parcel of publicly owned land to private contractors; the artists and neighbors gave presentations providing information about alternative parks, and they called meetings of the shop owners from around the site and groups of children and neighbors to come up with projects and debate them, thus creating a community of designs, or as they put it, a "collective production of desires." With all of their collaborations they were able to create traveling exhibits to spread the news about their proposal, sending them to Vienna, Berlin, and *Documenta XI* in Kassel in 2002. The culminating event, in Hamburg, titled *Improbable Encounters in the Urban Space*, brought the promoters of this project together with groups from across Germany and from other countries: Ala Plástica, from Argentina; Sarai, from Italy; Expertbase, from Amsterdam.

Second example: in Argentina, Roberto Jacoby, an artist associated with the avant-garde at the Instituto Di Tella in the 1970s who has preferred since then to make not physical artworks but interventions on the street, on the phone, and in the press, which he calls "media art." In the 1990s he started a network of some seventy artists, musicians, writers, and nonartists—a group that eventually grew to five hundred—for trading objects and services. All this was announced on a website, and everyone who joined received an allotment of Venus coins (named after the program) that they could use to pay for the goods and services they were exchanging on the network. The idea, as Jacoby explained it on the project website, was "to bring into existence a place not 'outside' of 'society' but endowed with the elements that society itself promotes," raising not so much a social critique as "a practical inquiry into the monetization" of social relationships (Laddaga 2006: 94).

In his comparative study of both movements, Reinaldo Laddaga (2006: 22) argues that they were trying to produce a "cultural ecology" in which artists formed alliances with everybody else in order to produce "experimental ways to coexist." These artists made their critiques not from outside of or in opposition to established society; rather their goal was to situate themselves in the interactions and in the disagreements, to make controversies visible through the uses and meanings of social representations.

Some of these artists of dissensus or social experimentation have also continued to act in the art world. They don't believe in the binary notion that once made hegemonic art out to be the opposite of alternative art, because the movements and institutions that represent these options aren't compact, self-contained universes. It is at this moment that it is worthwhile to take a look at the anthropological studies that record their internal diversity and external ties. We need these detailed descriptions to be able to specify what it is we're talking about when we refer to the art field.

The Mystery of Art and the Secret of Auctions

The sociologist Sarah Thornton has researched the contemporary logic of what she continues to call "the art world." She carried out ethnographic observations and some 250 interviews in six cities and five countries. She covered scenes that are supposed to be representative of how the art world operates, such as an auction in New York and a seminar at the California Institute of the Arts, "an incubator of sorts" where a very select group of students learn the trade and show their works to top-notch critics (2008: xvii); went to Art Basel to study how that event structures art circulation and consumption internationally; visited the studio of Takashi Murakami to observe how labor is organized and how negotiations with curators and gallery owners are carried out there; analyzed how the jury for the Turner Prize and the team that produces the magazine *Artforum International* work in order to understand the role of prizes and specialized publications; and attended an art historian convention as well as the Venice Biennale.

Her research is guided by the principle that the so-called artistic field should be studied through transnational networks and by correlating in cross-disciplinary terms the settings where it develops. But this global scale is not easily perceptible: "The contemporary art world is a loose network of overlapping subcultures held together by a belief in art" (Thornton 2008: xi). As her book demonstrates, diverse notions of art—and of what it means to believe in art—are held among artists, gallery owners, curators, critics, collectors, and auctioneers. Most artists don't attend auctions, and it bothers them when their works are treated as merchandise. At the art schools they speak of works "whose financial worth is—at this moment, anyway—negligible" (43), and teachers can be split into those who ask their students to develop projects independent of the market and those who encourage their students to subvert it. The prestigious California Institute of the Arts, founded by Walt Disney, maintains direct and indirect ties with Hollywood, so that graduates "who don't support themselves through sales or teaching can work in the ancillary industries of costumes, set design, and animation" (60).

What do galleries and art fairs believe in? Most don't bother with anything beyond commerce, advertising, and public relations. A few fairs include roundtables with critics, philosophers, sociologists, anthropologists, artists, and curators. Galleries tend to pick what they call a market niche, which could be an era, a set of five countries, or a group of artists. A fair brings together art from various eras, names that have been selling in the millions for years as well as dissident works, iconic works, and works introducing conceptual designs that have never been seen before. Even the fairs that don't hold roundtables bring together experts, gallery owners, art dealers, and a handful of historians and critics, who exchange knowledge and discoveries in the midst of "the fair's confusion of visual stimuli and social interaction" (Thornton 2008: 96). Thornton uses a phrase to describe the collector David Teiger that sums up what she observes in many of these individuals as she follows their hectic performances: "He enjoys being a player in the power game of art" (100). She quotes Poe, a gallery owner: "The subtle notes in artworks are drowned out by the cacophony" (98). Jeremy Deller, a British artist who has won the Turner Prize, says upon leaving the fair, "The amount of art in the world is a little depressing. The worst of it looks like art but it's not. It is stuff cynically made for a certain kind of collector" (104).

The art world includes situations in which this confusing abundance seems to fall into order. The stories told by the judges on art prize juries almost always emphasize the difficult balance among factors that influence their evaluations. Evaluations of what? Prizes are announced as if they are awarded for a work or for an artist's career. The judges, however, confess that they take into consideration the backgrounds of artworks, the market repercussions of awarding a prize (the big prizes tend to double or triple the prices for artworks), the expectations of the media, and how the communities of artists, curators, journalists, and museum directors will judge the judges for the decisions they make.

The institution that awards the prize is itself being judged, as the distinction may augment or diminish its prestige. Thornton's ethnography of the Turner Prize reveals the many ways in which Tate Britain carefully attends to the economic and media distortions it causes, including at the William Hill betting shop, which specializes in betting on cultural events such as the Oscars and the Man Booker Prize and accepts bets annually on which four artists will be nominated for the Turner. When Thornton (2008: 130) did her study, one of the judges, Andrew Renton, stated that "'to give the Turner nomination to someone who is straight out of art school is utterly irresponsible,'" but also that it "'shouldn't be a midlife-crisis prize.' The Turner Prize honors artists on the cusp between what the art world would call 'late emergent' and 'early mid-career.'" The prize was given that year, 2006, to Tomma Abts for her "geometric abstractions that tease the viewer with hints of figuration. 'My work hovers between illusion and object, and it reminds you of things,' she explained. 'For example, I create a daylight effect or a feeling of movement. Some shapes even have shadows'" (121–22). An artist of imminence. Laura Hoptman, senior curator at the New Museum in New York, agrees: "[Abts] has cracked a nut that artists have been working on for eons—how to paint the inchoate" (123).

Another agent putting order into the vicissitudes of art is the glossy art magazine, which sets itself up as an arbiter of the other actors in the art world. The best of these magazines are determined to guard the autonomy not only of art but also of their own publication. According to Tony Korner, the publisher of *Artforum*, "The one essential thing—it cannot follow the market. Nor should it try actively to influence the market" (Thornton 2008: 152). The huge circulation of *Artforum* (sixty thousand copies, 35 percent of which are sold outside of North America), its leading role among professionals, and its construction of a discourse independent of art collectors and dealers mean that appearing on its cover or being reviewed in its pages is as great a distinction for an artist as many prizes. Its interaction with the market is no minor matter, as evidenced by the fact that the number of pages completely devoted to advertising is double that for articles, reviews, and other texts; the September 2009 issue devoted 217 of its 326 pages to ads for galleries and museums. An advantage of this is that these paid pages offer readers a monthly selection of images and information about what is on exhibit almost everywhere in the world. The same issue also includes articles by Thomas Crow, Claire Bishop, and other prestigious authors about that year's Venice Biennale, making the magazine's nickname, *Adforum*, with its implication that the journal is nothing but an advertising forum, a bit of an exaggeration. The byzantine criteria for laying out the ad pages (the Marian Goodman gallery always goes next to the table of contents; there are constant battles over which ad gets to go next to MoMA's) are, as the editors acknowledge to Thornton, the result of negotiations with those who can pay for the pages, the drawing of hierarchies for what can be put on display, and the visual and fashion echoes of the layout. *Artforum* hesitated for years before accepting fashion ads; though the staff "didn't think jewelry was 'the right signifier,'" they finally "admitted Bulgari when the company became a key sponsor of the website" (163). The upshot of all this is a politics that defines the references of a "community of feeling," to use Rancière's term, in a wider world than that of art. Thornton doesn't draw this conclusion, but she does recall how, in an episode of *Sex and the City*, "we realize that the relationship between the characters played by Sarah Jessica Parker and Mikhail Baryshnikov is starting to falter" when we see Baryshnikov's character "reading a copy of *Artforum* in bed. Likewise, when Bart Simpson becomes an artist and opens a gallery in his treehouse," we can tell that he is a success when he appears "on the cover of *Bartforum*" (145).

Those who insist on defining art and creativity as uncontaminated are being challenged by studios where artists such as Damien Hirst give orders to a hundred collaborators. Takashi Murakami's company, Kaikai Kiki, makes art and also designs items for clothing and handbag stores, television networks, and record companies. The images on Murakami's paintings and sculptures aren't radically different from the standard line he manufactures for Louis Vuitton. It's true that his paintings attract more attention, but they are also created collectively. Several assistants paint them according to Murakami's directions, a photographer records each coat of paint with a digital camera, and when the artist arrives from one of his other studios in Japan or New York, he reviews each point in the process, perhaps deciding to return the work to an earlier state. "Murukami told me he was working on thirty or forty different projects that day. 'My weak point—I cannot focus on just one thing. I have to set up many things. If just looking at one project, then immediately get the feeling it [is] boring'" (Thornton 2008: 196). He compares his work process to video gaming and his works to manga. He thrives on Japanese popular culture and devises lots of ways to insert it into contemporary art. And what about Louis Vuitton? What does it mean to put a boutique inside the Museum of Contemporary Art in Los Angeles? Murakami "referred to his Louis Vuitton work as 'my urinal.'" The artistic director of the Louis Vuitton company went along with the allusion: "'I'm a big fan of Marcel Duchamp and his readymades,' he said coolly. 'Changing the context of an object is, in and of itself, art'" (212).

Art biennales have been called the stage on which globalization is displayed as homogenization. Thornton's description of the Venice Biennale, however, reveals a diversity of artists, curators and collectors, museum and gallery directors, magazine staff documenting the biennales, artists who have never been invited, and tourists. If we add politicians and businesspeople, we can see that in so many senses, both intra- and extra-artistic, the collective action that Howard S. Becker studied as a distinctive feature of the art field is a key factor for art to exist and be seen. These actors cooperate and compete just as collectors at an auction do. The most influential biennales, such as the Venice Biennale, attempt to encompass the globalization of art, but they modify their agenda with each edition. Biennale directors are named two or three years in advance, and they travel and do research in lots of countries to broaden and renovate the already exuberant spectrum.

Robert Storr, director of the fifty-first Venice Biennale in 2005, declared himself "'beholden to the Biennale because I will make shows out of what I've seen for some time to come.' His conclusion after visiting five continents: 'The dire predictions of global homogenization are just not true. There's a lot of shared information, but people do wildly different things with it'" (Thornton 2008: 229–30). We have seen, in the discussion of Sierra's and Muntadas's works at the Venice Biennale, a pair of contributions at the 2003 and 2005 Spanish pavilions that commented ironically on the ability of national pavilions to represent the art of one country at a global event. Sierra blocked entry to the "Spanish territory" of art to everyone who didn't have a Spanish national identity card. Muntadas burst into the Giardini, the "friendly garden" where dozens of national pavilions coexist, with the results of his research into the Biennale, founded in 1895, in order to depict it as "a theme park" bearing anachronistic witness to an earlier stage in the articulation between the internationalized economy (Venice as an economic and naval power), the art market, and tourism.

The closest thing to a world or national heritage site at the Biennale is the thirty pavilions (the maximum number is variable) on exhibit in the Giardini. The list of countries that have pavilions, like the list of sites that UNESCO has declared part of a world heritage, forms a geopolitical map of culture. Two-thirds of the pavilions belong to European nations and get the best locations; five belong to American countries (United States, Canada, Brazil, Venezuela, and Uruguay); and two to the "Far East" (Japan and South Korea). Egypt is the only African and Islamic country represented. In his printed material, Muntadas emphasizes how nations have changed their presentations with every geopolitical earthquake: the facelifts given to the Belgian and Spanish pavilions after World War II, the echoes of changing borders in the placement of pavilions, the actions that made the 1968 protests visible ("Biennale of the bosses, we'll burn down your pavilions!").

Two of the most frequent critiques of the Venice Biennale concern the close proximity of different architectural styles, turning it into a sort of Disneyland, and the no longer tenable thesis that each pavilion can represent a national school or style. Others, however, maintain that many attendees continue to recognize national feelings: "Nationalism is one of the things that gives the Biennale tension and longevity," said Philip Rylands, former director of the Peggy Guggenheim Collection (Thornton 2008: 235). Acts in which artists and their projects take over pavilions to problematize the sense of nationhood or the role of the nation in history are contended to be sources of dynamism: when

"Hans Haacke chopped up the floor of the German pavilion" in 1993; when "Luc Tuymans premiered a series of acclaimed paintings about the Congo to make a statement about colonial history" in the Belgian pavilion in 2001 (243).

How does the declared intention of some biennales to speak about the state of the world relate to the social condition of art? Several concepts or metaphors have been used to characterize what the Venice Biennale has become: "a form of circus" (Andrea Rose, quoted in Thornton 2008: 238); "the avant-garde in a goldfish bowl" (Laurence Alloway, quoted in Thornton 2008: 252); "The Giardini as a readymade. . . . Part of these pavilions function as consulates: the soil is Italy, but each pavilion acts as a kind of consulate or embassy, though I can't imagine them having refugees" (Muntadas, in Muntadas and Wigley 2005: 275, 277–79).

From Field Ethnography to Social Theory

What part of the hard theories about the art field or art world, or of relaxed, "lite" theories such as relational aesthetics, still stands up after a reading of this ethnography? Many of the facts it presents justify a continued recognition of an art world that is relatively autonomous, at times incestuous. At the same time, in each space studied—not only those where commercial relationships prevail, such as auctions and fairs—artistic practices are open to ties with outside actors, who influence their dynamics. Some of the people from the artistic mainstream whom Thornton (2009: 177) interviewed assert that even art circuits that depend on sizable investments and commercial operations constitute "a neutral ground where people meet and interact in a way that's different from their class ghettos."

Auctions, fairs, museums, and biennales do not all have the same degree of autonomy from or interdependence with the socioeconomic and media spheres. Even in the most "contaminated" of these, such as auctions and fairs, we can find collectors and critics who like "artists 'who are on a slow burn'" and are bothered by the fact that the field is now continually pumping up the "'hurry-hurry collectors who go to the hurry-hurry galleries to buy the hurry-hurry artists'" (Thornton 2009: 90). The first transnational ethnographies on contemporary developments in art, by making possible comparisons among countries, groups, and forms of social involvement, have recorded a number of behaviors that do not add up to a single trend. Against this background, theories about the autonomy of art that arose from national analyses (Becker's study of music in the United States, Bourdieu's on French art and literature) now look like records of a modern stage that is being reconfigured. In this globalized restructuring, relational aesthetics seems like the rushed reformulation of a curator-critic interested in making a splashy contribution to the analytic crisis of art by using a biased selection of works while ignoring social complexities.

While Thornton's book condenses the composition of her ethnography into "seven days in the art world," it reveals a vast trove of information that actually took her five years of fieldwork to accumulate. Reducing the story to seven days was a skillful narrative trick. The most interesting problem about the book isn't Thornton's concession to journalistic style but the same one faced by ethnographies that are published as academic works: they are too confident that description will tell readers everything they need in order to know what's going on. Though the book's bibliography includes authors who have rethought art theory (Becker, Bourdieu, Hal Foster, Raymonde Moulin), the story it tells leads to no theoretical conclusions. As happens when ethnography stops at description, it doesn't problematize what informants say in the social relations it observes. It merely suggests these complexities with a few ironic phrases.

There are several significant absences in Thornton's analysis. She doesn't include any studies of the artworks or of their audiences, nor of the structure of the audiovisual and digital media that cover art. (She examines only one written medium, *Artforum*.) She doesn't spend much time on the economic structure of the art markets or give references showing how publications and money condition artists' autonomy and dependence. The boundedness of the "art world" as the object of her study is never questioned. We know, however, that this world exists not only through those who participate by running it or discussing it but also through the behaviors of those who reject it or are rejected by it. To be and not to be a part of it: these are, as we have seen, mobile conditions. Just as many who are active today in the art scene have only recently arrived there and may leave it tomorrow, a high percentage of the viewers are artists who are never going to win prizes or get exhibits, art school students and teachers who disagree with what is put on exhibit at the biennales but who take what is displayed there into account in an ambivalent or negative way and participate in the game. Later they translate or rebut these hegemonic trends in the national circuits to which the circulation of most of what artists produce is restricted. The question left hanging is how to move on from an ethnography of the hegemonic art world to some broader kind of conceptualization that can situate it in worldwide social processes, where we might find more than "a loose network of overlapping subcultures."

Thornton's book presents a family portrait of people who competed successfully during the five years she studied them. To ascertain the degree to which the art world still exists, it isn't enough to show the disagreements and diverse participation styles of the people who pull the strings in New York, London, and Venice. Even there we can see—and this is one of Thornton's merits—that the borders between those who fully belong, those who have a foot in the door, and those who are excluded are frequently shaken up: she not only made the smart decision of choosing a Japanese artist for her visit to a studio; at the Venice Biennale she also took note of the presence of León Ferrari, Francis Alÿs, and Félix González Torres, interviewed Cuauhtémoc Medina, and realized that there was something up with the Ukrainians. But she didn't ask herself whether these rebellious movements, which had a different resonance at the São Paulo and Johannesburg biennales, blurred or contradicted the so-called art world. Is it still a world?

CHAPTER FIVE

>

UNSURE LOCALIZATIONS

We live in the age of unframed art. Art has come off the canvas, refuses to represent a country, aims at making society without religious or political pressures. Nonetheless canvases are still being painted, nations (both central and peripheral) still exist under globalization, global society is broken, and interculturality can't be attained through homogenizing totalizations. Is making postautonomous art possible?

In the previous chapters we worked through these critical junctions in the theoretic intersection between aesthetics and the social sciences. In this chapter we will listen to the artists, or rather to their works: how they create them in an era that claims to be postnational and intermedial and that is poorly represented by grand religious or political narratives. I've chosen three artists from the periphery: Antoni Muntadas, Cildo Meireles, and León Ferrari. By different routes, all three have entered the mainstream, getting exhibits at the Venice Biennale or at MoMA in New York, all the while maintaining conversations with their home societies without feeling obliged to adopt their cultural or artistic traditions in a literal way.

One of the changes initiated by the twentieth-century avant-garde and adopted since by thousands of artists has been to jettison the pretension of insularity—the idea that their work has some autonomous, protected field of its own—as well as the opposite reaction: leaving the museum, slamming the door behind them, while idolizing public or popular spaces. The three artists I analyze belong to a broad current of artists who create works that circulate as unexpectedly through the streets or across the TV screen as they do through galleries and biennales. They throw banks and money circuits into the mix or combine bomber jets with crucifixes. The juxtaposition of canonical representations of Hell with photographs of concentration camps in Ferrari's works tells us something we couldn't have learned by reading separately about the history of Christianity, the history of capitalism, and the history of art.

Insertions into Circuits:
Antoni Muntadas and Cildo Meireles

Workers in dissensus are also translators between different cultures and different ways of knowing. The metaphors that join together the chains of meaning that the disciplines separated are devices of *transfer* and *translation*: Antoni Muntadas gave his most significant series of works the title *On Translation* because, as they have circulated among cities and countries, from cities to media, from artwork to performance, they have cast doubt on what it means to circulate and to translate.

Interculturality appears in many forms: as migrations, as tourism, as exchanges of goods and messages. These forms don't always facilitate communication, as seen in free trade accords that deal only with the commercial aspect of trade. Even in the European Union, a region that assigns a high priority to cultural linkages with its educational, media, and art programs (MEDIA, Eurimages, EUREKA, Erasmus), anthropological and sociological studies show that the weaknesses and failures of European integration are due in part to the fact that citizens perceive top-down accords by politicians and corporate executives as distant from their own interests. Despite the creation of a single currency, a flag, and a European anthem and the proclamation that a "European audiovisual space" exists, these symbols seem to have created little sense of community (Abélès 1996; Balibar 2004; Bonet 2004).

Journalists devote little space to economic arrangements, which they admit to finding difficult to translate into the language of newspapers.

Analysts concerned about social participation wonder whether the technical complexity of the Europeanization of politics "is not contradictory to the ideal of a democracy based on transparency and the ability of each person to access what it at issue in a debate" (Abélès 1996: 110).

Muntadas put the cultural weakness of European unification on view when he created a carpet measuring four by six meters bearing the image of the European flag (twelve stars on a blue background) and displayed it in twelve public spaces of the European Union. In an opera theater in Thessaloniki, a library in Copenhagen, the Calais city hall, and a school in Frankfurt, people walked across the flag with an indifference they would not have felt had it been their own national flag. It was only in an art museum that the public carefully walked around the flag rug, treating it as a work of art. One detail in which Muntadas departed from the official flag was a visual allusion to these circumstances: in the center of each star was an embroidered image of one of the coins from the twelve countries that made up the European Union at the time.

The artist's work, like a research project, leads to conclusions similar to those reached by Marc Abélès in his anthropological studies or by Étienne Balibar (2004) in his philosophical and sociopolitical research into the difficulties of building a European sense of citizenship—proof that articulating economic interests is quite different from building transcultural identities rooted in everyday practices.

Museums, biennales, and art books contain works that denounce, explain, and try to defetishize the role of money in capitalism. Can the temples and sacred scriptures of art be demystified? In 1919 Marcel Duchamp was already questioning—with his *Tzanck Check*, a check he painted to pay his dentist bill—the links between art, artists, and money outside of the protected grounds of culture. We know, from Duchamp's work to the more recent pieces by Cildo Meireles, that it isn't a matter of turning art into politics or economics. Far from taking the facile route of setting a political manifesto to music or images, these artists want to dismantle the discursive connections and devices in language and visual communication that mediate in money movements. Thus Meireles's *Insertions into Ideological Circuits*, such as his *Zero Cruzeiro* and *Zero Dollar*, try to position themselves at the starting point, the zero point, the instant just before existence: the place of the market's imminence.

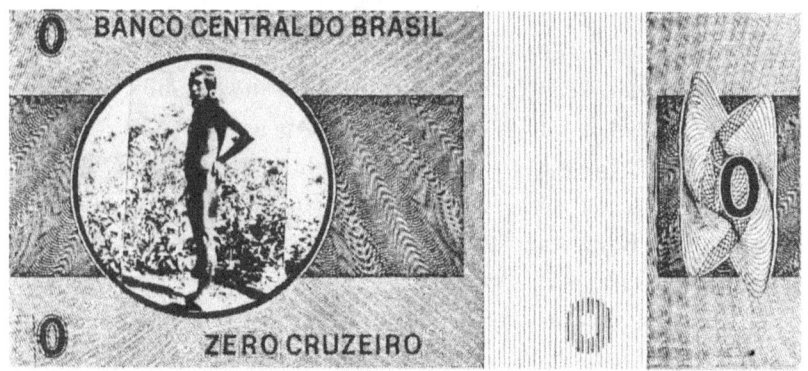

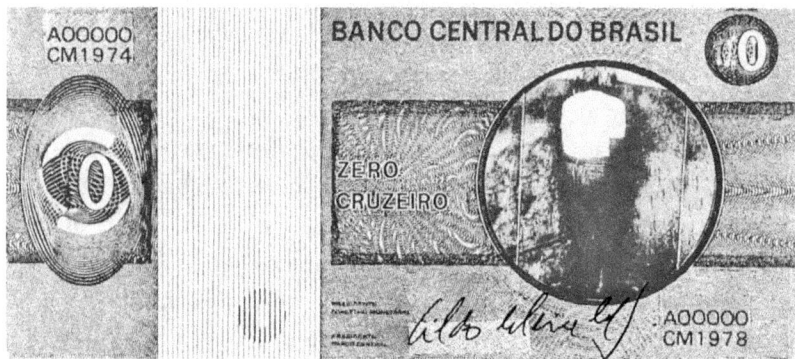

FIGURE 5.1 Cildo Meireles, *Zero cruzeiro*, 1974–78. Screen print on paper, unlimited edition, 6.5 × 15.5 cm.

Instead of dealing in political rhetoric, Meireles opens up "a newly minted political consciousness," writes Maaretta Jaukkuri (2009: 37), and "leaves us facing the border zone" of an "imminent danger." This involves "a method of sublimation that doesn't belong to the tragic-heroic paradigm" of political activism (37). Meireles seems more satisfied with his *Zero Dollar* because the *Zero Cruzeiro* risked miring his work in an argument over Brazil's chronic inflation and limiting its meaning by restricting it to a single country. "In reality, what I was interested in commenting on was the abyss that exists between symbolic value and real value, something that is continually, permanently at work in art" (Meireles 2009: 78). The objective was to get "the people to take the

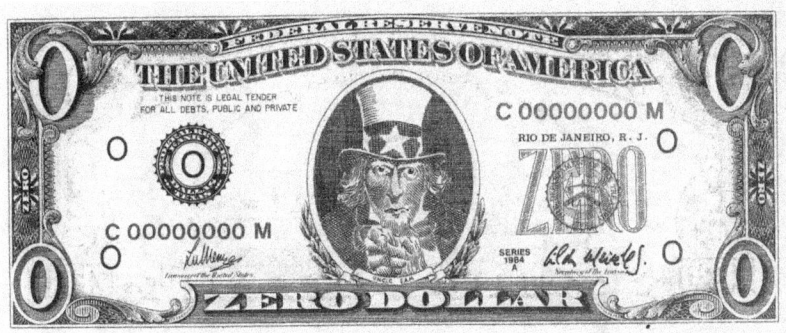

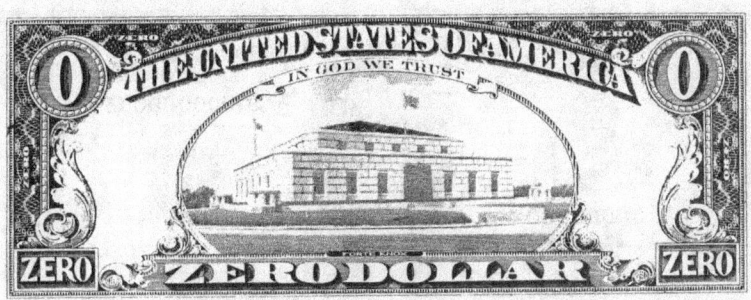

FIGURE 5.2 Cildo Meireles, *Zero dollar*, 1974–78. Screen print on paper, unlimited edition, 6.5 × 15.5 cm.

banknote and ask themselves: what is a cruzeiro? What language is this?" (74).

Much as he used his banknotes to provoke a question prior to any established economic and political circuits, he printed slogans in permanent ink on Coca-Cola bottles ("Yankees go home," "What is the place of art?") to avoid the risk of creating museified art. Instead of making a readymade by bringing a common object into a museum in order to canonize it, Meireles took an industrially mass-produced consumption product, inserted something handmade into it, and reinscribed it into the circulation of everyday goods. These were not simply objects used to represent and critique a way the market functions; they were

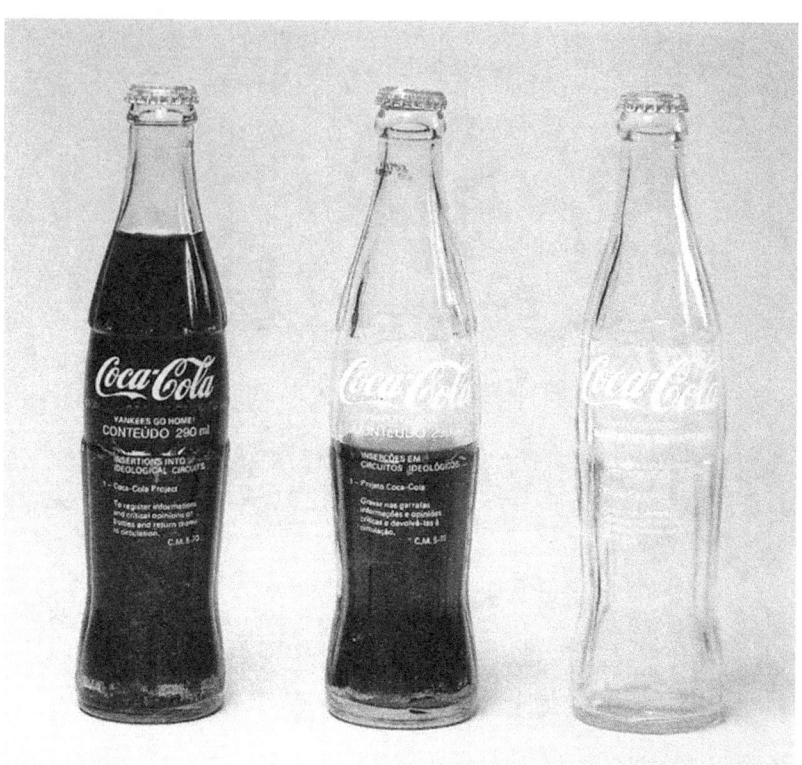

FIGURE 5.3 Cildo Meireles, *Inserções em circuitos ideológicos: Projeto Coca-Cola* (Insertions into Ideological Circuits: Coca-Cola Project), 1970. Text printed on glass bottle. Height: 25 cm, diameter: 6 cm.

objects destined to continue forming part of the structures that they questioned.

On a sheet of paper mimicking the signs that announce exchange rates, Muntadas superimposed an image of a thousand-dollar bill, placing underneath it an hourglass that could barely be seen because over it he printed, in heavy letters, the question "How long will it take for a $1000 to disappear through a series of foreign exchanges?" Most of the names of countries and currencies it lists are illegible, concealed under twenty-two flags from several continents; the cold black-and-white enumeration of exchange rates is euphemized by the colorful symbol of each country. Underneath, the title of the piece: *On Translation: The Bank.*

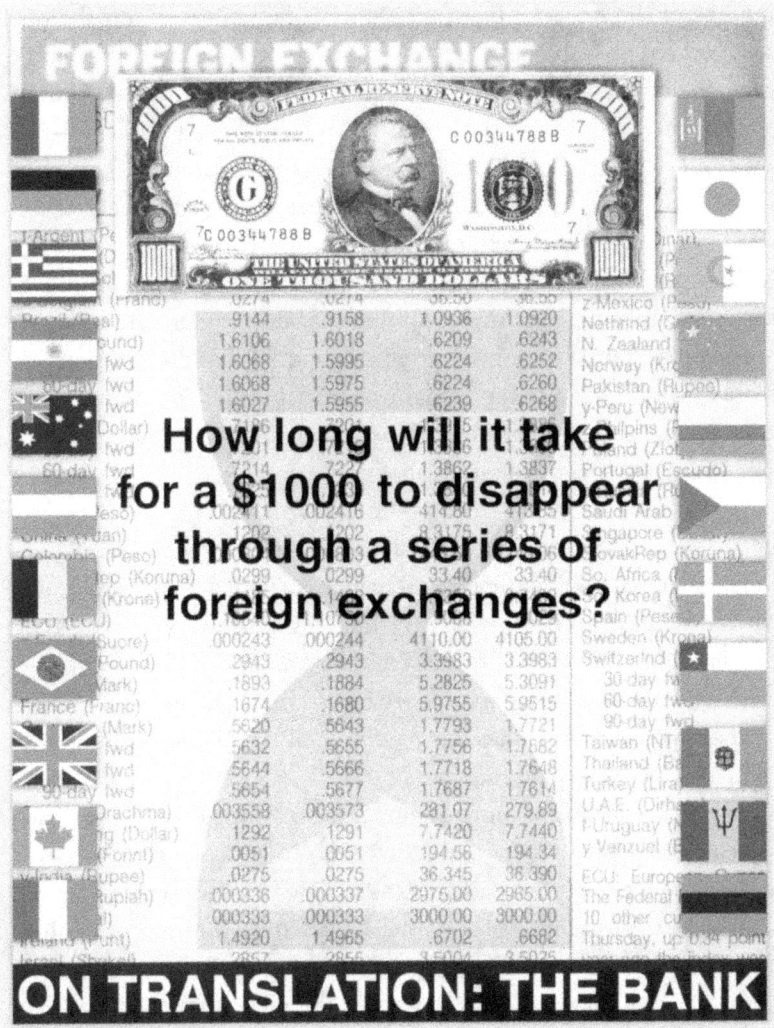

FIGURE 5.4 Antoni Muntadas, *The Bank: Inside the Counting House*. Collage, 1997–2002.

The ironic question that this work—created for the collective exhibit *The Bank: Inside the Counting House*, displayed in an abandoned Chase Manhattan Bank branch office—poses about how quickly money evaporates in exchange transactions contrasts with the steady chromatic eloquence of the national flags: monetary transactions as translation, losses incurred as cash goes from one currency to another as the equivalent of the devaluation of symbolic actions between countries. Unlike the operation performed with the European flag—a rug to step on—the images in *On Translation: The Bank* express the durability of nations, not as resistance but as setting. They accompany the question about the dissemination and dissolution of money.

Jesús Martín-Barbero reminds me that imminence can also be found in the marketplace, in its uncertainties that economics cannot manage to regulate. What does money tell us about? What does it refer to? Detached from labor and the actual use of real things, from any social relations less abstract than those of the financial sort, perhaps it refers only to emptying society of public meaning.

What are the mass media? Three decades ago the first generation of critical media studies replied that a newspaper isn't a place where a group of journalists inform the citizenry; rather it is a place where a mass of clients is sold to advertising firms. This was the moment when people started noticing that newspapers were being financed less by subscriptions than by commercial advertisements and thus were beginning to depend on those who paid for ads.

Today the definition is more complicated. A more diverse set of actors means that newspapers and television networks (including news programs) now serve predominantly as settings for entertainment and mechanisms for influencing the vote, humiliating bothersome politicians through video scandals, and accumulating profits from all these sources. It is only too easy to suppose that the media have become omnipotent constructors of "reality." This regression to the theory of manipulation in current studies of video politics, though more sophisticated than the conspiratorial version of the 1970s, pays too little attention to a more radical effect: the emptying out of the public sphere. As the pact of verisimilitude with the media erodes, their relationship to viewers and readers becomes more closely linked to the register of entertainment, a stage on which society—collective ways of desiring or representing— continues to be constructed, but is stripped of what public sentiment once entailed: taking the commonplace for granted, in a shared form, through social interaction (Rabotnikof 2005).

While some movements see art as demanding payback for the media's deceptions or emptying the public space, making such demands tends to be a situational job, and the artistic way of acting in the social realm appears not to be very effective in this regard. Just as art is impoverished when it mimics the language of certainties and "political correctness," it also fails to advance when it is devoted to demythifying media operations, a job that is already being done by hundreds of people in communications studies and by the alternative information networks on the web. The most disturbing works are those that display the emptying of the public sphere and the frenzy that can be ginned up by media indoctrination campaigns.

Several art, literature, and video works call for readings from the intersection between media circuits and urban space. The piece *Sala de Control (Control Room)*, created in 1996 by Muntadas in his hometown, Barcelona, consisted of installing nine video monitors that displayed scenes transmitted by surveillance cameras, some of which were trained on different areas of the city while others were placed inside and on the roof of the building where the monitors themselves were on display. Yet another monitor played the taped opinions of people from the neighborhoods that were being filmed; a separate screen projected slow-motion images of buildings being demolished and imploded in the same areas. The city as a place of appropriation, reappropriation, destruction of *spaces* and the city as a system of communication and circulation of *flows*.

The unfolding of the urban in spaces and flows, more obvious in the metropolis, corresponds to the loss of the sense of boundaries among the people who live in the city. This makes it hard, even for people who live in the same city, to have a narrative of shared social life. Meanwhile the systems of communication and surveillance (radio, television, hidden cameras) simulate mending a view of the whole by gazing in every direction. The complementary play between the city as a territorial space and as a communications circuit is notable for defining the urban in current sociological theories such as those of Manuel Castells and Saskia Sassen. The imbalances and uncertainties created by unregulated urban sprawl seem to be counterbalanced by the television journalists who recount from their helicopters where a car crash or a crime took place and which roads you can drive on and so make the destructured space your own.

Muntadas imagined that, by changing the orientation of a few cameras, turning them to face the public, making their information visible, he could help give citizens back control over their city. I would say that such actions by artists with respect to surveillance don't generate real changes, but they do serve to make the procedures of disorganization and control visible.

The same interpretation fits another work by Muntadas, *Words: The Press Conference Room*, a parodic re-creation of a political press conference. At one end a microphone-covered podium, illuminated by a circle of light against the backdrop of a wall, underlines the inexistence of whoever was supposed to be giving explanations and taking the consequences. A path carpeted with the front pages of newspapers from around the world ties the podium to a television placed at the opposite end, on the floor, on which politicians speak redundantly until their words begin to run together. In the middle, chairs covered with white sheets point out the ghostly nature of the audience. Politicians who won't show their faces or put their bodies forward, who aren't there— they emerge only from the televised fiction, speaking for no one.

The circularity of *The Negotiating Table*, described in chapter 3, illustrates the impossible completeness of intercultural translations. The table's uneven legs, "corrected" at floor level by stacks of books on the circulation of images, which in turn both name and conceal financial firms, create another *mise-en-abyme* circle of translations. The flag-turned-carpet also refers to the floor. Communications descend from the ethereal realm to everyday urban life, from the ineffable to the visible, when television messages and the recordings of surveillance cameras are forced to interact with the voices of local people.

Transculturations *en abyme*: there is no negotiating table, regardless of how perfectly round, that can stop the cracks in the economy and keep them from spreading; no transnational flag can succeed as a reconciling

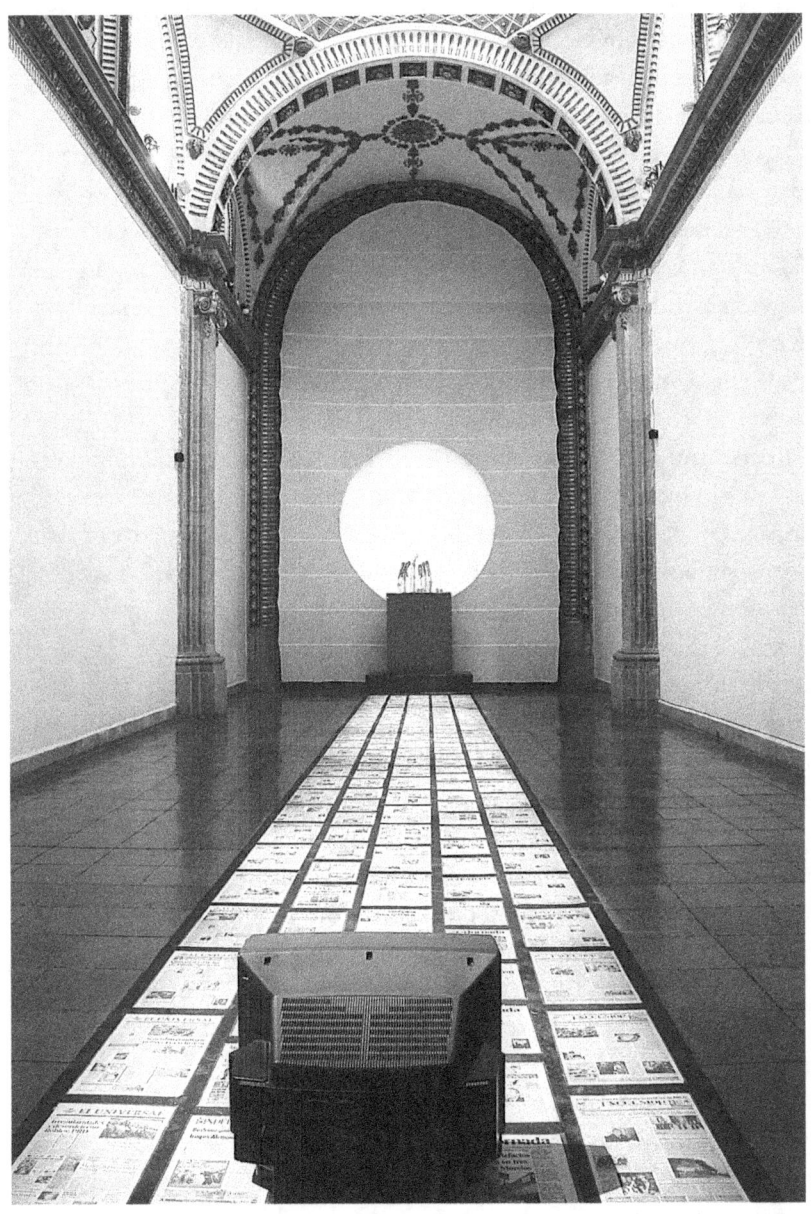

FIGURE 5.5 Antoni Muntadas, *Words: The Press Conference Room.* 1991–2004.

image, neutralizing the fierce competition between exchange rates that is hidden behind the national flags. Muntadas's trajectory leaves open questions about how to translate the sign systems and codes we use to try to understand each other. It is exasperatingly dubious whether translations can make cultures or nations audible to each other.

Art doesn't present itself as a repertoire of responses, not even as a jab at seeking them. It is rather the place where questions and doubts are translated and retranslated, where they hear their ringing echoes. *On Translation* is a project that is replicated in many countries and languages, never the same way. What does it tell us, in the end—that all we have left is the ability to drift, to wander on from version to version? Are we also dissipating in these operations, like the thousand dollars as they are exchanged from one currency to another?

I can't find the dissolution of the self that is so celebrated by postmodernism in the collected works of Muntadas. Although the nomadic slippages of *On Translation* could induce us to see them as part of that deconstructive landscape, in which all subjects are imaginary, a succession of mirrors or simulacra, his references to identity are not entirely unstable or delocalized. Muntadas names diffuse, transnational agents that are difficult to apprehend, but in the end they are agents. The bank is the agent that translates cash, and its translations do not always lead directly into ruin: some people get rich. The negotiating table is circular but unbalanced, and the maps that blanket its surface evoke the inequality involved in traveling from country to country. I agree with Javier Arnaldo: "Translation functions as a nexus of asymmetric relations between parties" (Muntadas 2002: 46). Continuing to replicate this project keeps it from becoming a (finished) work, maintains the opening to the abyss, to the unexpected. But I feel a moment of doubt when I describe these transculturations as en abyme, like the infinite repetition of images in facing mirrors, because they also connote disappearing into a vacuum.

In the abyss, echoes still ring. Like applause in society. The version of *On Translation* prepared for Bogotá in 1999 presented color digital images of anonymous hands clapping, and above them black-and-white snapshots of situations of physical, media, ecological, military, economic, and sexual violence from different countries. We don't know whose hands are clapping, but many of the violent situations can be identified. The viewers in Colombia could hear the echoes this show made in many situations all around them.

Muntadas's decision to place his works in the contexts of the city or the nation where he was acting, following the art or media discourses of those contexts, reveals his consideration about the sites where he put on his exhibits, his resistance to perceiving them as mere nonplaces. In these acts of interlocution, in his personal insertion into the destinations of his works, I find much more than an echo of a preconceived work that need only traipse around the world. There's someone here who has doubts about what properly ought to be said in each place and who set himself the task of interacting with the language, the codes, the conflicts, and the questions of that drama, that point in the itinerary. Translation is an attempt to connect the experiences of artists, institutions, and audiences from different cultures: placing the need for translation, and its insufficiency, at the center makes manifest the lack of a unifying narrative; insisting on the possibility that we might share something in common means refusing to accept the emptying out of the public sphere or the conciliatory simulations of the media.

Redistributing the Way We Count: Alfredo Jaar

Faced with the lack of an integrating narrative, faced with the media's simulacra, it is possible to put on display the abyss between symbolic and real value, as Meireles does, or to construct translation devices in the style of Muntadas. Wondering what to do when faced with the pain of society and when faced with the distortions of the media has led to a third strategy: coming up with a different way to document events.

From the middle of the nineteenth century to the middle of the twentieth, photography and film had the role of recording and communicating wars, the everyday lives of people far away, and the decisive events in disconnected cultures. When these jobs were taken up by television and the Internet, photographers and film and video makers began to learn that images can think and speak in different ways. How can you give a different intensity to things everyone has already seen? Can you mitigate the cruelest disconnect between narratives: the global disinformation that selects certain massacres and ignores others? Jean-Luc

Godard's *Histoire(s) du cinéma* (1998) and the essays on photography by Alan Sekula and Martha Rossler are examples of efforts to renew the documentary vocation of photography and film.

In his work *Untitled (Newsweek)*, Alfredo Jaar displayed *Newsweek* covers from April 6, 1994—when the massacres in Rwanda began—to August 1, 1994—when *Newsweek* made the genocide its cover story for the first time. Next to each cover Jaar noted what had taken place that week in Rwanda that *Newsweek* had neglected to report on. Three weeks after the end of the slaughter that left nearly a million people dead over the course of less than one hundred days, to the indifference of the international community, Jaar traveled to Rwanda, interviewed some of the survivors, and photographed the massacre sites and refugee camps. He tried many ways of organizing this material but always felt that he was failing. One device he tried was selecting photographs of different aspects of the destruction and burying them in black boxes, which he then piled up, like a cemetery and an archive. On top of each box he placed a description of the images it contained, such as this one:

> Gutete Emerita, 30 years old, is standing in front of the church. Dressed in modest, worn clothing, her hair is hidden in a faded pink cotton kerchief. She was attending mass in the church when the massacre began. Killed with machetes, in front of her eyes, were her husband Tito Kahinamura (40) and her two sons Muhoza (10) and Matirigari (7). Somehow, she managed to escape with her daughter Marie-Louise Unamararunga (12), and hid in a swamp for three weeks, only coming out at night for food. When she speaks about her lost family, she gestures to corpses on the ground, rotting in the African sun. (Gallo and Jaar 1996: 59)

Jaar thought, "If the media and their images fill us with an *illusion* of *presence*, which later leaves us with a sense of absence, why not try the opposite? That is, offer an absence that could perhaps provoke a presence" (59).

Another work that resulted from this documentation was *The Eyes of Gutete Emerita* (1996), made of a huge pile of slides that, viewed from close up, all showed the same image: the eyes of a survivor whom he had interviewed.

The artist decided against showing piles of bloody corpses or children missing limbs, that is, none of the images that voyeurism would call for. Instead of displaying what the news magazines had concealed, Jaar stages its absence, the scandalous distraction of *Newsweek* by all the things it found more interesting for its covers: the deaths of Jacqueline Kennedy and Richard Nixon, the anniversary of D-Day, a campaign for American values. The boxes that enclosed the photographs, a work titled *Real Pictures*, displayed names that bore (hi)stories. "The reality they show is that of names that have a story. And we must first be sensitized to that story, that capacity for each name to have a story. The names have to be made visible, the silent bodies have to be made to speak. It is not a question of removal, but of redistributing the way we count" (Rancière 2007: 75).

At times it is said that the media have to select images because too many of them can blind us, make us insensitive. Jaar chooses not to compete with the excessive numbers of views of the massacres, to show not the massive deaths but rather the eyes that have seen that spectacle. The *image* can't be reduced to a presentation of what is visible; it can also appear in words, in the poetic movements of displacements and condensation. The gaze that these object seek is one that might alter the conventional relationships between the multitude of images and the excess of words, between the image, the word, and silence. The artist isn't competing with the media to supply missing information but constructing spaces where we can see and think in a different way.

As a student of communications and society, Jaar learned about the procedures the media use to select images, but as an artist he made works that propose a different way of seeing. Rancière, as a social thinker, reflects on what it is that the artist does and about the worry, first raised in the late nineteenth century, that too many images of social pain can desensitize us:

> It was the time when physiology was discovering the multiplicity of stimuli and neural circuits in place of what had been the unity and simplicity of the soul, and when psychology was turning the brain into a "polypary of images." The problem is that this scientific promotion of number coincided with another one, that of the people

as the subject of a form of government called democracy, that of the multiplicity of anonymous individuals whom the proliferation of reproduced texts and images, of shop windows in the commercial city, or of lights in the city as spectacle, turned into fully-fledged inhabitants of a shared world of knowledge and enjoyment. The old division separating the select few dedicated to the work of thinking, and the multitude, believed to be buried in sensory immediacy, ran the risk of getting lost. In order to separate scientific number from democratic number, it was necessary to give a new form to the ancient opposition of small and large numbers, of the higher world of ideas and sensory multiplicity. It would henceforth be the opposition of two nervous systems, of two organizations of the sensory multiplicity of messages. (2007: 72–73).

The perception then began to spread that the dangerous excitement of so many images would produce

appetites unwisely unleashed, pushing the masses to attack the social order; or conversely an exhaustion of the race, weakened in the face of the enemy, or submitting to tyranny. Lamentation over the excess of images was at first a picture of democracy as a society in which there are too many individuals, too many consumers of words and images, all crowded together, preventing our gaze and thought from assimilating broader perspectives. (73)

The Museum beside Itself: León Ferrari

Pleasure or denunciation? Artists are used to hearing two calls: those from the art "field," demanding that they guard the autonomy and political asepsis of their works; and those from the political "field" or movements, urging them to be socially responsible. In the twentieth century many artists heard these two appeals as a choice. Like other artists disillusioned by avant-garde actions in the 1960s in Argentina, León Ferrari abandoned the galleries in 1966 and worked for the next decade with collectives such as those that produced *Malvenido Rockefeller* (Unwelcome Rockefeller) and *Tucumán arde* (Tucumán Is Burning), a visual and textual documentation of an Argentine province impoverished by the closing of sugar refineries, which was exhibited in trade union offices.

Three decades later the continuation of these underground practices and their simultaneous mainstream canonization led from the choice between aesthetics and politics to a question that isn't easy to answer: How is it that an artist who has been recognized only in his own country and by a small handful of foreign Latin Americanists for the better part of half a century should suddenly, at the age of eighty, find his works promoted by galleries in New York and Europe, put on display at MoMA and the Reina Sofía, circulating through seven biennales in one year, and winning the Golden Lion at Venice? How is it that his most recent works and other works that cost $1,000 or $2,000 two decades ago should now be selling for $80,000 and $150,000? How is it that this artist should, at the same time, become the accidental leader of a pro–human rights, anticensorship movement?

I'm going to try to give a partial answer by analyzing Ferrari's works and his insertion into multiple circuits. His trajectory also displays an intermedia practice, but in a different sense from that of Muntadas. Andrea Giunta and Liliana Piñeiro (2008: 10) describe the experience of watching him work in his workshop:

> Using a gutta outliner, he writes St. Alphonse's words about the infinity of hell on an extensive piece of fabric, where the texts bundle up and the ink he writes with runs and drips, turning the phrases into an unintelligible smudge. At the same time, and with his other hand—or between words—León ties wire, smears plastic mice in glue, fills holes with polyurethane, and mounts the crystals of his magical aerial sculptures. A walk around his workshop is a unique experience that brings us into contact with a complex, humour-filled type of work. Ferrari mixes materials and topics: biblical and poetical quotes; paper, fabric, wire, videos, and polyurethanes; love and sensuality, the madness of big cities, the horrors of war, or the greatest of cruelties disguised as kindness.

Languages and materials have no autonomy in his explorations. A key device is getting everything to intertwine. When he uses metal, wood, wire, oils, acrylics, maps, blueprint paper, block-letter stamps, and plastic images bought at a religious articles store to make calligraphic drawings, collages, or stagings, he doesn't limit himself to the expressive qualities of each material; he seeks to have each intercept the others, making them say something different from what they habitually express. A first answer to the question about his delayed resonance can be found in the "othered" materials his works feature: the montage of martial and sacred imagery, the surprising eroticism in unexpected scenes, the radical skepticism that doesn't bar the occasional happiness. Rancière's (2005: 47) statement about the "clash of the heterogeneous" as a feature of critical art applies here: "It aims at sharpening at the same time our perception of the play of signs, our consciousness of the fragility of the procedure of reading those signs, and the pleasure we experience when we play with the indeterminate."

Is he transgressive? It's more complex than that. He takes off, in effect, from structures that we all consider paragons of order—floor plans, city maps, chessboards, the reiterative untidiness of the jungle—and messes with their rules. The black king sleeps with a white queen, sometimes on a chessboard besieged by dozens of confused little men, at other times in carefully made beds surrounded by thousands of domestic items, musical notes, random letters of different sizes, everything that can be said in the union or separation of a couple. On blueprint paper measuring 100 by 280 centimeters, he designs streets or floor plans for buildings in which twenty-seven bureaucrats sit at a series of desks surrounding a bed; others coexist with furnaces and Volkswagens in a single room. Objects from different rooms visit each other, home life spills out into the street, and the whirl of public life piles up inside the houses.

The heliographs he exhibited at *Documenta XII* form part of a series of constructions made from conventional graphic signs: architectural forms, urban designs, highways, or a simple agglomeration of cars and stereotyped human figures. Since he made them in São Paulo in the 1980s, in them we can detect references to that congested metropolis; since he was living there with his family, exiled by the persecution of the Argentine military dictatorship, these structures are usually read as a metaphor for that stifling political climate. But these dense labyrinths tell us more than that.

Obsessive designs may tranquilize some people. On Ferrari's maps and plans, the way they mix together and pile up looks like they are exacerbating failed arrangements. If poetic or ironic humor lent warmth to other works of his, here the unlimited reproducibility of cars and human dummies suggests the desperate confusion generated by "strategies" of ceaseless expansion, which are so destructive of diversity and meaning.

Nevertheless Ferrari's critical thinking doesn't mean he is an ill-tempered or cynical artist. His pieces making fun of the unique, unrepeatable, exceptional work of art make the argument that serialization isn't a dark and fatal destiny. By multiplying we can construct difference, open ourselves up to the unknown. True, his frenetic and strict images hint that the poetry generated by mechanical and electronic reproduction tends toward the desperately baroque; critics, however, are more likely to deem it a parody than a creative transformation.

Ever since his most famous work, *La civilización occidental y cristiana* (Western and Christian Civilization)—an image of Christ crucified on an American fighter-bomber—was removed from the Instituto Di Tella exhibit in 1965, Ferrari has been the frequent target of censorship, insults, and threats. There were two particularly low points. In 2000 his exhibit *Infiernos e idolatrías* (Infernos and Idolatries) at the Centro Cultural of Buenos Aires, which combined Last Judgment images by Bosch, Giotto, Michelangelo, and Brueghel with toasters and frying pans in which plastic saints were "cooking" and toy birds placed to look like they were defecating on the religious images, generated waves of emails to the Spanish embassy demanding that the exhibit be shut down, as well as protests by nuns and Catholic fanatics at the doors to the cultural center, who chanted the rosary while hurling garbage and tear-gas canisters into the gallery. Ferrari declared in an interview that they had completed the artwork.

In 2004, at a retrospective of his work at the Centro Cultural Recoleta in Buenos Aires, in addition to the seventy thousand people who came to see the exhibit, the way he revised sacred iconography "attracted" some who do not usually visit museums: these impassioned visitors destroyed works of art; a Mass of Propitiation "for the rights of God" was offered at the Iglesia del Pilar, the church next door to the cultural center; the Corporation of Catholic Lawyers demanded that Buenos Aires fire the city's secretary of culture under whose authority the center had mounted the exhibit; and five corporate sponsors withdrew their support.

"What is most offensive?" asked the writer María Moreno (2004). "The virgins with cockroaches and scorpions? The saints in the frying pan? . . . No doubt it was Michelangelo's *Last Judgment* being shat on by three canaries through the grating of their cage floor." According to Ferrari (2000: 13), these crosses between religious and historical images are disturbing because they reveal that "the West feels a singularly double passion for cruelty. On seeing Jesus crucified, they weep for two thousand years and reject it; on seeing the suffering of those whom the one tortured on the cross condemns to torture, they understand, justify, and encourage it. Cruelty is unjust when Jesus suffers from it for a few hours and a just punishment when it means that millions will suffer for all eternity."

Ferrari's work questions religious and political oppression along with their modes of representation. His collages superimpose crowds adulating Hitler or the gesticulating dictators of South America with the images of Hell enshrined in the Sistine Chapel and the Last Judgments by Giotto, Brueghel, and Dürer. No one is unaware that the church was complicitous with the dictatorship of Francisco Franco in Spain, or that priests accompanied members of the Argentine military on the airplanes from which they threw their victims, still alive, into the water of the Río de la Plata. But Ferrari's images attain a new level of eloquence by expressing both the humorous and the sinister sides of the sublime.

A judge shut down the exhibit at the request of the Asociación Cristo Sacerdote (Association of Christ the Priest) and in response to a message by Cardinal Jorge Bergoglio declaring the show blasphemous, which was read in every church in the Buenos Aires diocese. The Buenos Aires city government appealed the decision, and the higher court ordered the exhibit reopened, arguing that "freedom of expression should protect critical art; and when art is critical, it is bothersome, irritating, and provocative" (Ares 2005). Ferrari thanked Cardinal Bergoglio for giving his exhibit free advertising, which effectively increased the number of visitors and landed the conflicts between religious repression and political and cultural rights on the public agenda in a way that the habitually polite pretences of the media and society never do.

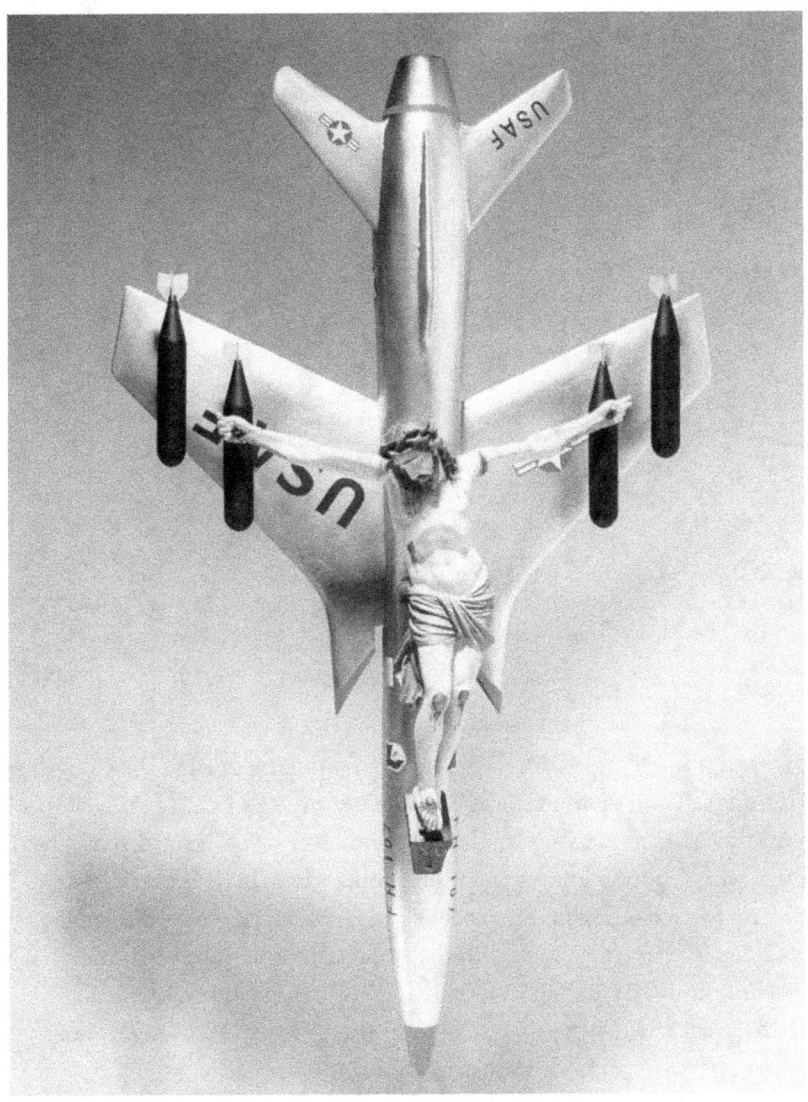

FIGURE 5.6 León Ferrari, *La civilización occidental y cristiana* (Western and Christian Civilization), 1996. Plastic, oil, and plaster, 200 × 120 × 60 cm. Collection of Alicia and León Ferrari.

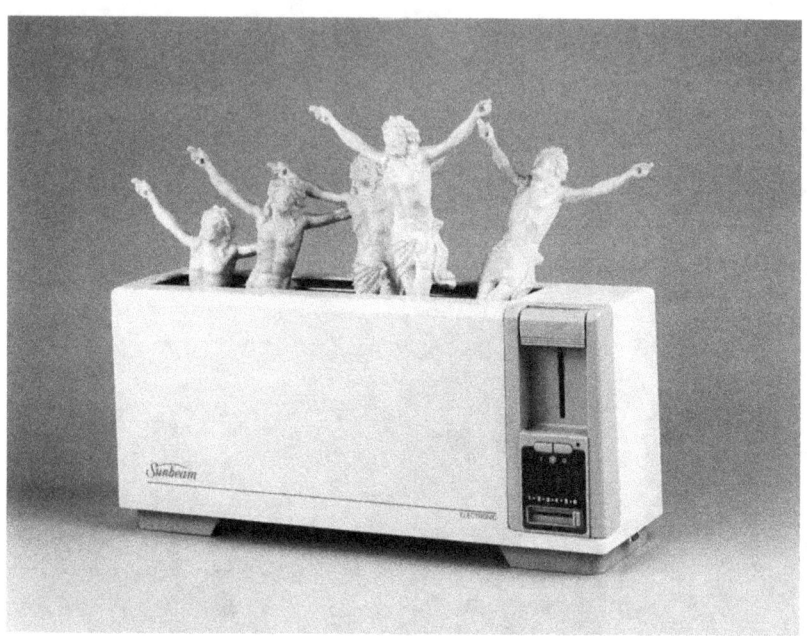

FIGURE 5.7 León Ferrari, *Tostadora* (Toaster), from the series *Ideas para infiernos* (Ideas for Hells), 2000. Electric toaster with plastic Christ figures, 29 × 35 × 10 cm. Collection of Alicia and León Ferrari.

Ferrari is much more than a provocateur. Sticking to what the Church attributes to God, to what makes God an extremist—being against condoms and abortion, using "Hell, that semi-Nazi idea" as a threat—he argues with God; he knows the Bible well and challenges the repeated autos-da-fe of Jews, witches, heretics, homosexuals, and political opponents. He wrote two letters to the pope, asking him to work on "the cancellation of the Last Judgment" and to "extend the repudiation of torture proclaimed in the Catechism to the Beyond" by doing the necessary paperwork to have Hell suspended (Moreno 2004).

It doesn't help to think of Ferrari's work as that of a transgressor or subversive, if we bear in mind the will for organizing and containment displayed in his boxes, cages, and architectural plans. Classic reflections on paintings maintain that frames demarcate and contain. Nearly a century ago José Ortega y Gasset ([1921] 1963: 310) wrote in his essay

"Meditación del marco" (Meditation on the Frame) that he saw in the framing of a canvas evidence of the separation of the aesthetic object, its autonomy with respect to "the real." If someone looking at Ferrari's creations still continued to imagine him as an avant-garde artist seeking the insularity of the work of art, all it would take to disabuse him of that notion would be to take him to see Ferrari's studio crammed with pots, frying pans, plastic toy soldiers, Santería knickknacks, and newspaper clippings.

Like other artists of his generation (I'm thinking of Luis Felipe Noé), Ferrari makes the noisiest manifestations of reality explode into his works: torture, battles between gods, men, and demons, institutional hypocrisy, the violence enshrined in Scripture. But these explosions are contained when he represents or narrates them using the techniques of collage or montage. True, we aren't used to seeing the sacralized (and optimized) Hell of Christian iconography turned into a metaphor for German or Latin American concentration camps. But that irreverence is moderated by its packaging—by the boxes surrounding, the bottles enclosing the symbols of the conquest and the forced evangelization of the Americas, the cages holding the pigeons that can transcend them only by dropping their excrement onto the Inquisitorial pile below.

> Your mannequins, León, are loose, out in the open. Their only limitation is the profile of the human figure and the written figure. But why so many rectangles in so many of your pieces?
>
> Almost always rectangles. . . . As an element, the box . . . is handy. A rectangle never stops you, never bothers you, because it's so familiar, and boxes sort of take after that; you can use their volume.

How can you make yourself heard in a cacophonous world? Fundamentalist religions try to always say the same thing, politicians cheapen meaning when they talk, and lovers complain that they can't find the right language for their experiences, between the clichés of romantic kitsch and their powerlessness to name the unnamable. The media parody them all.

Ferrari is trying to construct an eloquent language for naming the ruins and sufferings of the world, which we all know already from the television and the Internet. His aims are to upset the usual mainstays, make fun of the oppressors as well as the representations that glorify them, and confuse a city's public and private spaces—public streets and the privacy of homes—on an enormous map where all the scales of social life intermingle.

I find the keys to Ferrari's resonance in these strategies. It lies not in directly confronting the powers that be but in the revealing gaps that are described without letting the humor paper over the tragedy. To achieve this, he understood—unlike many political artists—that in addition to questioning Western values, as Giunta (2008: 90) put it, he had to problematize "the canon, the value of the unique object, and the limits of taste."

This isn't about the artist who becomes transcendent by suffering and dying young, or about the artist who keeps surprising the public and the media with splashy new ideas every season, or about the one who retires from view to guard his secrets from the world's folly. Ferrari gathers cockroaches, politicians, plastic saints stamped "Made in China"; he argues with the priests who interpret this confusion and try to establish order on earth by separating toy heavens from toy hells; he demystifies them by not just setting loose the dictators, the serpents, the Christs, and the fighter-bombers but by arranging them on suggestive canvases or in neat boxes.

What we're left with is so "orderly" a version of our current disarray and a correlation so closely fitted to our paradoxical religious sources that they make traditional narratives about communities saved by brotherly love sound like apocryphal gospels. Something of the sort is also going on with his work in relation to art history: a simplified reading of avant-garde artworks has interpreted them as transgressive gestures meant to carry the art beyond the frame, the exhibit outside the museums, find meaning for art again in politics, the revolutions of customs, and the imaginaries. While Ferrari shared the disappointment over these frustrated attempts, he is now doing just the opposite: because of the public debate generated in Buenos Aires over the question of whether his exhibit had to be shut down, the judges, politicians, human rights activists, and people who believe that true culture is made in the churches were all forced to go to the museum. Turning the biblical invitation around, it wasn't "Come unto me" but rather "Come into the museum." Not to see the world-famous architect or even the artist. When they arrived, they found that everything having to do with sex, politics, and iconoclasm was contained in boxes, bottles, canvases, and objects as everyday as blenders. The artist wasn't there.

Convinced that he should continue with the discretion, the subtlety, with which he reinterpreted Pop and Dadaism and reinvented sacred art, he keeps working in his studio, creating unexpected forms in polyurethane and writing letters both to the powerful and to those he loves. He paints and writes, faithful not to any Scriptures but to his obsession with frenzied maps, to his tremulous hand spelling out incomprehensible calligraphies on mannequin bodies—because "writing on the body is like caressing a woman," he says, "and also not understanding her. Caressing, but not understanding."

Multiple Localizations and Digital Media

In this era of postautonomous art, artists are redesigning their creative programs in order to situate themselves flexibly in what remains of the art fields and in other spaces and networks. New economic, media, and critical windows broaden their horizon without entailing the radical delegitimization of museums and galleries. This expansion of practices also changes the realms of theory, criticism, and cultural politics.

Critics find that they must transcend the "four successive circles of recognition" noted by Alan Bowness (1989: 88): those of other artists, art dealers, curators and critics, and the public. When it comes to the critical fate of artworks, we must also include media networks, the horizons and failures of sociopolitical actions, and the broader cultural controversies with which artists and institutions interact. It is a matter of reconceptualizing the role of art beyond museifying and biennalizing it.

A similar redefinition is going on with the territorial relationship established between art and the nation and with the concept that led scholars to write national histories of art. We need to rethink the visibility and communicability of the arts without yielding to absolute delocalization or merely returning to nationalist glorification. Global circuits are powerful, but they don't cover everything. Migrations grow larger and they draw forcefully on our imaginaries, but in many regions ethnic, national, or simple local identities continue to be meaningful. After the impact of postmodern thought on anthropology, philosophy, and aesthetics, idealizing travels and making "nomadism" a key to understanding all humanity, today we draw distinctions between the displacements of tourists, labor migrants (documented and undocumented), soldiers invading foreign countries, natives going into exile, artists and curators who attend several biennales each year, and the majority of artists whose work circulates only in their own countries. The homogeneous aestheticization of such diverse travels—as in the case of Sebastião Salgado, who collects images of migrants from forty countries and several continents in his show *Éxodos*—gives rise to an "abstract, global solidarity that undoes the specifics of the exploitation of the subject" (Ramos 2003: 71). As we've seen with regard to the unjustifiable abstraction that represents the notion of "world heritage," artistic actions cannot reconcile the world by annulling differences and inequalities. Nor can they deal on their own with national or ethnic identities unless they want to take on the fissures and contradictions.

Instead of merrily adopting a diasporic perspective as epistemic model, both the social sciences and art found it more fertile to conceptualize their actions in "a world where the great majorities not only never move but never want to move" (Grimson 2009: 18). Most migrants, writes Alejandro Grimson based on sociological and anthropological studies, "are migrants out of resignation, not out of impulse or desire," and calling all our contemporaries nomads is mainly due to an "aestheticizing of theory" (18). Perhaps we need, in megacircuits as well as in the medium and small scale," to follow Daniel Mato's (2007) advice and analyze not deterritorialization but "transterritorialization" or "multilocalization." I would add, for my part, the "unsure localization" of many cultural processes. In this notion I see an attractive poetic and hermeneutic potential for producing and communicating art.

Moreover the idea of unsure localizations is in sync with changes in the notion of place in the digital production and circulation of images. Spreading images digitally and reproducing them on screens should reduce, but not eliminate, the canonization of exhibit spaces such as museums and biennales and create other ways to access and socialize artistic experiences. It should also put art on a relatively equal footing with other areas of visual culture.

Chapter Five

>

Online museums transcend their physical locations, and at the same time they can visualize and measure the number of visitors their pages receive by country. The places where images are received and consumed can be traced by collecting and storing user data. Then again, mobile devices such as the iPhone and iPad give you access to the cultural offerings of your own city and of many others around the world. These are just some of the new interactions between museums as buildings, artists as the mediators or translators of their collections, and the spectators who can now assemble their own archives and ways of seeing.

Videos, the Internet, the World Wide Web, and digital devices make it possible to rethink the job of museums, as Manuel Borja-Villel suggests, not as proprietors of artworks but as custodians who facilitate their circulation, not by defining their collections based on the scarcity of Picassos or Pollocks in the marketplace but as shared collections and archives. Criticism should therefore deal not only with artworks but with images, not only with images but with the events that take place as they circulate, as they interact with and are reappropriated by diverse audiences.

What keeps art alive isn't that it has become postinstitutional, postnational, and postpolitical. One of the ways art continues to play a part in society is by working with imminence. Imminence isn't a threshold that we're about to get past, as if one of these years we'll be completely global, intermediated, and able to live together interculturality with a minimum of politics. Art exists because we live in tension between what we desire and what we lack, between what we would like to name and what is contradicted or disagreed upon by society.

>

CHAPTER SIX

THE DEATH OF PUBLIC SPACE

Survival Tactics

The theory of fields of art and literature was formed in the era when we conceived of the world as modern and tied together in a narrative. Modernity was posttotalitarian and in some countries was democratically organized, in others a project or simply the desire of a minority. There were no dictators, and when they did burst onto the scene, it was just a matter of getting rid of them and reestablishing free elections, political parties, trade unions, and social movements. Among the human rights being defended were cultural rights: freedom of expression and free communication of ideas, access to education, information, and creativity. The state was asked, in the name of the common interest, to promote the equitable distribution of material and symbolic goods to the entire population.

Defending art and the sciences as autonomous—that is, secular—fields called for managing things using criteria intrinsic to creative activity and knowledge production. Interference by religious and political forces was rejected, because it was confidently believed that keeping art and science independent would make them more productive. There was also an assumption that society was going to incorporate each activity—economics, politics, education, and cultural production—into development organized by the state, which guaranteed or promised the general welfare.

Incomplete Visions: From Solidarity to Espionage

These principles of social organization were gradually transferred to a globalized narrative. This entailed moving from solidarity among a nation's citizens to "Proletarians of the World, Unite!" and, more recently, to the fantasy of global citizenship. There also came the new "corporate solidarities" of entrepreneurs, employees, and consumers who identify with the transnational factory that sells a brand of beverage or car in dozens of countries. The final stage of this narrative is that of networked solidarity, made possible by NGOs, Internet sites, and other more or less real, more or less magical ways of belonging to transnational communities of consumers of music, brand-name clothes, or techniques for physical and spiritual health.

During the first stages of modernity, the independence of the cultural fields and the notions of national and world heritage made sense. Their effectiveness declined as global interdependence and the international circulation of culture advanced. As we know, a world government never came about, and the United Nations never succeeded in establishing itself even as a democratic forum where national governments (many of them undemocratic) would arbitrate their political, economic, and intercultural conflicts according to their shared interests. International organizations couldn't get countries generally to stick to indispensible ecological policies or balance trade between rich and poor countries. Nor has UNESCO been able to come up with a globally effective program for protecting cultural heritage. (Let us recall its inability to stop the destruction of Iraq's Qur'anic Library, the National Archives, and the Archaeological Museum during the U.S. invasion.)

As for the cultural industries and intangible heritage, UNESCO sponsors conferences, research, and programs on saving traditional music forms, languages, and rituals, but its actions tend to stop the moment a clear position must be taken on collective rights and free access that goes beyond copyright. After its failed attempts in the late twentieth century to establish a world information "order," UNESCO left decisions on intellectual property, freedom of expression, and other communication rights in the hands of organizations that deal with international trade: the World Trade Organization and the World Intellectual Property Organization. Only a handful of European countries have kept laws and policies in place to protect their common interest in these strategic matters of contemporary culture.

At a time when the public questions of culture, those that have to do with people's rights, welfare, and access to information, have been left behind—or forgotten—under the commercial hegemony of multinational corporations, the development of art has come to depend on networks of economically powerful leading galleries, museums, biennales, and fairs. Their power is concentrated in a few countries in the Northern Hemisphere, all competing to sell and to attract investments—some investments coming from the art world, others from the oil, computer, banking, and arms industries, or from organized crime.

The same model would apply to the publication "field," if we replaced galleries and museums with the holding companies that have absorbed national publishing houses and talked about book fairs (Schiffrin 2000, 2005) and digital networks instead of art fairs. As I write these words, Google is multiplying the number of accords it has signed with libraries and publishers (more than ten thousand editors and authors from over a hundred countries) in order to continue adding to the millions of books it already has made available in nearly forty languages. Is this a matter of opening up access to world knowledge? Or a corporation sweeping away authors' rights? Or is it a new global structure for distributing scholarship, art, and entertainment? Millions of books include art images, the heritage safeguarded in museums and private collections, the reproduction of which has up until now depended on getting the proper authorization. Other than a few judicial settlements and a few voluntary transfers of rights by the "content creators" or content owners, other writers, screenwriters, artists, video artists, and authors of all sorts feel powerless in the face of this agile, deterritorialized machinery, which makes it possible to reproduce hundreds of texts and images a minute, at the same time making the decisions of many individuals and publishers meaningless.

I'm not forgetting about alternative globalizations. Artists and writers who are still thinking as citizens create independently and come up with their own opinions, do exhibits more for artistic goals than for commercial or media ends, defend cultural policies in their countries, and test out Internet solidarity networks. Public institutions survive, as do independent organizations such as NGOs and associations of artists, theater professionals, cultural promoters, and journalists and networks of cybernauts who distribute creativity and gather information from beyond the commercial circuits.

Gustavo Lins Ribeiro has drawn on the anthropological literature and his own research to show the powerful cultural and aesthetic innovation that has entered the systems and networks of economic globalization "from below," created by Chinese immigrants hawking their wares in Portuguese in the streets of Brasilia and Ciudad del Este, by African street vendors in New York and Washington, and by Arab, African, and Korean peddlers in so many European cities. An architecture of transnational "connecting mechanisms," where languages, habits, and trade cross paths, makes visible the processes in which globalization is still read as simple top-down oppression (Ribeiro 2006: 246). Occasionally these economic and cultural networks generate movements that defend minority rights, backing indigenous groups, the urban poor, and women suffering discrimination.

Nevertheless the increasing appropriation of the public stage by private mega-actors gives them an overwhelming ability to redesign the spaces and circuits where most people get their information and their entertainment, where resources are accumulated, symbolic value is shaped, and works and practices are appraised. This isn't about a simple triumph of privileged minorities over subjugated majorities. We're looking at a process of restructuring—or, according to some, radically breaking down—public space, leading to an extended period of social discontent and disorder. Reactions range from theoretical critiques to local uprisings, from giving a skeptical reception to hegemonic promises to searching for different ways, beyond legal structures, to satisfy basic needs and find meaning. In short, we're facing the death throes of what remains of the art fields and the so-called welfare state—everything that was modern in the organization of social life. Here I will point out two structural features of this new situation: the dismantling of the opposition between inclusion and exclusion and the transition from the politics of living together in harmony to survival tactics.

Beyond the Contrast between Inclusion and Exclusion

During the first stage of the modern era, from the Enlightenment through the middle of the twentieth century, society was imagined as a comprehensible and increasingly integrated whole, insofar as it was progressively coming to include every sector. The state was the guarantor of this inclusion and of the coherent structuring of an ever more participatory society.

Liberal pluralism was based on the proposition that social cohesion and dissent weren't incompatible. As social organization and personal practices were secularized, dissidence came into favor. On the younger fringes and in artistic movements, rebellion and innovation were perceived as legitimate, and they bestowed prestige. Ruptures between adults and youth were thought of as the renovation of a social order that in the end, over the long run, would appear continuous. Conflicts between academic art and the avant-garde were also conceived, as Pierre Bourdieu expressed it a few years ago, as a dispute within the art field in which the participants, by the mere fact of taking part, were demonstrating their interest in continuing the game and reproducing the field by renovating their life options. Nowadays many sectors wish not to be included or feel that they don't form part of any national or social project that could transcend their group interests. They tend to look at inclusion only as an opportunity to take advantage of resources. They don't rule out a job in the formal economy or in a cultural institution, but they can flexibly combine such jobs with informal practices.

This mixed use of both inclusive and informal or even illegal resources can be seen in the new generations' aesthetic consumption habits and in their artistic production. The volume of books, music, clothes, and entertainment they obtain outside the formal market is evidence of low levels of integration or of plain disintegration. When I analyzed the contents of a number of videos on YouTube, as well as the violent rituals of spectacles, I found that the areas of confrontation or of transgression have grown. The same is true when it comes to graffiti, tattoos, the loud, invasive volume of music, and even with regard to cases of direct aggression; such behaviors are sometimes interpreted as ways of occupying differentiated territories—neighborhoods, local dives—and as stage settings for the young people and artists who defy the pretensions of a social order that leaves them on the outside. Their riotous or crude acts, which some adults perceive as a deliberate show of "bad taste," can be read not so much as rebellion as in terms of the radical theatricalization of the quest for difference and forms of disintegration. We see this in their music and their vehement recitals that exclude older generations, as well as in young people's writing, chats, texts, emails without punctuation or written in all caps and abbreviations: a form of writing that alters the order of grammar and sometimes of communication because it occasionally seeks inscrutability, as graffiti has long done. But graffiti is a more marginal and minority form. Linguistic transgression on the Internet has spread to all social classes and seems to be a distinguishing feature between the generations that is also expressive of the lowered effectiveness of education.

There is a significant generation gap between adults who still trust public institutions, even when they criticize them, and the flexibility with which vast sectors of the youth appropriate goods and resources from diverse sources. In the countries that provide state institutions devoted to youth and government aid programs for students or artists, the divergence between official policies and the behavior of the young is remarkable. On one side, government actions intended to deal with the youth try to provide things that the labor market will not offer, that families neglect, or that schools fail to give; on the other, we find that young people aren't very put off by the social disturbances or the barely structured relationships that seem so incomprehensible to governments and institutions for the youth.

The flexibility seen in young people of every sector also shows up in the way artists are changing their behaviors and values. Studies on transformations in the art field in Latin American countries show that music groups, visual artists, and videographers apply to every office at hand. In Mexico they ask for state-sponsored fellowships; if Televisa or private foundations offer any sort of favors, they'll take them; and some go so far as to take cultural financing from drug traffickers, not worrying about the source of the funding, its effects, or the inconsistency among the resources they are using. Similar things are happening in Brazil, Colombia, and other countries. Distinctions that earlier generations drew between public and private, legal and illegal, are vanishing. We perceive a remarkable versatility for moving around, given a scant but very diverse range of resources, and a different set of worries about survival and social development from the ones that artists had to deal with twenty years earlier.

This malleability of behavior is sometimes read as lack of persistence, as opportunism, or a result of the destructuring of the public sphere, from a modern liberal sociological or philosophical viewpoint that conceives the articulation between the public and the private, between the individual and the social, as a compact whole. By contrast, anthropological studies that use a narrative method to record a subject's distinctive positions observe that in present-day societies a single individual will frequently choose to identify with different organizations or contexts, with seemingly opposing behaviors, in order to accomplish his or her aims (Maines 1993; Vila 2009; Watson 2003). That is what I discovered when I asked a few artists to narrate their careers. They included in their life narratives their participation in galleries, museums, and biennales, as well as in independent groups that criticize those institutions; or, as we will see in a discussion of Carlos Amorales, in addition to listing their participation in the artistic fields, they might speak about their involvement in *lucha libre*, a rock group, and formal and informal networks.

It's no accident that so many writers and visual artists are attracted to rock and other musical genres where performers experiment with new ways of forming groups and communicating and which offer a more democratic redistribution of cultural power. They grow there with aesthetic "imbrications" that include artistic productions, behaviors, languages, and political stances, objects, downloading and linking online, institutions, urban spaces, and the media. Young people live in plural worlds, and in their creative practices they use heterogeneous sources that might seem contradictory to older people who adhere to unified narratives. As Maritza Urteaga (2009) has shown, this universality can be observed among young people from many nations; migrants, from young middle-class Arabs who use Western consumer goods while remaining devoted to their Islamic faith to indigenous Purépechas studying at Mexican universities, maintain communitarian values and adopt contemporary, transnational aesthetic referents with a "reflexive habitus."

For this point it is worth citing at length Urteaga's (2009) ethnographic description of "trendsetters," especially those she calls "specialists in expression":

> These are young people born in the city, aged 21 to 32; they are unmarried, have no children, and live with their families of origin or share an apartment with a relative. They specialize in a few expressive activities with a markedly generational stamp that transcends their class origins (the lower limit is the lower middle class): they are concentrated in creative careers such as design (graphic, clothing, industrial, architectural, fashion, jewelry, furniture, etc.), advertising, architecture, communications, fine arts, film, and video, and they make incursions into other specializations to spark their creativity and complement their training, such as acting, speech, cultural promotion, photography, silk screening, visual and audio art, among others. Their cultural products are artistic and functional for modern life in the city, and their creative labor is for a certain segment of the market. They have no quarrel with commercialization and believe that they can be creative in the commercial world and can live from what they work on and make creatively. . . .
>
> Trendsetters are particularly situated between those who generate and those who spread new lifestyles and ways of working. Though they share certain conceptions of work with the avant-garde—such as pleasure and gaining aesthetic satisfaction as innovation—what sets them apart or marks them as distinctive is their combination of creativity and enterprising abilities, which I have termed "enterprising passion." That is, they are capable of taking the risk of pursuing (in the entrepreneurial sense of the word) new ideas and of spreading them to new audiences and markets by associating with other creative people to work, create, and plan. They associate with others in very diverse ways, but what they have in common is forming self-directed collectives around creative, entrepreneurial projects that end when the projects are complete. They live, work, and form their entertainment circuits from the Historical Center to the Polanco, Condesa, and Roma neighborhoods, the historically urbanized zone of Mexico City. They consider themselves "city dwell-

ers" and feel that the source of their inspiration lies in the ethnic and social diversity of the city center, not in the periphery of the middle and upper classes or of the poorer sectors. Their appropriation of urban space is metropolitan; their leisure activities take them to places ranging from traditional urban, abandoned, and underground spots to more commercial locations or cultural centers where a diverse group of young people and personalities converge. They value the city for making it possible to meet people very different from themselves.

Several studies on these sectors of society show that these youth do not see themselves as excluded people seeking inclusion. They don't aspire to careers in corporations or public organizations. These "trendsetters" employ their creativity in transitory, shifting projects, whether in fields called creative or in design, computer science, or lifestyle activities. Does their ethos herald a new "creative economy" in which the ties between work and leisure will change (Florida 2002), or are these novel ways to resituate themselves in an increasingly precarious labor market (Lazzarato 2008; Lorey 2008)? More research is needed to evaluate their role in the megastructures of social reproduction.

From Peaceful Coexistence to Survival

The anthropologist Marc Abélès (2010: 1), whose critical views on European unification I cited in chapter 5, writes that though the people of his generation were born "into a world that was divided in two blocs after enormous bloodshed," they still believed, even "after the death camps, after Hiroshima," in some form of progress and in a balance within terror. In the early twenty-first century, he observes, our relationship with politics has changed as we have moved "from a tradition that places harmoniously living together (convivance) as the highest aim of social beings" to an era when our worries about *survival* orient our choices in the public space (14).

Two reasons for this change stand out. One is the *scale change caused by globalization*—in expectations, in our ability to identify the origins of problems, and in "the conditions of being together" (Abélès 2010: 11). The 1973 oil crisis (start of the collective representation that the planet's energy potential could run out), technological accidents such as the 1986 Chernobyl catastrophe, disasters in megacities, and the "violent intrusion of otherness into our world" that took place on September 11, 2001 (43), are some of the events making us live in uncertainty and caution, in "a world without promise" (16). What was the upshot of the rational projections that inspired studies of futurism and political volunteerism in the 1960s? They began to vanish as a result of the powerlessness of nation-states threatened by roiling ethnic conflicts, overconsumption, "the proliferation of nuclear weapons, and mafia-orchestrated trafficking" (51–52). These other actors seem to adapt more easily to globalization than do nation-states or international organizations.

The other reason for our changing view of the future and of politics is the *opacity and anonymity of the institutions where power is concentrated.* In the current global restructuring of meaning, citizens are feeling radically shocked by the decisions that affect our daily lives. Where do the powerful live? Clearly, few actions can be identified with specific territories. How much good does it do us to learn the names of our country's leaders and legislators and spend our time keeping up to date about their programs and disagreements, when the reins of power are located much farther away? In the IMF or the World Bank, in secret summits of a few heads of state or of CEOs from undiscoverable corporations? Their statements, which invoke the enigmatic marketplace as the ultimate source of rationality, can't help us pin down causes or explanations. Nor can conceptual constructions that give this unfathomable entity names such as "the cosmopolitan regime" (Beck 2000) or "empire" (Hardt and Negri 2000).

Power keeps growing more opaque, but we citizen-consumers are becoming more and more transparent because social surveillance systems know what we eat, where we shop, what our sexual preferences are, and how we react to political unrest. Tweeting and uploading personal images to Facebook was seen at first as playing around, trading photos, random thoughts, and music. And also the personal artistic creativity that doesn't fit in galleries or museums, or that we don't care to have people see in those venues. Suddenly we find out that it isn't just our 970 "friends" who know about our private lives. Our stockpiles of information are also visited by political intelligence services, companies that want to find out what their employees won't tell them at work, and competitors who want to sideline a politician, an artist, or another candidate for a job they are after. Facebook had the profiles of 300 million users by September 2009, nearly 5 percent of the world's population, and there are also other sources of information: "It is common for bosses and team leaders who want to analyze their workers' skills and labor productivity to turn now not to search engines such as Google, but to the new social networks. According to a recent study of the employment website CareerBuilder, in which Microsoft is a minority stakeholder, some 29 percent of employers use Facebook to check whether or not a job candidate is appropriate for a position. Another 21 percent prefer MySpace, and 26 percent use the professional network LinkedIn" (Alandete 2009: 27).

The mysterious nature of the current power structure is perhaps the major cause of citizens' powerlessness and lack of interest in politics. Add to that the abstract nature of global affairs, all the failures that affect us, no matter how far away they are, and the opacity of the largest political actors, and we end up in an uncertain register of the social. Before, a lack of security was conceptualized from a standpoint of coexistence and the task of controlling it was left to the state. Growing instability and uncertainty have made survival our main concern. Our relationship with the future has likewise changed: we have gone from prevention, which implies acting in relation to known contexts, to precaution. It is no accident, Abélès (2010) notes, that our confidence in the great political institutions has fallen in this world, while the NGOs, organizations devoted to economic or ecological survival, have prospered, given their visible actions in concrete places.

This argument may explain the family resemblance we sense when we compare the performances put on by Greenpeace or Amnesty International with those by artists and cultural movements. All of them work by taking fragments of the world, giving a certain visibility to the imminent, and showing how action can still be taken, even from an incomplete view of things. Just as some NGOs (Attac, for example) reject the World Trade Organization, while others seek to help establish national and international regulatory processes, there are some artists who decide to do without institutions and others who interact with both institutions and social movements. The question they both face, in the challenge to prove effective, is how to make the transition from fleeting events to structural changes. But should we put this question to artists, or is their effectiveness of a different order, residing in experiences with the power of imminence?

To answer this question, we'd have to rethink two notions—resistance and alternative actions—that remain almost intact despite changes in the exercise of power. In this age's restructuring of meaning, there are some aspects of social life that have been thought about more thoroughly than others, in spite of being related. Strikingly the concept of power has been modified much more than that of resistance. After Foucault, though not only he, the idea arose that power is distributed multidirectionally. We no longer think of power working from the top down, like a pyramid, but as distributed. But we also got past Foucault's simplified notion when we realized that concentrations of force still exist.

In the field of visual arts, the series Paris–London–New York is broken. There is no one art capital. Beijing will never take the place of New York. Several cities have concentrations of power, which they mobilize in different directions. This isn't necessarily due to acts of resistance but rather to restructurings and alliances. Thus the concepts of power and the ways it moves have been complicated, while notions of resistance show an amazing inertia. No matter where we look, at economics, art, or politics, we find neither bipolarity nor unipolarity but a complex and unstable distribution of focal points where power is exercised. This dispersal generates the first problem for building resistance, opposition, or alternative movements, especially if you want to insist on using modes of organizing power that worked for the popular forces at another stage of capitalism. What we've seen over the past few years is that resistance takes many forms—sometimes biased ones that can see only the environment, or ethnicity, or gender—but they hardly ever form a united and effective front for transforming structures. This may be one of the reasons why much of what we are seeing today comes out of the opposition between inclusion and exclusion—or between the hegemonic and the subaltern, as we used to say. The word *resistance* seems poor and thin to me in relation to the multitude of behaviors that arise when people search for alternatives.

The Disturbing Beauty of the Nonnarrative

Artists such as Santiago Sierra, Antoni Muntadas, and León Ferrari create works and performances that we can interpret in the framework described above. They are reinventing their language in order to talk about a world that is contradictory or in decay. The narratives they confront, however, are still identifiable. They face them openly, setting all orthodoxy aside, but they produce the meaning of their works in dialogue or in conflict with global institutions and narratives. Sierra strips the Spanish pavilion bare at the Venice Biennale and questions his claim to represent a nationality by leaving the pavilion empty and shutting it off to foreigners. Ferrari organizes his collages by short-circuiting the narratives and practices of Christianity, capitalism, and the dictatorships in order to make their collusion visible. In his successive versions of *On Translation*, Muntadas displays the difficulties of articulating the meanings that are being displaced at a time of interactive globalization. All three work by combining diverse formats in their works and their exhibit sites, which is one reason why they multilocate in galleries, museums, biennales, newspapers, digital networks, and urban settings.

In this chapter and the next, I'd like to give some examples of artists in whose works we can find no identifiable social or political narratives, or only resignified remains of them, in a visual display that resists any totalization. My aim is to show that we are looking at more than a narrative turn.

How does an artist like Carlos Amorales work? He uses, in part, the same strategies described above. He exhibits in museums, biennales, and galleries; he is also involved with the world of lucha libre, with his Nuevos Ricos band, which produces music and performance art, and he uses animation and video techniques. His open, fluctuating way of situating himself in his artistic practice makes for malleable ties to institutions, habitual art circuits, and their iconographic orders. In talking about the stiff visual culture of Mexican muralism, "where everything from primitive man to communism is expressed," Amorales told me that it is "an enormous comic book" leading to "an enormous conclusion about world history."

So he chooses a different method: "I did a series of forty watercolors that are lyrical and that shift between formal compositions and constructing characters." It's all about a vocabulary, about making a "liquid archive." His project on *luchadores*—building up a body of images and documentation on lucha libre matches, taking photographs of objects and characters, doing drawings based on them until he had compiled a collection of 1,300 images—led him to think about the archive as something equivalent to the luchador's mask, as a tool rather than a work.

As an artist, he doesn't just paint, sculpt, or create images. A large part of his studio work consists of collecting or inventing images that go into his archive, which he may use later on or not. We might say it's an archive oriented toward the future, not the past; not for safeguarding, but for creating or re-creating.

Moreover it isn't his personal artist's archive, one that he alone will use. Many of the drawings were done by his collaborators. Their later use may be assigned to a graphic designer or a musician, as was the case when Amorales produced *Dark Mirror*. He participated in the composition and final staging of the animation, like an orchestra conductor, energizing the participants, coordinating and sharing responsibility for the process and the product.

Take a look at the variety of works this artist has produced over the past decade—stills, animations, videos—and you'll run into a singular sort of narrative about the monstrous and the apocalyptic, represented by flying things (birds, butterflies, airplanes), wolves, skulls, and trees. The same elements also inhabit the works of other visual artists, filmmakers, and writers, but Amorales combines them and gives them a tone that identifies his way of dealing with terror. They don't frighten, don't moralize, don't assign blame and redemption.

What is it they do? They suggest decay, uncertainty, and a disturbing vitality or serenity. We see a bird, sleeping or watching, perched on a branch of a black tree that has hanging from it ten black skulls with energetically red eyes (*The Bad Sleep Well*)—all of this crisscrossed by fine, delicate lines that nervously string the elements together, as if to calm the scene down. Where does it take place? We don't know. It isn't in the cemeteries or piles of burning bodies that we've seen in so many movies about political and military terror (Alain Resnais's *Night and Fog*,

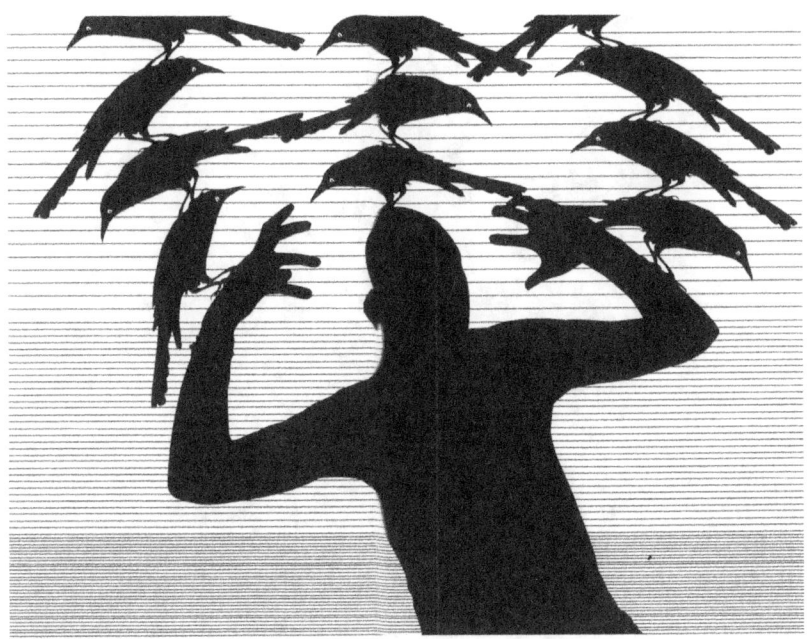

FIGURE 6.1 Carlos Amorales, *Dark Mirror* (from *The Bad Sleep Well* 03), 2007. Paper collage, 45 × 60 cm. Courtesy of the artist and kurimanzutto, Mexico City.

for instance), and it isn't in the borderland between art, jewelry, and fashion that Damien Hirst's diamond-encrusted skull flirts with.

Is it a nonplace? Again, no. We're already familiar with the criticisms that have been leveled at Marc Augé's notion of the nonplace: airports and shopping malls aren't nonplaces for the people who work in them every day. Amorales's pieces containing "characters" from supposed nonplaces—nearly unidentifiable landscapes, birds, and stereotyped humans—refer to contemporary tragedies: plane crashes, terrorist attacks, ecological disasters. But nothing is represented literally; it is as if the works spoke of a nebulous mood of the times.

This author—the strong term fits—isn't afraid of clichés. He says that he likes their clarity and impact. But a cliché for him is like a mask for a luchador: "a protocol for the communication that I seek with the public" (Amorales 2007: 66). To avoid literalism, he superimposes cliché on top of cliché, getting them to work in unexpected ways: planes fly

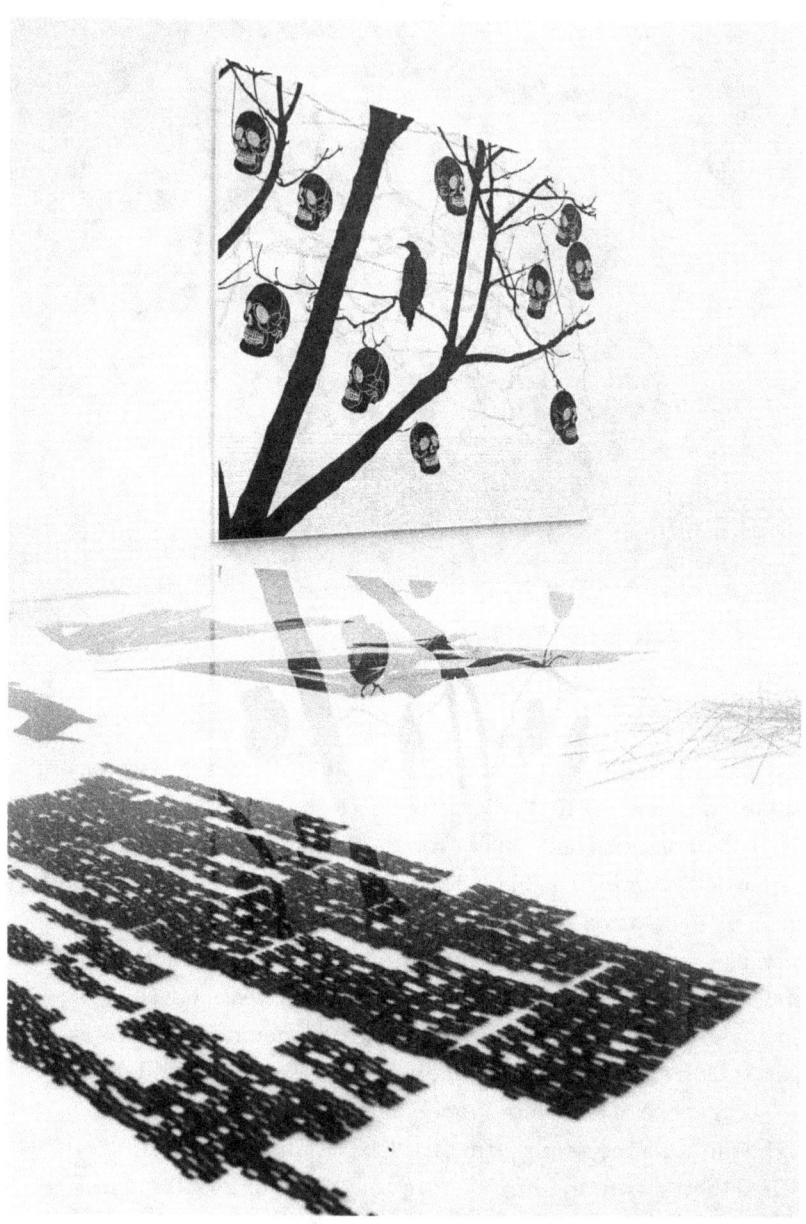

FIGURE 6.2 Carlos Amorales, from *The Bad Sleep Well* 11, 2004. Oil on canvas, 150 × 200 cm. Collection of Daros-Latinamerica, Zurich.

at low altitude, among the trees; in the "octopus monster," one figure inhabits another. The clichés are (con)fused; they have a sense of being re-creations, making them uncomfortable and uncertain yet still recognizable.

These are figures, icons, disoriented or only half-oriented, made by someone who belongs and doesn't belong to Mexico, where he was born, and to the Netherlands, the country where he studied art and which he represented at the 2003 Venice Biennale. His shifting sense of belonging gives meaning to his aesthetic decisions. "If I do something in a European language, I lose half of myself, but if I do something entirely in a Mexican or Mexicanized language I also lose half of myself. So what I'm seeking is a compromise between these two forms, where they can coexist. And I think that's exactly where mystery is created" (Benítez Dueñas and Barrios 2007: 102). Allusions to contemporary events in a Gothic language with purist lines and a surreally heterodox atmosphere. Graphic art, necessarily created from clichés, but dreamt like a nightmare.

"What is your notion of beauty?" Hans-Michael Herzog asks him.

"It is that moment of contradiction that an image can have, of absolute seduction and absolute repulsion, like something that makes a lot of sense but loses it, and opens up a space for you." This is why his works haven't turned into an allegory or a narrative of the world we live in. They are instead about "creating the possibility for a spectator to associate, inside a composition of images, his own idea." "Creating something that is beautiful, but without knowing exactly what it says, can be very disturbing, disquieting, and I like that" (Amorales 2007).

He also uses digital media for the same ends. As we know, advanced reproduction technologies accentuate the indeterminacy of the places where objects and images are produced. We use similar printers, formats, colors, and projectors in both central and peripheral countries. The process of creating innovations is speeding up as much as that of disseminating them. We can all upload our creations onto YouTube; we can all search for them.

Yet the differences between North and South persist. We don't all have the same kind of access or the same abundance. Many of Amorales's projects deal ironically with this situation, for example, the simulated maquiladora that was his contribution at the Venice Biennale. The public—made up of artists, intellectuals, critics, journalists, art lovers, and tourists—was confronted with the assembly-line production of material in one of its most oppressive forms: the audience in the prosperous north of Italy was invited to participate in a maquiladora like one of those located in Jakarta or El Salvador, representing long-distance exploitation.

Carlos Amorales's Archive of Interruptions

Another example is piracy, which exists on every continent but proliferates most in developing or underdeveloped countries. Amorales played with this imbalance as part of his art and recording project, Nuevos Ricos (www.nuevosricos.com). Together with the other band members—the musician Julián Lede and the graphic designer André Pahl—he created a website for editing rock bands from Mexico, the Netherlands, Russia, Colombia, and Germany. They give away the music and the accompanying graphics. Unlike the way things are going in the music industry, where albums are pirated and then sold at low prices in informal markets, they have broken through to a wider audience thanks to the free downloads. The industrial media (including the megalabel EMI) decided to reissue the same albums "legally," with copy control embedded. To complete the circle, Nuevos Ricos used covers designed by pirate record producers for their own albums, so that the pirated versions were introduced into the circuit of "formal" stores. They also took advantage of the "cool" aura these alternative products had gained among European youth, buying pirated copies at wholesale prices and then exporting them at Euro prices to make up for their economic losses from the pirating.

Amorales welcomed the fact that, on one occasion, the pirate industry appropriated images he had used for the cover of a Nuevos Ricos album: "I never got to meet the people who transformed my images and reprinted them with a copying machine to sell them illegally. Those people remained anonymous, but the results were out there on the street. The new covers had modifications that I'd venture to call improvements on my originals: they took decisions to make the pirated CDs more effective. It moves me to think that in this case I never asked for such an appropriation: it happened through the channels used by an informal economy" (Benítez Dueñas and Barrios 2007: 226).

I invited Carlos Amorales to participate in a collective exhibit titled *Extranjerías* (Foreign Statuses) that Andrea Giunta and I curated in July 2009 at the Espacio Fundación Telefónica in Buenos Aires. We wanted to deal mainly not with the people who cross borders and change countries but with other types of estrangement, such as moving from analog to digital, from the lettered city to the world of screens, where young people act as natives and we older people have a hard time learning the new language. We were interested in the metaphorical *extranjerías* (foreign statuses or estrangements) created by acts of segregation among people close to each other or cultural phenomena that defy our ways of perceiving and evaluating. Amorales made *History of Pirated Music*, an installation in which he randomly handed out a thousand CDs about and among the figures of made-up characters, questioning the relationships between original and copy, between his visual lexicon and his participation in the rock group Nuevos Ricos. His practice as a visual artist ranged from images painted on CDs, enigmatic characters who dance, and the music that envelops the installation: "Being able to operate in environments that aren't strictly part of the art world," or between various arts, institutions, and circuits that have nothing to do with art, makes it possible, according to Amorales, "to belong to several spaces at once, to belong and go away." Or to use and leave behind: the visitors could take the CDs and listen to them on a sound system that was part of the installation.

When a maquiladora is constructed at a first-world art biennale, is the material labor carried out there labor, art, or entertainment? When pirated music infiltrates formal record stores, who are the pirates and who are foreigners to the system? As for his rotoscopes, the drawings he makes from photographs—what are they, in the end: drawings, photos, animations, or something else? Amorales uses these ambiguities as material for his presentations: "Sometimes I think that, instead of talking about drawings, photographs, or designs, it would be more to the point to speak of them as 'smudges.'" He prefers to call them "spider webs," which are like smudges in the form of nets.

Even with these scattered component elements, there are situations

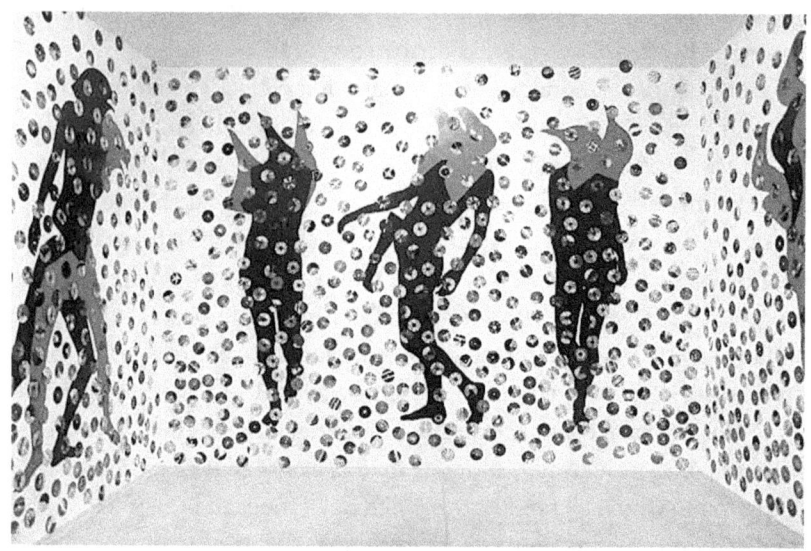

FIGURE 6.3 Carlos Amorales, *Historia de la música pirata (Necrópolis)* (History of Pirated Music [Necropolis]), 2009. Installation, various media, cut vinyl on wall, CDs, marker, and sound system.

that suggest association, productivity, and narratives moving forward. There are also apocalyptic deconstructions. There is almost always a combination of human, animal, machine, and something posthuman or prehuman. The prevailing stylization is soft, tending toward severe; it never becomes severe because it also looks tragic, as with the black figures, terrified and terrifying. But something in their rhythm or their way of playing or narrating tells us it isn't tragic. What is it?

These are signs situated in between society and nature. What we find is a work that could be a topic for semiotics, sociology, and anthropology. But it evades them. Its signs are grouped outside the usual grammar. They nevertheless allude to social relations we're familiar with, although when these luchadores, or these cards from a deck that Amorales invented, or these "human trees" show up, they don't tell us what we're used to seeing: it's a real lucha libre, a free-for-all.

It's hard to approach his oeuvre with a sociological gaze because he is one of the Mexican artists whose works can least plausibly be forced to represent his country, or society in the broadest sense. His works aren't antinationalistic or global either. Nor is his shaken iconography a prediction of some future era. Or if it is, it puts the prediction in the form of a question: "Why fear the future?" The whole set of drawings, playing cards, and videos that formed the exhibition under that title cannot be read as part of the history of art or of a tradition-bound tarot deck.

Few works manage to ignore their frames of reference entirely. The men, the women, the animals, the planes, and the trees in Amorales's works don't form part of any rigid social structure. Possible threats aren't read through the conspiracy plotline; they are signifiers awaiting their signified meaning.

As with other foreigners, there is a temptation to ask Amorales for his passport and find out, once and for all, where he's coming from. Or to go onto his Facebook page. I have read interviews and articles that trace his possible origins to the Mexican cult of death, to theories of postproduction (Allen), to Hitchcock's use of terror and birds, to Ulrich Beck's concept of a risk society, to Derrida, or to Lacan. I haven't yet found anyone who associates his notion of the archive with Foucault, or his "liquid drawings" and "liquid archive" with Zygmunt Bauman's generous application of the term *liquid* to describe society, love, art, and everything he knows. But Amorales's own language would support such connections.

Some of these links may exist, but I'm afraid that finding so many affiliations may sometimes be a way to exorcize the "disturbing strangeness" of his work. (We already know about the uncanny or *Unheimlichkeit* in Freud, but this doesn't mean that we can grant Amorales a psychoanalytic lineage.) If we want to tie him to Foucault, we shouldn't do so through the notion of the archive—"the law of what can be said, the system that governs the appearance of statements as unique events" (1972: 129)—but through Foucault's perceptiveness in detecting "the incidence of interruptions" (4).

Faced with someone who seeks "to be able to be a foreigner, just not in another country, but rather in a different profession," and who keeps exhibiting these disconcerted and disconcerting works, it seems that instead of finding precursors for him, it would be better to pay attention to what he forgets and what he repeats, to see whether he is starting up or proposing a discontinuity in the gaze and thought. His works deserve the sort of praise that is hard to justify: they interrupt visual conventions.

I had my doubts about including this analysis of Amorales in this book. How could I edit it? On that point, the dialogue between him and his designers, Mevis and Van Deursen, is instructive. They tell the story of how they worked with twelve offset plates and how each plate showed a different element from the archive. Without seeking any particular composition, they superimposed them randomly on a single sheet of paper. Amorales recognized that they had come up with combinations of images and ways of using color, size, and repetition that never would have occurred to him. "I like to imagine the archive as a language that I'm not the only speaker of. . . . [I'd like for] other people to speak that language, to corrupt it and invent dialects" (Benítez Dueñas and Barrios 2007: 226).

>

CHAPTER SEVEN

HOW SOCIETY MAKES ART

Spectacle, spectacularization, spectator: this series has become key to the process of making art. It is one of those areas where we see that art cannot really be autonomous, where hopeful attempts to establish definitive, a priori meanings for artworks break down. Creative projects are complete only when they gain the recognition of those who view them. As Nathalie Heinich (1998: 27–28) reminds us, in the same period when Marcel Duchamp declared that "it is the spectators who make the pictures," the anthropologist Marcel Mauss was explaining that it was the sorcerer's clients who made his magic powers effective, because they believed in them. It isn't the nature of a magical action that defines it but rather the way it is recognized individually and collectively; similarly, artistic quality is contained not in a work but in the movement that completes the viewer's gaze. From the perspective of some artists and theorists, the question isn't "What is art?" but "What can it do?" (Popelard 2002).

Since the 1960s, the statistical research methods that have long been used in the English-speaking world to understand consumer preferences by nationality, sex, education level, and socioeconomic status have been applied to art museums. The aim has been to improve communications and adapt exhibit floor plans to meet the viewers' expectations.

When marketing surveys and consumer studies were applied to cultural processes, they provided evidence of the many meanings that works of art can acquire. As soon as we do more than merely count the number of museum tickets or books sold, we find that there is no such thing as "the public." Readers and museum visitors modify or re-create meanings in all sorts of directions that authors and curators could not have foreseen.

Many have wondered whether it makes sense to use the tools of sociological and communications studies research in order to get at an understanding of access to art. Can we really compare the behaviors of consumers of cars or food with those of visitors to museums or purchasers of paintings at auction? Here again the question of the specificity and autonomy of the art field arises. When several European museums asked Pierre Bourdieu to study their visitors, the answers to these questions began to change on the part of both social scientists and art historians and theorists.

Let me mention two discoveries that Bourdieu, along with Alain Darbel and Dominique Schnapper, first presented in their book *L'amour de l'art* ([1960] 1991), and that Bourdieu later developed in his own book *Distinction* ([1979] 1984).

First, museum attendance is stratified by income and education level. The massive difference in attendance between farmers or manual workers (less than 1 percent visit museums), managers and directors (43.3 percent), and professors or art specialists (51 percent), together with the family and social formation of "dispositions toward culture," reveal that aesthetic practices arise not from disinterested tastes but from the combined accumulation of economic capital and cultural capital.

Second, when survey data are linked to qualitative material obtained in interviews and observations, we find that museum attendance and criteria for appreciating the art are not arbitrary. Their statistical regularity, organized by social group, shows that people's social positions and the different courses they took to learn culture are manifested in them as dispositions for liking or rejecting art. Their social conditioning enables them to orient themselves in a museum and evaluate the works of art. In this way we arrive at a subtler analysis of the points of agreement and disagreement between art preferences and other frames of belonging and drawing distinctions: reading habits, music preferences, food customs.

Bourdieu's own research presented data for understanding that the art field intersects with other processes: the democratization of society and culture, the growing access to secondary and higher education, and of course the expansion of the communications industries (though he underestimated their place in society). Nevertheless its trajectory exemplifies the difficulties that a sociology interested in constructing macronarratives has in being open to the ways different groups and communication processes adjust their behaviors.

One contribution of sociological and anthropological studies of art reception has been to make visible the multiple mediations standing between artworks and spectators. Some mediators, such as museologists, curators, dealers, collectors, critics, and journals, form part of the art field. Other intermediaries do not belong to the field, and their goals are not centered on art: cultural policymakers, politicians, investors in all other areas, journalists, and people with an occasional interest in art can play a part in its diffusion and recognition, but their loyalties are inscribed in logics that are not those of the art field. Regarding Duchamp's urinal, Heinich detected six steps mediating between the object and its reception: (1) its displacement into an art context (the 1917 Society of Independent Artists exhibit at which Duchamp attempted in vain to display it); (2) its defunctionalization; (3) the signature, R. Mutt; (4) the date; (5) the title, *Fountain*; and (6) the photograph of it by Alfred Stieglitz that was published in the journal *Blind Man* and later reproduced endlessly. The transformation of the object, images, words, and institutions all played their roles in making it so that this readymade (like other works) would ultimately be canonized as art by its audiences: specialists, dealers, collectors, the media, and the public.

It has become crucially important to take into account the roles of these actors—members of the art family and outsiders alike—in this era when the production, communication, and reception of art has spread into so many areas of social life. It is precisely at this time that public audiences have begun to be seen as effective parts of the artistic process. This is why the emergence of spectators throws light on how the field is being restructured and relocated in society as a whole. I am not going to deal with the specter of theoretical and methodological problems covered by the sociology of art publics and art reception, which has been well systematized by, among others, Jean Claude Passeron and Emmanuel Pedler (1991) and Heinich (2001). I will confine myself to a few significant points in order to address the question of postautonomy art.

First, just a warning that this turn to studying the audience may not be an opening to what exists beyond art in society but rather a tactic to reaffirm the self-referencing and self-justification of those who make up the art world. We could see the unstable logic of art fairs and auctions as attempts to embrace the most diverse tendencies in the market. With varying degrees of subtlety, and paying attention to the economic dynamics of supply and demand or to the variations in symbolic differentiation, the point is to understand the rationality of art consumption, of each group's behavior, in order to make the commercialization of the artworks more efficient.

In settings where aesthetic interests are assumed to prevail, as in the case of museums, audiences are usually invoked without questioning the mechanisms that reproduce the field's internal inertia and drive away the uninitiated.

The Venice Biennale chose the slogan "The Dictatorship of the Viewer" as the title for its 2003 show. That title did not describe the exhibition's theme, given that a crowded and heterogeneous biennale like the Venice never has a thematic core, or if it does, it is designed so vaguely that almost anything will fit it: in 2003 the Venice Biennale was divided into sections titled "Delays and Revolutions," "Clandestine," "Individual Systems," "Zone of Urgency," "The Structure of Survival," "Contemporary Arab Representations," "The Everyday Altered," and "Utopia Station."

Despite the declaration of the general director Francesco Bonami that he was seeking pluralism among the spectators through the diverse geographical origins of the curators in charge of each section, many works could have been switched from one section to another without anyone's noticing, since they reflected the ways the artists and curators of various nationalities submitted to the dominant global trends. The impression left by a tour of every section, especially those in the Arsenale, was that the 2003 biennale marked a high point in the dictatorship of the curators. Nothing in the selection and layout of the works or in regard to interactions with the visitors changed the fact that the people who were touring the biennale were assigned the predominant role of observers. I heard several artists express their dissatisfaction with the diffuse narratives in which their works had been placed.

The Audience Completes the Artwork

In reality, however, what gives artworks this fickle existence is the way they are alternately accepted and rejected by members of the art field and other social actors. Umberto Eco's (1978: 214) observation with regard to texts also applies to paintings, sculptures, and installations: they are "lazy machineries" that viewers must bring to life and that await their cooperation. Artists can try to anticipate their audiences, seek them "gastronomically" in order to arouse pleasure in them, but they cannot neutralize the unforeseeable creativity of those who will be viewing their work. Historians and critics usually draw distinctions between the intrinsic meaning of a piece, its critical fortunes, and its media impact. But cultural meanings accumulate slowly, fighting by many means to establish their place. So this is not so much a matter of marketing aimed at seducing clients as of understanding the audience according to the theories of active reception, usage, and the pragmatics and politics of symbolic processes.

This shift to an emphasis on reception and the viewer isn't confined to art. It results from the repositioning of artists and institutions as society and politics have shifted. It was the questioning of cultural institutions, the critique of the capitalist economy and political authoritarianism, that turned our gaze toward art reception and viewers and toward the aesthetic potentials of social movements. The May 1968 events in Paris, Berkeley, Mexico City, and other cities, together with the urban, youth, ethnic, feminist, and antidictatorship movements of Argentina, Brazil, Chile, Uruguay, and other countries around that time, moved cultural initiatives out of museums or theater halls and into dialogue with new interlocutors. In addition to spectators they sought creators and participants. Artists joined forces with labor unions and political groups on the left to redesign the art scene and communicate their messages in spaces that were open to all. Some abandoned not only the institutions of the art field but art itself, understood as a distinct type of activity. Others pushed the categories of art to the edge of political propaganda and social action without dissolving into them; they constituted what in Chile was called "the advanced scene," where they refused to be illustrators for political discourse. As Nelly Richard (2004) has pointed out, sometimes they created "works" that, by marking a radical disruption of desires and bodies, served as alternatives to the disciplined styles of leftist parties.

Many of these movements languished in exile, underground, or in the economic doldrums. Even where there was no overt repression, they were demobilized in the 1980s and 1990s by the hegemony that declared neoliberalism the only way to think. Artistic irreverence faded into tenuous postmodern actions. The educational advances of the middle class and their incorporation into the consumption of goods with better aesthetic taste could be summarized, as a sociologist specializing in social movements has suggested, in the IKEA ad that showed a couple buying furniture for their home under the caption "May '68, we remade the world. May '86, we're redoing the kitchen" (Löfgren 1994: 48).

All the same, we have a poor understanding of how culture has changed historically if we reduce it to a choice between resistance and the domestication of aesthetic subversion. Culture has not developed in a unilinear fashion. I think of the process I know best, what happened during the period of Latin American dictatorships and especially during the open democratization of the mid-1980s. In those years there arose a social view of culture, accompanied by anthropological, sociological, and communications studies research, that rethought the involvement of the arts in society, both practically and theoretically. Books by Hugo Achugar, José Joaquín Brunner, Jesús Martín-Barbero, Carlos Monsiváis, and Silviano Santiago, among others, provided a new foundation for research practices, reflections on the social places of art, and the successes and failures of creating links among the art fields, the cultural field, institutions, and social movements. Three leaders in this process—Marta Lamas, Nelly Richard, and Beatriz Sarlo—deserve special mention. First, because they edited three journals that published many of the reflective articles that best expressed this rethinking (*Debate feminista* in Mexico City, *Revista de Crítica Cultural* in Santiago de Chile, and *Punto de Vista* in Buenos Aires). And second, each of the three did research that represented women's increased role in cultural and artistic leadership and in the reworking of theory. In Latin America this reorientation of art theory and cultural criticism—in dialogue with European and U.S. thought and following the new practices of artists, writers, movements, and institutions—was as radical as the linguistic or semiotic turn in cultural analysis.

Similar displacements can be identified on the European and U.S. scenes. Let me mention, as a comparable example, the innovative role played in aesthetics and the sociology of culture (in its typically most "masculine" area, theory) by women researchers whose work has been cited in many books, including this one: Mieke Bal, Susan Buck-Morss, and Nathalie Heinich. Along with such writers as James Clifford, Jacques Rancière, and others mentioned above, they have given visual studies what Buck-Morss (2011: 227) calls an "epistemological resiliency" to think about "the promiscuity of the image": "The force of the image occurs when it is dislodged from context. It does not belong to the commodity form, even if it is found—stumbled across—in that form, as it is so powerfully in advertisements."

Buck-Morss (2011: 233) notes that the architecture of cathedrals and mosques arguably created a sense of community through daily ritual, and "the mass readership of newspapers and novels" can be said to have formed the community of citizens; we should, then, ask ourselves: "What kind of community can we hope for from a global dissemination of images, and how can our work help to create it?"

As part of this transformation, there was a turn toward audience reception and social actors, as manifested in a profusion of research on cultural and audience consumption at universities, museums, and government and private organizations. Something else that speaks to this new emphasis is the spread of graduate programs in cultural management in European and Latin American countries, in which the analysis of art and culture is extended from movements among artists to the demands, habits, and tastes of their audiences (Nivón 2006; Orozco 2006; Rosas Mantecón 2009). But this inclusion of audiences is more than a quest for effectiveness in the reception, the control of resistance, or the legitimizing of a corporation or a state through cultural marketing. It implies a reflection on the activities of the targets of artists' actions, who may be not just consumers but participants in art production: "prosumers." It leads to social interactions at a time when anybody can create images with a camera or cell phone and distribute them on YouTube. It calls for rethinking what we mean by space and public circuits, how interpretive and creative communities are formed, and how else people make agreements not only about readings (as literary reception studies say) but about comprehension, sensitivity, and action.

What Art Achieves When It Is Rejected

Studies of audiences and reception in the visual arts usually make reference to the value of established, historical works (Panofsky, Gombrich), and they normally center on admiring behaviors. Both of these features tend to reaffirm what is regarded as valuable a priori within the art field: its predominant organization and aesthetics. They therefore exclude other experiences, points of view, and audiences with different competencies who also connect with artworks at times and can influence the dynamics of the field, if they have any economic or political power. Still, what matters most to us is to understand the permeability of the art world with regard to the world outside it. For grasping the postautonomous situation of art, it is key to see what happens when the history of art is at odds with the history of taste.

So far this book has dealt mainly with how artistic projects become part of other logics—logics of the market, the media, politics, or social movements—or are modified by them. We now need to consider autonomy and dependency with respect to the viewers. The prevailing attitude of audiences toward contemporary art is one of indifference. While a handful of museums—the Tate, MoMA, the Pompidou—get a half-million visitors or more when they exhibit Warhol or Bacon, and some four million or more visitors total every year, their biggest attractions are exhibits of artists from other centuries (Rembrandt, Van Gogh) and heritage spectacles (Tutankhamen, the Aztecs). The proliferating museums, biennales, and galleries devoted to contemporary art attract the "art world crowd" on opening day and then eke out modest attendance numbers on weekends if they have the resources to advertise to locals and tourists that they are offering something exceptional.

Indifference is hard to document. We study the people who do attend exhibits. National surveys on cultural habits tend to rank museums and art galleries among the least visited sites, and they lump together visits to contemporary art displays and those to the art of other eras, including exhibits of famous artists, which improve the statistics. In reception studies from France, Spain, the United States, and Latin America, visitors' admiration ends with Impressionism or some version of "realism," and a tiny minority enjoys Surrealism and the most familiar examples of abstract art. Most attendees say they are going to the museum for the first time, having heard about an exhibit from television or having been brought as part of a school trip or a sightseeing tour (Bourdieu, Darbel, and Schnapper 1991; Cimet et al. 1987; Heinich 1998; Piccini, Rosas Mantecón, and Schmilchuk 2000; Verón and Levasseur 1983).

Visitors' responses about how they value what is on display range from irony to rejection or surprise: "This is art?" "What does it mean?" Most rush past installations and experimental videos, judging them by the values of the everyday world and trying to mitigate their ignorance by comparing them to familiar things. They don't get the specialized information they would need to orient themselves in the ruptures and explorations of contemporary art from school, not even from a university education. Only a fringe group of art professionals and students, and a few others, are familiar with the innovative trends of recent decades.

What, then, is behind the sometimes spectacular impact that some contemporary artists have had outside the art field? There have been plenty of media scandals, protests, and arguments over whether this work or that deserves to be put on display in a great museum. It has been debated whether Christo has the right to wrap an object that forms part of a country's heritage, such as the Pont-Neuf over the Seine, whether León Ferrari should be able to display works that mock Christian iconography at a public culture center in Buenos Aires, how much nudity and homosexuality are acceptable in photographs, and what sense it makes to spend public funds on building private museums such as the Guggenheim in Bilbao and the Guggenheim branches that were planned and then abandoned in Buenos Aires and Rio de Janeiro.

The resonance of these debates in the press and on television, and the fact that actors who have nothing to do with the art field (politicians, businesspeople, bishops, sociologists, journalists) feel they must take positions, show that the interactions between the art world and other areas of social life are more intense than they have been at any time in the modern era. There are artistic practices that stimulate the public agenda, inspire debates about ways of knowing and representing social disagreements, and make us rethink the harmonious coexistence of life-styles and evaluation criteria.

In these contentious discussions, aesthetic questions sometimes come up: what do we mean by beauty, harmony, or taste? But most of the arguments are moral, political, religious, or civic. The values underlying the debates are justice, the national interest, how far the social order can be transgressed, and the rights of dissidents to protest. The disputes are organized not around singularity or innovation, the criteria discussed by aesthetics, but rather around a conformist view nurtured by the logic of the everyday world.

The partial victory that the art field gains when it emerges from the museum and sparks interest in artworks among nonartists is diminished when those works are received with religious, economic, or political arguments. Artists rarely get their aesthetic quests onto the public agenda or problematize the direction of the social conversation. They burst in on the scene with events that disturb long-lasting structures only for a short time. Taking stock of the rejection of contemporary art, Heinich (1998) concludes that societies (or the public authorities who represent them) ultimately respond to artists with nonaesthetic arguments that reaffirm their profane views and therefore their indifference.

In the face of these heteronomous judgments, which relativize the autonomy of art and the power of its representatives, the art field has some strategies of self-affirmation. The experts (curators, museum directors, dealers, critics) in charge of the artistic heritage, both material and symbolic, justify its value and its hierarchies intellectually. There are differences of opinion: the "moderns" prefer painting, sculpture, and photography, while the more globalized "contemporaries" promote performance art, installations, and videos. But in the end they are not mutually exclusive. From outside the art field, Heinich writes, arguments over aesthetics can seem inconsistent or look like personal attacks between enemies; from the inside, coexistence among divergent positions is carefully maintained in order to protect the autonomous survival of the "art world."

Heinich has studied several discursive and museological practices that reinforce the art world's self-sufficiency. One thing they do is use *mise en intrigue* on artworks—Paul Ricoeur's (1984) term for inscribing things in a story or narrative with temporal markers (before and after, precursors and followers) to give meaning to each piece of the story and to the narrative as a whole. Another is using *mise en énigme*—that is, problematizing the work, surrounding it with questions, doubts, and critiques of its apparent meaning, so that it's necessary to call on a hermeneutics different from what gives meaning to everyday objects, and thereby emphasizing how difficult it is to grasp its significance at first glance.

It isn't enough to analyze these practices as clever gimmicks that the experts use to justify their role and the singularity of their field. If we agree that art uses imminence, uses what exists in a virtual state and is constitutionally polysemous (that is, what flows into "reality" with different meanings), then a work of art has no intrinsic, essential meaning, and decoding it requires the labor of many. What factors should we take into account as shaping its meaning? George Dickie (1974) points to institutions. Arthur Danto (1997) emphasizes the artist's intentionality and the effects of interpretation. For his part, Nelson Goodman (1976, 1977) and, in his own way, Bourdieu (1996) highlight the context and devices that make certain object function as art. Unless we subscribe to a single philosophical theory, we should admit that there are many factors that affect the meaning of artworks and the boundaries of what we mean by art. The consequent relativism doesn't imply arbitrariness. The open configuration of the object does not allow us to say anything about it: there are specific contexts and actors that each have an impact on the construction of meaning.

We know how often rejection has benefited contemporary art. The abstruse nature of the artworks, vandalism by spectators, censorship and its repercussions in the media—all help make a work famous. There is no lack of experts who are interested in taking exclusive charge of managing the hermeneutics of imminence, and to this end they amass a body of rhetoric that walls off the enigma. In these swings between autonomy and dependence, spectators' attempts to understand intrinsic meanings from extrinsic positions recapitulate the ambivalent relations between the art field and the world outside it.

The spread of art beyond its field, the democratization of social relations, and the economic, political, or media reutilization of artistic works have led artists and spectators to live in intersection zones. The creators' innovation interacts with their audiences' understanding and incomprehension, with being rejected by institutions, and with attempts by institutions to assimilate them. There are no clear or lasting borders. With essentialist definitions of art left far behind, the desire to reaffirm the autonomy of spaces for exhibiting and canonizing artworks should admit that what is still being called art is the result of conflicts and negotiations with other people's views: "There is no definition that is not structural, relational, contextual" (Heinich 1998: 328). But the relational, situated now by this socioanthropological description of art, doesn't have the diffuse character of Bourriaud's aesthetics.

Where does recognizing the reception and contexts of art with the tools of the social sciences get us? We don't arrive at a simple, more rigorous definition of art's place in society just because we have a more coherent sociological theory. What makes Heinich's conceptualization productive is questioning at the same time the illusions of idealist aesthetics and the tools with which sociology has defined what an artwork is, who its audiences are, and how the mediations between artists and viewers operate. Art processes are epistemological places where art and society, aesthetics and sociology, rethink their ways of making and knowing.

Disenchantments: Between Art and Politics (Teresa Margolles)

Spectators and the communication of art are strategically important, not only because studying them allows us to delve into cognitive processes; communication and reception also lie at the heart of the ongoing debate about visual arts and politics. In the theater, spectators have been treated as protagonists since the time of Brecht, Artaud, and Pirandello in the first half of the twentieth century. With the "happenings" of the 1970s, visual artists used the lessons of theater to shake up the contemplative position of the viewer. Abolishing the distance between creation and viewer, between looking and acting, was sometimes a matter of entertainment, but in some cases the aim was for the aesthetic experience to lead to transformative learning experiences.

Some artistic practices of the past two decades shorten the distance to the viewers and share the power of creativity. Paintings and sculptures can be modified, videos allow for interactivity, objects are reconfigured in multimedia shows. The roles of sender and receiver are hybridized in performances and thus become interchangeable.

The abolition of barriers transcends art and often seeks to reflect on the state of the world. Martha Rosler's photomontages—by juxtaposing a trash can, an image of a dead child, and bottles discarded by protestors— combine consumer waste, political action, and everyday suffering, and evoke these disparate elements as parts of a single reality.

The papers and bed sheets, stained with blood and fluids from the morgue, that were exhibited by Teresa Margolles at the Miami and Madrid art fairs and in the stately, decaying Palazzo Rota-Ivancich on the Piazzo San Marco at the 2009 Venice Biennale, brought what had been kept private and concealed into the rituals of canonizing art. After experimenting for several years with materials and images taken from the morgue to produce videos and sculptural objects that allude to Mexico's "Gothic modernity" of political assassinations and disasters, Margolles exported them, hanging them on the walls of the palazzo and washing the floors day after day with a mixture of water and the blood of people who had been killed execution-style in Mexico. "The idea emerged from the question of who cleans up the blood left by someone who's murdered on the streets. When it's one person, it might be the family or a neighbor, but when it's thousands of people, who cleans up the entire city's blood?" (Margolles 2009: 90). When Mexico leads Iraq in murders due to the confrontations between drug traffickers and army forces (the government has recognized 22,700 deaths from 2007 to March 2010), when the infiltration of traffickers in the halls of politics and the police becomes too obvious to hide, while the government flails about trying to safeguard "the nation's image abroad," Margolles brings the evidence of criminality to the international public stage, and she brings jewelry confiscated from narcos in confrontations with the military to settings where the high price of art makes money suspicious.

What Else Could We Talk About? is Margolles's title for her exhibit in Venice: it dogged visitors, wouldn't let them escape a deep discomfort. The power of the exhibit lay partly in the fact that it reproduced not the original scene—a shootout, murdered bodies—but rather its imminence, in the smells, the washcloths soaking up red stains, the loud-speakers broadcasting the voices of witnesses. At her exhibit opening, Margolles set out cards designed to look like bank credit cards. One side sported a photograph of a person's burned and beaten head; the other side had the Biennale's logo and the caption "Person murdered because of links with organized crime. Card to cut cocaine."

Suggesting, insinuating, working with imminence rather than with literal representations is what gives these works value. "The referent of violence does not provide us with any context, since it features on a quasi-dematerialized level," according to the curator Cuauhtémoc Medina (2009: 78): the blood and dirt caked onto lengths of fabric; the "shards of glass . . . mounted as pieces of jewellery"; the "phrases that buzz around the killings [that] are 'tattooed' onto the walls or embroidered in gold thread over the blood-soaked fabrics" at the Biennale. The aesthetic act comes about by working on "all that's left" in order to show "what does not appear" (78). Simply spectacularizing pain and grief to keep the visitor from walking too quickly past a work, to keep a viewer from seeing it as just one more among the thousands of works at a biennale or an art fair, tends to be off-putting. The same is true of works that try to create a militant reaction: they fail in their political as well as their aesthetic objectives, and so do works made for educational goals that try to teach the spectator something new.

Taking the path of suggestion doesn't mean forgetting that the nation's social and economic breakdown prolongs the collapse of its geo-political structures, a fact that is well known in drug trafficking circles. Margolles suggested this in Venice, but perhaps her most eloquent work was what she did for the 2006 Biennial in Liverpool, that port city from which European merchandise is shipped to the Americas. "What would Mexico send back?" she wondered. She decided to pave a pedestrian street with the glass of windshields shattered by slayings in northern Mexico.

> One time when I was in the morgue, I saw a girl who had been murdered in a car-to-car drive-by shooting. Her body was covered in glass shards that had come from the car windows. I tried to remove them with some tweezers, a nearly impossible job that I worked on

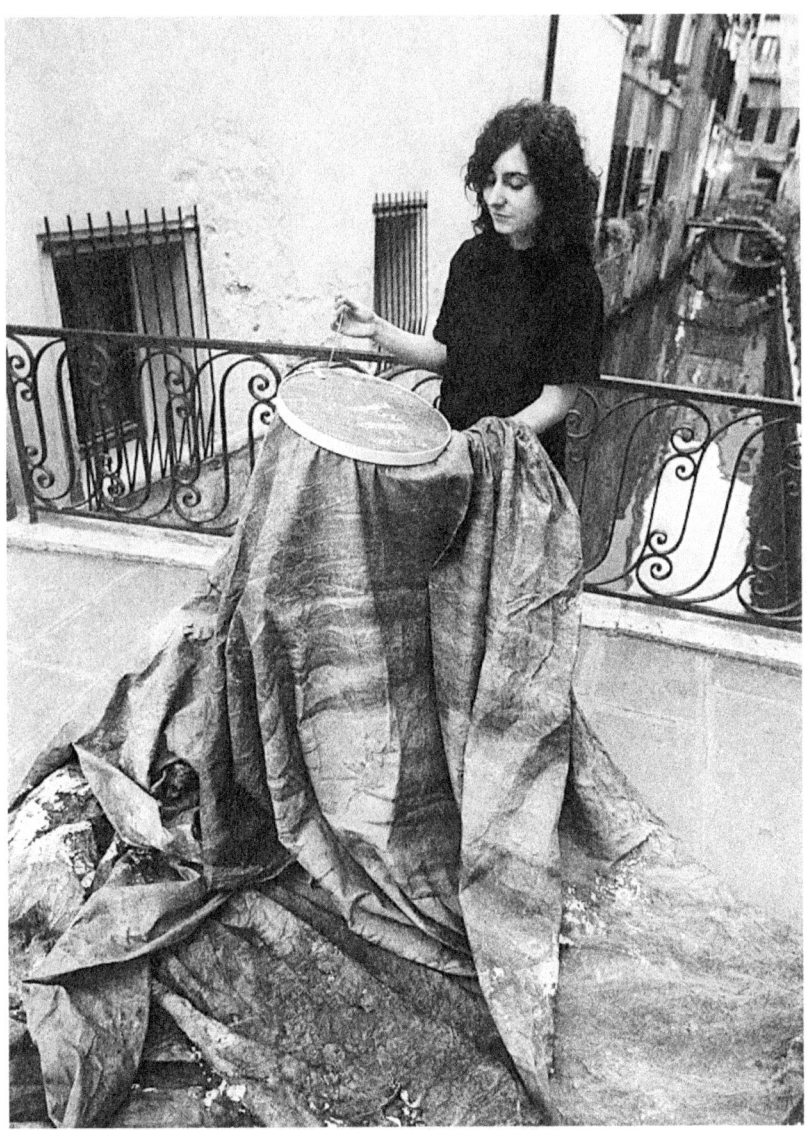

FIGURE 7.1 Teresa Margolles, *¿De qué otra cosa podríamos hablar? Bordado* (What Else Could We Talk About? Embroidery), 2009. Joint activities on the streets of the city of Venice with people embroidering with gold threads fabrics soaked in blood collected from execution sites on the northern border of Mexico.

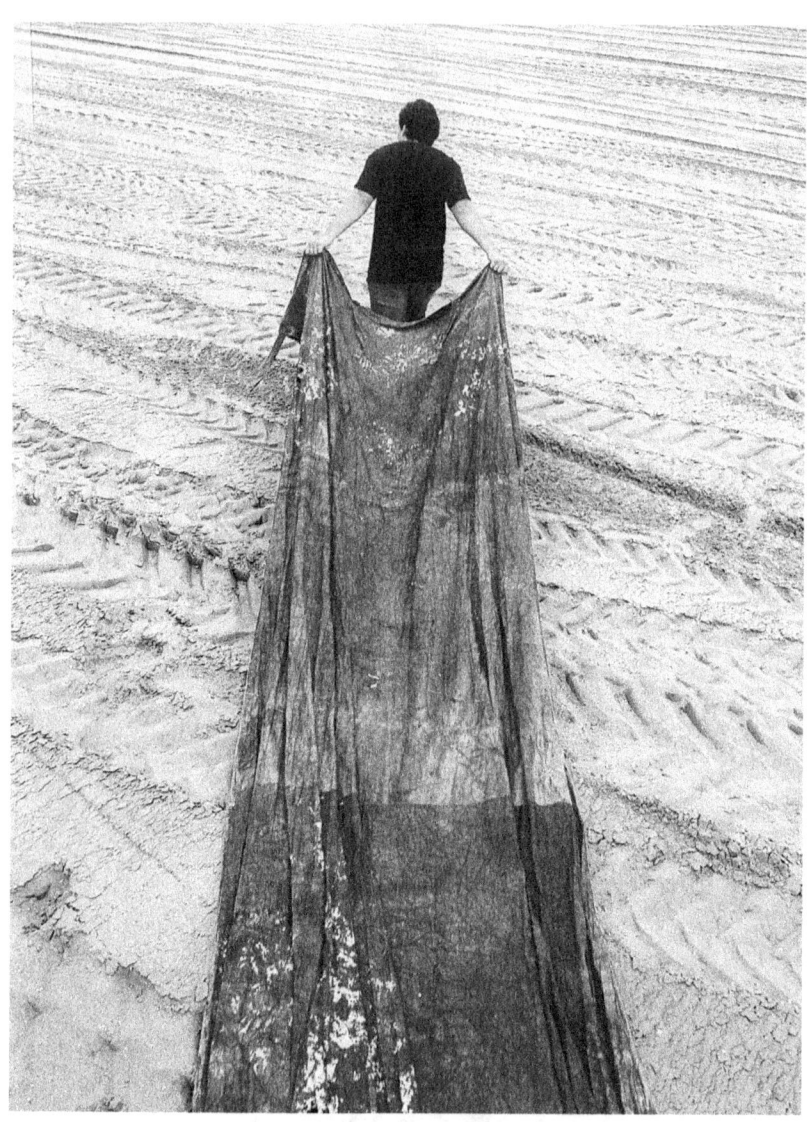

FIGURE 7.2 Teresa Margolles, *¿De qué otra cosa podríamos hablar? Bandera arrastrada* (What Else Could We Talk About? Dragged Flag), May 2009. Public action in Lido Beach, Venice, done with fabric soaked in blood collected from execution sites in Mexico.

for hours. That led me to think about the rest of it: pieces of glass that were taken from a dead body and put into a plastic bag. Shards that touched a body and entered into it and that, as they were removed, were stained with blood or bodily oils. After there's a car-to-car drive-by execution on a public street, the body and the car are removed from the scene of the crime for further forensic studies. But the shards that came from the shattered windshields are not—they stay there in the street, clustering in the cracks in the asphalt, in its fissures, and are integrated into the urban environment. They are brilliant sparks—areas that shine by night because of so much ground up glass. They sparkle as a result of murder. Those forgotten, ignored shards form the rest of it. (Margolles 2009: 86)

Could imminence be what it takes to keep the museum or biennale visitor from rushing past, like a reader leafing through a fashion magazine or eager to turn from the cruelty of the police blotter in the newspaper? But not just any sort of imminence. According to Rancière (2009: 32–33), "postmodernism lite" and frivolous conceptualist dematerialization pretend to be critiques, but all they take from Marx is the well-known formula, "All that is solid melts into air." They are thrilled by liquid and gassy things. They are ventriloquists of Marx, according to Rancière's *The Emancipated Spectator*, bent on turning reality into illusion and illusion into reality: "This post-Marxist and post-Situationist wisdom is not content to furnish a phantasmagorical depiction of a humanity completely buried beneath the rubbish of its frenzied consumption. It also depicts the law of domination as a force seizing on anything that claims to challenge it."

What we need to know, then, is what kind of critical work with imminence can break us out of the melancholy disenchantment with the world system in which critical interpretations themselves become part of that same system. First off, it is necessary to "de-fatalize" the secret that seems to conceal the mechanisms by which reality is transformed into image or shaped through the imaginary.

It was a mistake, according to the critic José Manuel Springer (2009), not to put on display at the Venice Biennale the jewelry that Margolles created from the broken glass of ambushed cars, keeping it locked up instead in a safe built into the building. Those shards of broken glass transformed into necklaces and bracelets convey hints, just as the fake credit cards for cutting cocaine do, of reflections generated by the complacent games between consumption and crime, drifting into fetishism. Revealing the evidence that the media haven't made conventional about the partnership between crime, money, luxury, and power may demonstrate that the complicity between economics and drug trafficking results in death.

A second point about imminence that I must clarify is that it is not a mystical state of contemplating the ineffable but rather a dynamic and critical disposition. Faced with the disorder of a world with no unifying narrative, the temptation arises, as it does in fundamentalist systems (and, in a different fashion, in relational aesthetics), to withdraw into harmonious communities where each person occupies his or her own place, ethnicity, or class, or into an idealized art field. The sublimation of protected spaces tends to be associated with the desire to resolve emotionally what economic competition has "corrupted." I conceive of imminence as the experience of perceiving in the existing reality other possible ways of being that make dissent, not escape, a necessity.

The emancipation of the individual in the modern age has resulted, according to Rancière, from breaking the correlation between occupations and skills. I would add that technology and migrants' transnational mobility have destabilized the relationship between our birthplaces, our jobs, and the practices by which we move from place to place. It is impossible to escape this uncertainty in communities whose integration has been slowly eroded by modernity.

Let's look at what this implies about artistic communication, the concept of the spectacle and that of the spectator. An important task for the art critic is deconstructing the illusion that there are inexorable mechanisms that transform reality into image, into a certain type of uniquely true expressive image. The danger of forgetting the transition of actual into imagined things, which tends to happen in the media on "reality" shows and on news programs that use fictionalization, can be avoided by an art that conceives of the pact of verisimilitude and criticism in a different way.

The spectacularization offered up by the media (and by art exhibits that stick to the rules of spectacle) is devoted to neutralizing social dissent or to convincing us that some magical political power—that of a hero or of a community of survivors—can avoid it. Who put the media and the arts in charge of organizing the sensible in a way that lessens the discrepancies between the perceptible and the thinkable? This sort of confusion only serves the interests of those who would benefit from a placid common sense that accepts the current distribution of skills and handicaps, of employment and unemployment.

Artists' actions test different ways out of this bewitchment. One is the education model: displaying photographs of the victims of a dictatorship or an ethnic cleansing in order to make the concealed visible and provoke our indignation. When we find out that this sort of denunciation has little effect, we learn that there's no automatic continuity among the revelation of hidden facts, the images and the means by which we communicate them, and spectators' perceptions of and responses to them. The reason for these failures is that an aesthetic of mimesis persists in certain zones of contemporary art. Art doesn't turn us into rebels by shoving repulsive facts into our faces, nor does it mobilize us because it has gone after us outside the museum. Its critique, and not merely its indignation, might infect us if the art itself would let go of forms of language that are complicit in maintaining the social order.

What we need is a different model in which art avoids becoming a generalized form of life or creating total works, as in certain acritical fusions with mass assemblies or movements. Nor is it a matter of turning spectators into actors, as in the activism of the 1970s. The practical effectiveness of art, according to Rancière (2008: 62–63), is a "paradoxical efficacy" (*efficacité paradoxale*): it doesn't arise from the suspension of aesthetic distance, but from "the suspension of any determinable relationship between an artist's intention, a sensible form presented in an art venue, a spectator's gaze, and the state of a community."

Rancière's circuitous statement about this paradoxical efficacy seems at first glance to restore the autonomy of art. He says that aesthetic efficacy is achieved when a Florentine virgin, a Dutch tavern scene, a fruit bowl, or a readymade appears separate from the form of life that gave rise to its production. Such a work no longer has meaning as an expression of royal, religious, or aristocratic domination but rather in the framework of visibility provided to all artworks by the common space of the museum. The efficacy of art comes from a disconnect between artistic meaning and the social goals to which the objects had originally been devoted. Rancière gives it a twist and calls this disconnect "dissensus." By dissensus, he does not mean "the conflict between ideas or feelings. It is the conflict of many realms of sensoriality" (2008: 66).

At this point he makes the link between art and politics. Since he conceives of politics as "the activity that reconfigures the sense frameworks within which common objects are defined," breaking the order of the senses that naturalizes a social structure, art is connected to politics because it acts at "a moment of collective enunciation that redesigns the space of common things" (2008: 66). The aesthetic experience, as an experience of dissensus, is opposed to the mimetic or ethical adaptation of art for social purposes. Without functionality, artworks make it possible, outside of the network of connections that determine a preestablished meaning, for viewers to turn their perceptions, their bodies, and their passions toward something completely different from domination.

Aesthetic experiences thus point toward creating an unexpected landscape of the visible, new subjectivities and connections, different rhythms of apprehending objects. But they don't do so in the same way as the activity that creates a "we" with possibilities of collective emancipation. Artists and writers have to resist everyone who wants to subordinate their many ambiguous stories to History, as Juan Villoro wrote with regard to the anthropologists who praised *Pedro Páramo* because they appreciated the way the novel had "captured" the language of the Altos de Jalisco. It is blindness to think of the novel's narrator as "a skilled reporter taking down the colloquial language in shorthand" in order to represent History rather than someone who uses ghosts, voices, and rumors to create an allegory about the people who have been exiled from history (Villoro 2000: 22).

Art forms a fabric of dissensus filled with snippets of objects and feeble occasions for subjective statements, some of them scattered and anonymous, that do not lend themselves to any specific calculation. This indeterminacy, this unpredictability of effects, corresponds in the perspective I propose to the status of imminence in the works or artistic actions that cannot be grouped into political metanarratives or collective programs. We seek an open, unpredictable relation between the logic of redescribing the sensible on the part of artists, the logic of communication in their works, and the several logics of appropriation by viewers; the point is to avoid a set correlation between the micropolitics of the creators and the constitution of political collectives. Artists help change the map of what is perceptible and thinkable and can spark new experiences, but there is no reason why heterogeneous modes of sensoriality should lead to an understanding of meaning that can motivate transformative decisions. There is no direct, mechanical line that goes from viewing a spectacle to understanding society and from there to a politics of change. In this zone of uncertainty, art is suited not so much for direct action as for suggesting the power of what hangs in suspense. Or of what has been left hanging.

It was easier to believe artistic projects that had social goals when national narratives still achieved an appearance of continuity between sensibly presenting commonly held facts and interpreting their political meanings. The globalization of communications and economics has multiplied sense repertoires and their representations, while narratives are jointly incapable of containing and interpreting this diversity. The dissensus between realms of the senses lacks realms of understanding that could simultaneously encompass the commodities that have been disorganized by financial speculation and the national political systems that have been eroded by global trends with no governing structure. There are strategies of homogenizing advertisements and of highly successful globalized media iconographies—Disney, manga—but they are incapable of creating governability or a social sense that can build consensus on a large scale. Why should we ask art to do it?

This last reflection leads me to make an objection to Rancière's work. I agree with him that there is no future in looking at art as a mediator between the goals of renovating our sensory perceptions and transforming society. The inability of art to do that sort of mediating work was demonstrated in the period when the autonomization of the art field coexisted with different strains of political voluntarism—from Constructivism and Surrealism to the militancy of the 1970s. What happens when art becomes nonautonomous by taking part in the dynamics of the economy, the media, fashion, or social thought?

The aesthetic actions that aim to change the references of what is visible and expressible—that aim to get us to see what is hidden or get us to look at it in a different way—are not exclusive to the arts. They also take place in the media, in urban renewal, in advertising, and in the framework of alternative politics: this is one of the keys to our fascination with innovative advertising and with television shows lampooning political personalities and sclerotic narratives of society. The "creatives" in these fields, as their name suggests, also create sensory dissensus from time to time. Communications studies have shown that fashion and the messages that fashion sends contribute to women's liberation. Research on consumption demonstrates that it can be both a setting for commercially disciplining habits and distinctions and also a place of creative innovation and intellectual discernment: consumption is good for thinking.

Now and then Rancière stops to wonder about this new condition of the arts. He recalls, as an example of artists who infiltrate the networks of domination, the performances of the Yes Men when they used false identities to crash a business conference, Bush campaign events, and a television program. Their most eloquent action had to do with the Bhopal disaster in India. One of their members managed to pass himself off to the BBC as an spokesman for Dow Chemical, which had bought a controlling share of Union Carbide. He announced during a prime-time broadcast that the corporation recognized its responsibility and was committed to compensating the victims. Two hours later the corporation reacted and declared that its only responsibility was to its shareholders. That was the desired effect.

Rancière (2008: 82) is correct when he says that "these direct actions in the real heart of domination" leave us wondering whether or not they empower lasting collective action against domination. They also foster distinctions, he argues, between reality and fiction. "There is no real world outside of art. There are folds and more folds in the common fabric of the sensible. . . . There is no such thing as the real in itself, only configurations of what is given as our reality, as the object of our perceptions, of our thoughts, and of our speech. The real is always the object of a fiction, that is, of a construction of the space where what can be seen, what can be said, and what can be done are joined together" (83–84).

Sure. But we still face the question of how to think about "political" actions, in the sense that Rancière gives them—activities that reconfigure the frameworks of the senses within which common objects are defined—when those who carry them out aren't the people recognized as artists but the architects who modernize cities, the creatives of advertising or fashion, the designers of political ads and not the politicians themselves: those who are usually seen as reproducing common sense and the dominant fictions.

So, are you saying that the agents of revolution are the ad men?

No. I'm trying to think about what the political is, where the place is from which cultural and social changes are produced. I'm trying to understand what it means that social and political agency are more widely distributed than we are used to acknowledging.

>

Can There Be a Postautonomous Aesthetic?

This book set out to look at the void left by the exhaustion of (the) modern aesthetic(s). It has also criticized the idealization of fragmentary and nomadic works and their fleeting prestige in the postmodern canon, including the neocommunitarianist installations and performances that "justify" relational aesthetics. Doesn't the postautonomous aesthetic invent a new arbitrary canon when it concentrates on "embedded" works and actions, whereas a good measure of what people recognized as artists do remains independent of economic, media, or political coercion, and critics evaluate their work by criteria unfettered by those contexts?

Above all, the purpose of this book isn't to come up with a new aesthetic. It doesn't establish a set of rules about what kind of art ought to be done. It attempts to describe the current landscape of art practice by observing what is going on with certain art studios, artworks, museums, auctions, audiences, theories, and critics. We come to a few conclusions about the circuits in which art opens up to linkages that lie beyond its own field. We show that this opening, as well as the challenges of outside actors, make the autonomy of the art world problematic. Instead of proposing that art should be dissolved into design, politics, the market for items of distinction, or popular culture (as has so often been argued), I have been interested in understanding the changes in the way artists and other participants in the field act and how the networks that reach out beyond the art fields and their changeable behaviors are constructed.

By devoting many pages to examining a few artists and their works I have formed not a canon but a corpus of documents. Even among the artists selected I have distinguished between different tactics and relate them to varied contexts. León Ferrari makes collages with political and religious discourses and also abstract and purely playful works; he has exhibited in union halls, museums, human rights organizations, art fairs, and biennales. Cildo Meireles's "insertions" in ideological circuits are, strictly speaking, acts carried out in circuits of market goods, museums, reflections on the media and even on social theorizing about art. I don't deny the interference of the subjective-collective disposition that we still call taste in my selection of certain artists, but my choice was also based on these artists' capacity for thinking with images. Part of what attracts me about contemporary art is the power with which many artists reflect on society wordlessly.

Nor do the artists selected here work as a canon, because they differ in their works with regard to social narratives. Ferrari, Antoni Muntadas, and Santiago Sierra have chosen different processes and narratives to develop their questions. The stylistic differences between their works depend in part on whether their targets are the alliances between dictatorships and Christianity, authoritarianism in political communications or intercultural translation, exclusivist nationalisms, or exploitation. Carlos Amorales removes himself from historical and national framings; his apocalyptic or festive lyricism gives expression to works that don't refer to any identifiable geopolitical conflicts.

I admit that I'm also interested in works by other artists in which imminence isn't the main device behind the aesthetic effect. We need other notions—beauty, provocation, violence, the predominance of form over function, debasement, memory—to name phenomena that appear in art today. Sometimes these other experiences, like the works of Teresa Margolles, can be distinguished from police reports of violence or debasement because the way she leaves them in a state of imminence gives them aesthetic meaning and prompts a different sort of reflection.

Tensions between Structure and Creativity

Anthropologists tend to find it easier to talk about artists' behavior than about their artworks. Nevertheless it is a good feeling to see their works challenge our habits of perception and our haste to interpret them. I go to Meireles's exhibit at the Museo Universitario Arte Contemporáneo in Mexico City and again see his "insertions into circuits," his *Zero cruzeiro* and *Zero dollar*, his manipulated Coca-Cola bottles, and other pieces that I've seen in photographs. Entering the exhibit, we have to take off our shoes before walking through a darkened room, across a floor covered with a fine powder—talcum or flour?—where some visitors ward off fear by tossing the powder, which we never identify, on themselves. Exiting the room dusted in white, we walk across a floor covered with broken glass, wearing our shoes again but tracing our way through a semi-opaque, semitransparent labyrinth, not knowing where it will lead.

I tried to understand what the narratives were—narratives of Christianity, of capitalism, of their own nations—that these artists were struggling with, not putting their pieces in too tight an order so as not to cut the struggle short, and not forcing them to fit a theory or a larger group where their energy would be attenuated. I wanted to avoid the aestheticizing or conceptualizing tactics that the Quai Branly Museum used to organize works from Africa, Latin America, and Asia into a single architecture, a single homogenized museological discourse, watering down their passion.

As I let myself get swept away by the lyrical watercolors, the luchador masks, the birds and the trees that Amorales has collected, what I find most disturbing isn't the chaos of his archive in a neutral, half-empty apartment, where he works at cutting and pasting or at combining figures on his computer screen. What unsettles me is the sort of ironic fury with which he cuts and pastes and goes back to designing, proofing, and correcting, not to find a better way to say something about a bit of the world or tell a recognizable story but to make these ten red-eyed black skulls more unsure, these birds flying off to who-knows-where more sinister, these disasters that never quite take place more festive.

Why begin each chapter with references to the aesthetic and social anthropological theories that have proposed new keys to reading these cultural movements in recent years? I wanted to see how the conceptual questions change and how we resist dropping the ones that have been useful to us up to now. There is no protected art world, and there are no general theories that can encompass all its diversity today. Not only because the autonomy of the field has fallen apart with the fluctuations in the auction market and the fleeting nature of biennales, those unsure locations that would be the arbiters of prices and the order in which we look at art. Museological theories and orders become disoriented signals. Even with the most programmatic artist I selected, Muntadas, or the cleverest, Sierra, you can tell that they no longer have frames for their pictures or exhibit spaces to hang them in. Nobody believes in being able to represent a country. We've left the era behind when aesthetic value amounted to a "field effect," a result of the creator's position of authority, the marketplace, and the viewers' credulity. The aesthetics that are now possible are those that accept untimeliness. The sociology of art becomes the ethnography of a landscape of cultural interactions, anxious ways of naming, that change over and over again. We are living in imminence and what we call art are the ways of working on this threshold. Not in order to enter a new territory, but to discover a tension.

Never in modern times has the structure of the art field been as determinative, as isolated, as some sociologists have claimed. But the interdependent ties between art and its context are more visible now that artists and their works are appearing on other stages. However, the many lines of evidence showing that the arts form part of the visual culture of society in general mean that one good theory alone isn't enough to describe the links between the art field and society. To gain a better understanding of this, we must both study the structural conditions of the art world and its social context and look at aesthetic works and projects in themselves, paying attention to the frameworks in which they refer to context, the wandering route of meaning through circulation and reception, being near the works and nimble in following their trajectories.

Another thing that makes it hard to arrive at a general theory of art is the fact that the practices of institutions and artists can't be summed up under just one logic, nor will they let themselves be caught in the opposition between museums that like to discipline and artists who like to transgress. It's true that most museums, auctions, and biennales are devoted to reproducing themselves as institutions. But no artists, not even the least accommodating, aim merely at throwing narratives into disorder: we've seen that the short circuits between the narratives of Christianity, the dictatorships, and capitalism have been fashioned by Ferrari into readable collages. In several of his works, the cockroaches attacking government offices and the hellscapes of war are contained in boxes or bottles. Muntadas's negotiating table has uneven legs that have to be leveled out with piles of books, but we can look at it without having it crash down onto us. Amorales's disturbing apparitions escape the interpretations that seek their origins in symbolism and suggest a randomness with some sort of meaning, or with forms that hint at one.

Making Society in a Different Way

The narratives of modernity have fallen, but the avant-garde illusions of postmodernism aren't convincing either. No matter how much they try to renew alternative pathways and freer circulation on digital networks, these ruptures have not placed us in a postinstitutional era. Though many artists refuse to represent their nations, to say that globalization has led us to a postnational age of carefree nomadism would be to forget that 97 percent of the world's people live where they were born and most artists have been heard of only in their own countries.

There are still hegemonic nations and networks of countries that structure art movements, which as a result can be analyzed by socio-logical and anthropological methods. Jet-set and peripheral artists and curators alike ground their artworks and exhibitions in their own man-ner of forming groups, representing minorities, and linking themselves into circuits whose power is concentrated in a handful of major cities. It doesn't get us anywhere to declare that we're living in a postpolitical age—we've seen that artistic practices make society differently, that they dovetail with orders of power and lose their singularity when NGOs in-vent similar performances and disrupt the logic of hegemony.

We should be cautious about slapping the prefix post- onto "autono-mous." The border between what is historically real and literary or artis-tic fiction may be ill-defined, and the supposed internal logic of the art field may have proved amenable to social influences, but there are still projects with aesthetic forms and intentions, there are still authors of projects with aesthetic goals, and there are still relatively differentiated spaces where fictional books and visual artworks circulate. As I said in the preface to this book, we can clearly see a movement toward post-autonomy in the form of a displacement from artistic practices based on *objects* to practices based on *contexts*—so much so that we can see the influence of this movement on works in social media, networks, and interactions. But simply declaring the abolition of differences between autonomy and dependency, between "reality" and fiction, won't help us understand the oscillations and ambivalences among them. Josefina Ludmer (2007) notes that "many texts today cross the border (the parameters that define what literature is) and remain outside and inside, in a kind of diasporic position: outside, but trapped on the inside. As if they were 'in exodus.'" It is this very state—being on the outside and on the inside, being a book or an artwork and being a piece of merchandise, being displayed in museums and in human rights organizations, calling yourself an author and doubting your own power—that I'm referring to when I talk about imminence.

Does the autonomy of art still matter? Simple ethnographic description reveals that it does, but with open formats. For one thing, we find it in the mystery of auctions, in the protected circuits of mainstream biennales, museums, and galleries, in the art journals and criticism that defend the practice of evaluating artworks by aesthetic criteria rather than the criteria for rating mass-produced industrial items. Then again, autonomy seems to be valued when we reject censorship and defend the independence of artists, critics, and institutions in the name of the public interest and the diversity of audiences. After the attacks by the Catholic Church on Ferrari's exhibit, arguing that it infringes on "the rights of God," and after the condemnations of gay-themed photographic exhibits and artist groups that give voice to human rights movements, proclaiming the autonomy to create and express art seems less like a scheme to protect artists' privileges than an effort to defend a common space where diverse positions can democratically debate social meaning. It has no absolute independence, but there are tactical autonomies. Along these lines, the emphasis on artists' work being with imminence is what distinguishes their productions from other works critical of social structures, as well as from expressly political actions that are aimed at changing the established order.

It still makes sense to distinguish between the effectiveness of political acts and of artworks; likewise it is both possible and necessary to differentiate the *quality* of the two types of actions. The imbrication of artworks and acts with "profane" media experiences has delegitimized the aristocratic posturing that speaks of quality as a kind of originality that defies social science analysis. But various authors reject the reductionism of those schools of cultural studies that value texts and artworks only in terms of how they represent social differences and contradictions. Some emphasize semantic density, others the way artworks question things or the possibility that they can be seen or read as supporting strictly aesthetic evaluations. In a book on the social and political interventions of Argentine artists after the socioeconomic disaster of 2001, *Poscrisis*, Andrea Giunta (2009: 122) speaks of quality not as the "adaptation to certain immovable principles of art, but rather [as] the challenge that some works issue to our senses and our intellects." She is therefore attracted to the artists about whose works "it can be convincingly argued that they disrupt the gratuitousness and superficiality that seem so prevalent today" (123). She chooses works that provide "a particularly intense experience," one "of defamiliarization," contrapuntal works that probe the dreams and failures of the age: "These works get us past the skepticism that the general state of art and its networks of power can produce in us" (128).

Taking up Claire Bishop's critique of relational aesthetics, cited earlier, Graciela Speranza (2007) defends the possibility of identifying aesthetic differences if we bear in mind "intentionality, the ability of a work to promote readings that make it intelligible, and the quality of the relations that the spectator weaves." If we ignore the question of aesthetic value, as some currents in cultural or postmodern studies do, according to Speranza, we allow our aesthetic decisions—which still exist and still have weight in society, in the economy, and in artists' practices—to remain "disguised in new selection criteria imposed by art institutions or the market." For similar reasons, Benjamin Buchloh argues that the central change that critical thinking needs to undertake today is to question "in aesthetic terms . . . the criteria of agreement with which curators, art historians, and critics should position themselves outside the monopoly system" (Bonami and Buchloh 2009: 20).

The Role of Art in Disorder and in the Loss of Narrative

One line of strategic reflection might be to argue about consensus and dissensus in relation to the problems of compatibility and incompatibility. A central concern in the economic, social, and technological changes of today, which involve all sorts of levels of development and orientations, is the problem of *compatibility*. Looking at the remaining socialist countries (Cuba, China), how can capitalist corporations and investments be made to coexist with one-party states in which there is no political competition? In postdictatorial processes like the ones we see in Argentina, Chile, and Spain, the idea is for democratization to move forward despite the inertia of authoritarian habits and hierarchies among the people and institutions of those countries.

Similarly the technological transformations that overlay the functions of readers, viewers, and web surfers follow development patterns that call for making different formats compatible: the paper book with computer texts and e-books, PCs with Macs, discs and videos with digital downloads.

There are plenty of discourses and practices that preach consensus, agreement, peaceful coexistence. We know that there are many new conflicts: entrepreneurs and governments that promote proprietary anticopying software and cut off Internet connections in reaction to free software and movements for the unpaid circulation of content on P2P networks; the commercial inertia of large institutions such as museums, biennales, and the major record labels, as opposed to networks that multiply the number of distribution points and redistribute the proceeds; the concentration of power in Northern Hemisphere art institutions with border controls that allow few names or artworks to filter in from the continents that have been subordinated in the modern age.

Until a few years ago artists of dissensus could find few ways to turn their protests into projects. Their works and their demands remained monologues heard only in their home countries. Technology networks facilitate the proliferation of stages, their multifocality and interconnection. Globalization, as we have seen, increases the percentage of

Africans, Asians, and Latin Americans in some of the great exhibit and art market events, especially on the web.

Confronting the persistent concentrations of economic power, there are *specifically artistic and cultural* ways to extend the spread of creativity in order to balance the exchanges between North and South, between actors from the center and from the periphery. Just as the relative autonomy of the art field is valuable in society for promoting innovation and social critique in the face of political or religious censure, taking the singularity of the international division of *cultural* labor into consideration can facilitate advances beyond the economic inequalities and global hierarchies of political power.

Sociology or Anthropology? Optimism or Pessimism?

Sociology and communications studies are giving us broader and broader frameworks, and they offer the tools needed for reading the new global relationships of interdependence. Anthropologists can better grasp the density of these interactions, and in recent years they have succeeded at giving more intercultural flexibility to their views. This book tries to show that combining these forms of training would be productive for doing a joint analysis of the near and the far, the heritage that would belong to all humanity, and the arts that globalize the local. The need to interweave distinct disciplinary focuses is already present in the cultural practices that do just that, such as the museums and biennales that try to be postcolonial and the artists who place intercultural translation at the center of their creative programs.

There is no narrative for a globalized society that can coordinate these disciplinary disagreements without conflicts or gaps. Or do it for social and intercultural disagreements. There are lots of doctrinal, religious, political, and even cognitive narratives that persist for a while as paradigms in the social sciences and humanities. As I've said with regard to World Heritage lists, these narratives tend to be anthologies of the answers that different cultures have come up with. The art that works with imminence has proved fertile for dealing with a different sort of question: What do societies do with what they find no answer for in their culture, in their politics, or in their technology? This ability isn't exclusive to art and literature. You can also perceive it in the creative sort of scientific research that pays more attention to surprising results than to things that reconfirm existing knowledge.

In this sense, art and science *make society*. They achieve this to the extent that they don't claim to offer new self-sufficient totalities but instead think and assist in recomposing structures, interactions, and experiences. Since it was our analysis of heritage that allowed us to appreciate this, both the aesthetic dimension of heritage and its cultural meaning and political management should deal not only with cultural items but with usages. When they are open to displacement, concepts travel, says Mieke Bal, and in both society and in art they grasp usages and meanings never foreseen in their original program. In this job of understanding displacements and the variations in objects and actors, anthropology has accumulated greater experience and flexibility. It is also beginning to overcome one of its historic limitations: moving from the local to comparisons between societies, from ethnography to social theory.

As we remake theory—a theory open to social disorder, with no single grand narrative—what we really need is the anthropological insistence on listening to actors, a great diversity of actors, spending time in qualitative matters, in the anxiety-producing density of facts. When I give talks in which I express the worry I share with Marc Abélès, that the world may be going from convivance to survival mode, or when I praise the works of Ferrari or Margolles, I've been asked to define myself: Am I an optimist or a pessimist? My answer is that neither pessimism nor optimism is a productive concept in social research. Personally I would prefer being antiskeptical, like lots of scientists interested in discovering a coherent rationality beyond the loss of meganarratives, the urgency of social demands, short-term economic and political speculation, and the fleeting vocation of many artistic experiences.

What Might Come

An aesthetic of imminence isn't an aesthetic of the ephemeral. At least, not a melancholy sort of ephemeral—that feeling of always thinking about what's been lost and living from an always inadequate recollection of memories. If imminence has anything to do with the ephemeral, it is with the ephemeral as an affirmation of life. Not in the Nietzschean sense, as an acceptance of the fickleness of life, but as a disposition toward what might come, as paying attention and waiting. Christine Buci-Glucksmann (2008: 28) takes off from a statement by Deleuze to the effect that we should rise to the occasion of what's coming, to characterize the unmelancholy ephemeral as an opening to the unknown, "something you can catch or allow to get away." An aesthetic of imminence is a way, other than taking the heritage route, to work with the sensibilities.

To the degree that we take into account the "hard" conditions revealed by social research, this opening to what might come should be connected to "actually existing," empirically testable processes. The postmodern embrace of the ephemeral as flow and flexibility, as we saw in our critique of nomadism, can hide the social vulnerability and aimlessness of a world that has knocked down the great narratives but has kept a concentration of great powers—the forces that limit our opportunities to be flexible, make discoveries, and innovate. Do we have to be reminded once more that the ability to innovate, to rise to the occasion of what's coming, is unequally distributed among groups and countries?

An aesthetic of imminence, being aware that art isn't autonomous, knows that the possibility of being open to new things, catching them or letting them get away, is linked to practices that don't take place in a vacuum, operating instead in the midst of unequal conditions under limitations that artists share with nonartists. By valuing imminence, the aesthetic disposition de-fatalizes the conventional structures of language, the habits of the professions, the canon of what is legitimate. But it doesn't magically eliminate them. It is merely our training for recovering our ability to speak and to do, getting out of preset frameworks.

The task of art isn't to give society a narrative so it can organize its diversity; it is to give value to the imminent, where dissensus is possible. Besides offering iconographies for living in peaceful harmony or manifestos for making a break, artists can participate by creating symbols and reimagining disagreements. The most interesting ways of making form prevail over function today are found not in the conformist designs of marketing and political advertising but in experiences for sublimating memory without erasing the drama and for enjoying the new forms of access.

Perhaps there is an ethics for this aesthetic without grand narrative.

Epilogue

‹

It would come about not by harmonizing the heritages of divergent cultures but by following the fusion deejays who are migrants or dissidents or outsiders in their own societies. Yet another avant-garde? No, we don't need either heroes or prophets. As artists, curators, critics, and audiences, we can be communities or networks that enjoy whatever is next.

WORKS CITED

>

Abélès, Marc. 1996. *En attente d'Europe*. Paris: Hachette.

———. 2010. *The Politics of Survival*. Trans. Julie Kleinman. Durham: Duke University Press.

Alandete, David. 2009. "Los arrepentidos del Facebook." *El País*. November 11.

Alÿs, Francis, and Cuauhtémoc Medina. 2006. *Diez cuadras alrededor del estudio/ Walking Distance from the Studio*. Mexico City: Antiguo Colegio de San Ildefonso.

Amorales, Carlos. 2007. *Carlos Amorales: Dark Mirror*. Zurich: Hatje Cantz.

Appadurai, Arjun. 1996. *Modernity at Large: Cultural Dimensions of Globalization*. Minneapolis: University of Minnesota Press.

Ares, Carlos. 2005. "El Cristo blasfemo de Buenos Aires," *El País*, January 5, accessed July 24, 2012, elpais.com/diario/2005/01/05/ultima/1104879601 _850215.html.

Artprice. 2008. *Le marché de l'art contemporain 2007/2008: Le rapport annuel Artprice/Contemporary Art Market: The Artprice Annual Report*. London: Art and Technology Press.

Bal, Mieke. 2002. *Travelling Concepts in the Humanities: A Rough Guide*. Toronto: University of Toronto Press.

Balibar, Étienne. 2004. *We, the People of Europe? Reflections on Transnational Citizenship*. Trans. James Swenson. Princeton: Princeton University Press.

Barboza, David. 2008. "The Many Faces of Yue Minjun." *Art Zine: A Chinese Contemporary Art Portal*. Accessed June 22, 2012. www.artzinechina.com /display_vol_aid111_en.html.

Barriendos Rodríguez, Joaquín. 2006. *Geoestética y transculturalidad: Políticas de representación, globalización de la diversidad cultural e internacionalización del arte contemporáneo*. Girona, Spain: Fundació Espais d'Art Contemporani, Col·lecció Premi Espais a la Crítica d'Art.

Beck, Ulrich. 2000. *What Is Globalization?* Trans. Patrick Camiller. Cambridge, UK: Polity Press.

Becker, Howard S. 1982. *Art Worlds*. Berkeley: University of California Press.

Benítez Dueñas, Issa María, and José Luis Barrios. 2007. *Carlos Amorales, Archivo Líquido: ¿Por qué temer al futuro? / Liquid Archive: Why Fear the Future?* Mexico City: UNAM.

Benjamin, Walter. 1968. *Illuminations: Essays and Reflections.* Ed. Hannah Arendt. Trans. Harry Zohn. New York: Schocken Books.

Bishop, Claire. 2004. "Antagonism and Relational Aesthetics." *October* 110: 51–79.

Bonami, Francesco, and Benjamin Buchloh. 2009. "Coexistence, Yes. Equivalence, No." *Parkett* 86: 18–22.

Bonet, Lluís. 2004. "Políticas de cooperación e industrias culturales en el desarrollo euro-latinoamericano." In Organización de Estados Iberoamericanos (ed.), *Industrias culturales y desarrollo sustentable.* Mexico City: Secretaría de Relaciones Exteriores and Consejo Nacional para la Cultura y las Artes.

Borges, Jorge Luis. 1964. "The Wall and the Books." In *Other Inquisitions, 1937–1952.* Trans. Ruth L. C. Simms. Austin: University of Texas Press.

Bourdieu, Pierre. (1979) 1984. *Distinction: A Social Critique of the Judgment of Taste.* Trans. Richard Nice. Cambridge: Harvard University Press.

———. 1996. *The Rules of Art.* Trans. Susan Emanuel. Cambridge, UK: Polity Press.

Bourdieu, Pierre, Alain Darbel, and Dominique Schnapper. (1960) 1991. *The Love of Art: European Art Museums and Their Public.* Trans. Caroline Beattie and Nick Merriman. Stanford: Stanford University Press.

Bourdieu, Pierre, and Hans Haacke. 1995. *Free Exchange.* Stanford: Stanford University Press.

Bourriaud, Nicolas. 2002. *Relational Aesthetics.* Trans. Simon Pleasance and Fronza Woods. Dijon: Les Presses du Réel.

———. 2005. *Postproduction: Culture as Screenplay. How Art Reprograms the World.* Trans. Jeanine Herman. 2nd edition. New York: Lukas and Sternberg.

Bowness, Alan. 1989. *The Conditions of Success: How the Modern Artist Rises to Fame.* London: Thames and Hudson.

Brea, José Luis. 2005. "Los estudios visuales: Por una epistemología política de la visualidad." In José Luis Brea (ed.), *La epistemología de la visualidad en la era de la globalización.* Madrid: Akal.

Buchloh, Benjamin. 2000. *Neo-Avantgarde and Culture Industry: Essays on European and American Art from 1955 to 1975.* Cambridge: MIT Press.

———. 2005. "Benjamin H. D. Buchloh entrevista a Gabriel Orozco en Nueva York." In *Textos sobre la obra de Gabriel Orozco.* Mexico City: CONACULTA, Turner.

Buci-Glucksmann, Christine. 2008. *Une femme philosophe: Dialogue avec François Soulages.* Paris: Klincksieck.

Buck-Morss, Susan. 2011. "Visual Studies and Global Imagination." In Chiara Bottici and Benoît Challand (eds.), *The Politics of Imagination.* Abingdon, UK: Birkbeck Law Press.

Chen Xiaorong. 2009. "Now, It's All about the Money." *China Daily.* April 13, www.chinadaily.com.cn/bw/2009-04/13/content_7670193.htm.

Cimet, Esther, M. Dujovne, N. García Canclini, J. Gullco, C. Mendoza, F. Reyes Palma, and G. Soltero. 1987. *El público como propuesta: Cuatro estudios sociológicos en museos de arte*. Mexico City: Instituto Nacional de Bellas Artes.

Clifford, James. 1988. *The Predicament of Culture: Twentieth-Century Ethnography, Literature, and Art*. Cambridge: Harvard University Press.

———. 1997. *Routes: Travel and Translation in the Late Twentieth Century*. Cambridge: Harvard University Press.

———. 2007. "Quai Branly in Process." *October* 120: 3–23.

Cruces, Francisco. 1998. "El ritual de la protesta en las marchas urbanas." In Néstor García Canclini (ed.), *Cultura y comunicación en la ciudad de México*, vol. 2. Mexico City: Grijalbo.

Danto, Arthur. 1997. *After the End of Art: Contemporary Art and the Pale of History*. Princeton: Princeton University Press.

Deleuze, Gilles, and Félix Guattari. 1994. *What Is Philosophy?* Trans. Hugh Tomlinson and Graham Burchell. New York: Columbia University Press.

Descola, Philippe. 2007. "Synthese." In Bruno Latour (ed.), *Le dialogue des cultures: Actes des rencontres inaugurales du Musée du quai Branly (21 de juin 2006)*. Arles: Actes Sud.

Dickie, George. 1974. *Art and the Aesthetic: An Institutional Analysis*. Ithaca: Cornell University Press.

Downey, Anthony. 2009. "An Ethics of Engagement: Collaborative Art Prices and the Return of the Ethnographer." *Third Text: Critical Perspectives on Contemporary Art* 23 (5): 593–603.

Eco, Umberto. 1978. "Lector in Fabula: Pragmatic Strategy in a Metanarrative Text." In *The Role of the Reader: Explorations in the Semiotics of Texts*. Bloomington: University of Indiana Press.

Edelman, Bernard, and Nathalie Heinich. 2002. *L'art en conflits: L'oeuvre de l'esprit entre droit et sociologie*. Paris: La Découverte.

Eder, Rita, et al. 1977. "El público de arte en México: Los espectadores de la exposición Hammer." *Plural*, July, 51–65.

Escobar, Arturo, and Gustavo Lins Ribeiro, eds. 2006. *World Anthropologies: Disciplinary Transformations within Systems of Power*. New York: Berg.

Escobar, Ticio. 2004. *El arte fuera de sí*. Asunción, Paraguay: CAV, Museo del Barro, FONDEC.

Ferrari, León. 2000. *La bondadosa crueldad*. Buenos Aires: Editorial Argonauta.

Fisher, Jean. 2009. "The Sleep of Wakefulness: Gabriel Orozco." In Yve-Alain Bois (ed.), *Gabriel Orozco*. Cambridge: MIT Press.

Fisk, Robert. 2005. *The Great War for Civilization: The Conquest of the Middle East*. London: Fourth Estate.

Florida, Richard. 2002. *The Rise of the Creative Class and How It's Transforming Work, Leisure, Community and Everyday Life*. New York: Basic Books.

Foster, Hal. 1996. *The Return of the Real: Art and Theory at the End of the Century.* Cambridge: MIT Press.

Foucault, Michel. 1972. *The Archaeology of Knowledge.* Trans. Alan Sheridan-Smith. New York: Pantheon Books.

Gallo, Rubén, and Alfredo Jaar. 1996. "Representation of Violence, Violence of Representation: Interview of Alfredo Jaar." *Trans* 3–4: 57–66.

García Canclini, Néstor. 1999. *La globalización imaginada.* Barcelona: Paidós.

———. 2004. *Diferentes, desiguales y desconectados: Mapas de la interculturalidad.* Barcelona: Gedisa.

———. 2007a. "Una pasión llamada Frida Kahlo." *Clarín, Revista Ñ.* July 21.

———. 2007b. "Frida y la industrialización de la cultura," *Reforma, Suplemento El Ángel,* August 19.

———, ed. 2009. *Extranjeros en la tecnología yen la cultura.* Buenos Aires: Fundación Telefónica, Ariel.

Geertz, Clifford. 1983. *Local Knowledge: Further Essays in Interpretive Anthropology.* New York: Basic Books.

———. 1988. *Works and Lives: The Anthropologist as Author.* Stanford: Stanford University Press.

Giunta, Andrea. 2008. "Perturbadora belleza." In León Ferrari and Andrea Giunta, *León Ferrari: "Todavía quedan muchos creyentes que convencer."* Buenos Aires: Capital Intelectual.

———. 2009. *Poscrisis: Arte argentino después de 2001.* Buenos Aires: Siglo XXI.

Giunta, Andrea, and Liliana Piñeiro. 2008. "León Ferrari, agitador de formas." In *León Ferrari: Obras/Works, 1976–2008.* Ed. Andrea Giunta. Trans. Mario Murgia. Mexico City: Editorial RM.

Godard, Jean-Luc. 1998. *Histoire(s) du cinéma.* Paris: Gallimard.

Godelier, Maurice. 2007. "Les métamorphoses de la qualification." In Bruno Latour (ed.), *Le dialogue des cultures: Actes des rencontres inaugurales du Musée du quai Branly (21 de juin 2006).* Arles: Actes Sud.

Goodman, Nelson. 1976. *Languages of Art: An Approach to a Theory of Symbols.* Indianapolis: Hackett.

———. 1977. "When Is Art?" In David Perkins and Barbara Leondar (eds.), *The Arts and Cognition.* Baltimore: Johns Hopkins University Press.

Grimson, Alejandro. 2009. "Fronteras y extranjeros: Desde la antropología y la comunicación—Cultura, identidad, frontera." In Néstor García Canclini (ed.), *Extranjeros en la tecnología y en la cultura.* Buenos Aires: Fundación Telefónica, Ariel.

Guasch, Anna María. 2003. "Los estudios visuales: Un estado de la cuestión." *Estudios Visuales: Ensayo, teoría y crítica de la cultura visual y el arte contemporáneo* 1: 8–16.

Guilbaut, Serge. 1983. *How New York Stole the Idea of Modern Art: Abstract Expressionism, Freedom, and the Cold War.* Chicago: University of Chicago Press.

Hannerz, Ulf. 1996. *Transnational Connections: Culture, People, Places.* London: Routledge.

Hardt, Michael, and Antonio Negri. 2000. *Empire.* Cambridge: Harvard University Press.

Heinich, Nathalie. 1996. *The Glory of Van Gogh: An Anthropology of Admiration.* Trans. Paul Leduc Browne. Princeton: Princeton University Press.

———. 1998. *Le triple jeu de l'art contemporain: Sociologie des arts plastiques.* Paris: Minuit.

———. 2001. *Lo que el arte aporta a la sociología.* Mexico City: Sello Bermejo, CONACULTA.

———. 2002. *La sociología del arte.* Buenos Aires: Ediciones Nueva Visión.

———. 2007. *Pourquoi Bourdieu.* Paris: Gallimard.

Hopenhayn, Martín. 2008. "Inclusión y exclusión social en la juventud latinoamericana." *Pensamiento Iberoamericano* 3, 2nd series: 49–70.

Huberman, Anthony. 2009. "Talent Is Overrated." *Artforum International* 48 (3): 109–10.

Jaukkuri, Maaretta. 2009. "Para curvarse con los ojos." In *Cildo Meireles.* Barcelona: Museu d'Art Contemporani de Barcelona.

Laddaga, Reinaldo. 2006. *Estética de la emergencia: La formación de otra cultura de las artes.* Buenos Aires: Adriana Hidalgo.

Latour, Bruno, ed. 2007. *Le dialogue des cultures: Actes des rencontres inaugurales du Musée du quai Branly (21 de juin 2006).* Arles: Actes Sud.

Lazzarato, Maurizio. 2008. "Las miserias de la 'crítica artista' y del empleo cultural." In transform (ed.), *Producción cultural y prácticas instituyentes: Líneas de ruptura en la crítica institucional.* Madrid: Traficantes de sueños.

Löfgren, Orvar. 1994. "Consuming Interests." In Jonathan Friedman (ed.), *Consumption and Identity.* Chur, Switzerland: Harwood Academic.

Lorey, Isabell. 2008. "Gubernamentalidad y precarización de sí: Sobre la normalización de los productores y las productoras culturales." In transform (ed.), *Producción cultural y prácticas instituyentes: Líneas de ruptura en la crítica institucional.* Madrid: Traficantes de sueños.

Ludmer, Josefina. 2007. "Literaturas postautónomas." *Ciberletras* 17. Accessed November 26, 2009. www.lehman.cuny.edu/ciberletras/v17/ludmer.htm.

MacCannell, Dean. 1992. *Empty Meeting Grounds: The Tourist Papers.* London: Routledge.

Mack, John. 2007. "Les métamorphoses de la qualification." In Bruno Latour (ed.), *Le dialogue des cultures: Actes des rencontres inaugurales du Musée du quai Branly (21 de juin 2006).* Arles: Actes Sud.

Maines, David R. 1993. "Narrative's Moment and Sociology's Phenomena: Toward a Narrative Sociology." *Sociological Quarterly* 34 (1): 17–38.

Margolles, Teresa. 2009. *What Else Could We Talk About?* Madrid: Instituto Nacional de Bellas Artes (Mexico), RM Verlag.

Martin, Stéphane. 2007. "Un musée pas comme les autres: Entretien." *Le Débat: Histoire, politique, société* 147: 5–22.

Martín-Barbero, Jesús. 2005. "Patrimonio y valores: Desafíos de la globalización a las herencias y los derechos culturales." Paper delivered at UNESCO roundtable Patrimonio y valores, Paris, June 15.

Mato, Daniel. 2007. "Importancia de los referentes territoriales en procesos trasnacionales: Una crítica de la idea de 'desterritorialización' basada en estudios de casos." *Estudios de Sociología, Araraquara* 12 (23): 35–63.

Medina, Cuauhtémoc. 2007. "Inundaciones, las artes como parte de la cultura visual globalizada." Paper presented at the workshop Conflictos interculturales, Centro Cultural de España, Mexico City.

———. 2009. "Materialist Spectrality." Trans. Gian Cristoforo Fregnan. *Des-bordes* 5: 69–86. Accessed August 8, 2013. http://www.des-bordes.net/0.5/en/pdf/cuadernillo.pdf.

Meireles, Cildo. 2009. *Cildo Meireles.* Barcelona: Museu d'Art Contemporani de Barcelona.

Méndez, Lourdes. 2009. *Antropología del campo artístico: Del arte primitivo al arte contemporáneo.* Madrid: Síntesis (Letras Universitarias).

Merleau-Ponty, Maurice. 1964. *Signs.* Trans. Richard McCleary. Evanston, Ill.: Northwestern University Press.

———. 1969. *The Prose of the World.* Trans. John O'Neill. Evanston, Ill.: Northwestern University Press.

Miller, Toby. 2005. *Global Hollywood 2.* London: BFI.

Mitchell, W. J. T. 2003. "Mostrando el ver: Una crítica de la cultura visual." *Estudios Visuales: Ensayo, teoría y critica de la cultura visual y el arte contemporáneo* 1: 17–40.

Moreno, María. 2004. "El león y los cristianos," *Pagina 12—Radar,* December 5, accessed July 20, 2012, www.pagina12.com.ar/diario/suplementos/radar/9-1868-2004-12-10.html.

Morley, David. 2006. *Media, Modernity and Technology: The Geography of the New.* New York: Routledge.

Moxey, Keith. 2005. "Estética de la cultura visual en el momento de la globalización." In José Luis Brea (ed.), *La epistemología de la visualidad en la era de la globalización.* Madrid: Akal.

Muntadas, Antoni. 2002. *On Translation.* Barcelona: Actar, Museu d'Art Contemporani de Barcelona.

Muntadas, Antoni, and Mark Wigley. 2005. "A Conversación between Antoni Muntadas and Mark Wigley, New York." In Antoni Muntadas, *On Translation: I Giardini.* Barcelona: Pabellón de España, 51ª Bienal de Venecia.

Musée du quai Branly. 2006. *La guía del museo.* Paris: Musée du quai Branly.

Nivón, Eduardo. 2006. *La política cultural: Temas, problemas y oportunidades.* Mexico City: CNCA.

Obrist, Hans Ulrich. 2003. "Orozco, Gabriel." In Hans Ulrich Obrist, *Interviews*, vol. 1, ed. Thomas Boutoux. Milan: Edizioni Charta.

Orozco, Gabriel. 2006. *Gabriel Orozco*. Exhibit catalogue. Mexico City: Consejo Nacional para la Cultura y las Artes, Museo del Palacio de Bellas Artes, Turner.

Ortega y Gasset, José. (1921) 1963. "Meditación del marco." In *Obras completas 2: El Espectador (1916–1934)*. Madrid: Revista del Occidente.

Ortiz, Renato. 2000. *O próximo e o distante: Japão e modernidade—mundo*. São Paolo: Brasiliense.

———. 2004. *Mundialización y cultura*. Bogotá: Convenio Andrés Bello.

Ortiz García, Carmen. 2004. "Celebración del fútbol y representaciones patrimoniales de la ciudad." In Carmen Ortiz García (ed.), *La ciudad es para ti: Nuevas y viejas tradiciones en ámbitos urbanos*. Barcelona: Anthropos.

Passeron, Jean Claude, and Emmanuel Pedler. 1991. *Le temps donné aux tableaux*. Marseille: IMEREC.

Piccini, Mabel, Ana Rosas Mantecón, and Graciela Schmilchuk. 2000. *Recepción artística y consumo cultural*. Mexico City: Instituto Nacional de Bellas Artes, Centro Nacional de Investigación, Documentación e Información de Artes Plásticas, Casa Juan Pablos.

Piglia, Ricardo. 2001. *Crítica y ficción*. Barcelona: Anagrama.

Popelard, Marie-Dominique. 2002. *Ce que fait l'art: Approche communicationnelle*. Paris: Presses Universitaires de France.

Price, Sally. 1989. *Primitive Art in Civilized Places*. Chicago: University of Chicago Press.

Rabotnikof, Nora. 2005. *En busca del lugar común: El espacio público en la teoría política contemporánea*. Mexico City: Universidad Nacional Autónoma de México.

Ramírez, Juan Antonio. 2009. *El objeto y el aura: (Des)orden visual del arte moderno*. Madrid: Akal, Arte Contemporáneo.

Ramírez, Juan Antonio, and Jesús Carrillo, eds. 2004. *Tendencias del arte, arte de tendencias a principios del siglo XXI*. Madrid: Cátedra.

Ramos, Julio. 2003. "Coreografía del terror: Justicia estética de Sebastião Salgado." In Álvaro Fernández Bravo, Florencia Garramuño, and Saúl Sosnowski (eds.), *Sujetos en tránsito: (In)migración, exilio y diáspora en la cultura latinoamericana*. Buenos Aires: Alianza Editorial.

Rancière, Jacques. 2004. *The Politics of Aesthetics: The Distribution of the Sensible*. Ed. and trans. Gabriel Rockhill. London: Continuum.

———. 2005. *Sobre políticas estéticas*. Trans. Manuel Arranz. Barcelona: Universitat Autònoma de Barcelona.

———. 2007. "Theater of Images." In Nicole Schweizer (ed.), *Alfredo Jaar: La Politique des Images*. Zurich: JRP, Ringier.

———. 2008. "Les paradoxes de l'art politique." In *Le spectateur émancipé*. Paris: La Fabrique Éditions.

————. 2009. *The Emancipated Spectator.* Trans. Gregory Elliott. London: Verso.

————. 2010. *Dissensus: On Politics and Aesthetics.* Trans. Steve Corcoran. London: Continuum.

Reguillo, Rossana. 2007. "Legitimidad(es) divergentes." In *Jóvenes Mexicanos: Encuesta Nacional de Juventud 2005.* Mexico City: Instituto Mexicano de la Juventud.

Ribeiro, Gustavo Lins. 2003. *Postimperialismo: Cultura y política en el mundo contemporáneo.* Barcelona: Gedisa.

————. 2006. "Economic Globalization from Below." *Etnográfica* 10 (2): 233–49.

Richard, Nelly. 2004. *Cultural Residues: Chile in Transition.* Trans. Alan West-Durán and Theodore Quester. Minneapolis: University of Minnesota Press.

Ricoeur, Paul. 1976. *La métaphore vive.* Paris: Seuil.

————. 1984. *Temps et récit.* Paris: Seuil.

Rosas Mantecón, Ana. 2009. "Ir al cine en la ciudad de México: Historia de una práctica de consumo cultural." PhD diss., Universidad Autónoma Metropolitana, Mexico City.

Rosenberg, Harold. 1972. *The De-definition of Art: Action Art to Pop to Earthworks.* New York: Horizon Press.

Sakai, Naoki. 2001. "The Dislocation of the West and the Status of the Humanities." *Traces: A Multilingual Journal of Cultural Theory and Translation* 1: 71–94.

Sartre, Jean Paul. 1976. *Critique of Dialectical Reason: Theory of Practical Ensembles.* Trans. Alan Sheridan-Smith. Atlantic Highlands, N.J.: Humanities Press.

Schiffrin, André. 2000. *The Business of Books: How the International Conglomerates Took Over Publishing and Changed the Way We Read.* New York: Verso.

————. 2005. *Le contrôle de la parole.* Paris: La Fabrique.

Sennett, Richard. 2006. *The Culture of the New Capitalism.* New Haven: Yale University Press.

Serra, Catalina. 2010. "Arte contemporáneo, arte a la baja." *El País.* April 14.

Smith, Bernard. 1988. *The Death of the Artist as Hero: Essays in History and Culture.* Melbourne: Oxford University Press.

Sokal, Alan, and Jean Bricmont. 1998. *Fashionable Nonsense: Postmodern Intellectuals' Abuse of Science.* New York: Picador.

Speranza, Graciela. 2007. "En construcción: Identidad y ficción en algunas novelas de hoy." Talk presented at the symposium Conflictos interculturales, Centro Cultural de España, Mexico City.

Springer, José Manuel. 2009. "¿De qué otra forma podríamos hablar? El pabellón de México en la 53 Bienal de Venecia." *Réplica 21: Obsesiva compulsión por lo visual* 566. Accessed August 5, 2012. http://www.replica21.com/archivo /articulos/s_t/566_springer_margolles.htm.

Thornton, Sarah. 2008. *Seven Days in the Art World.* New York: Norton.

Tupitsyn, Victor. 2004. "Post-Autonomous Art." *Third Text: Critical Perspectives on Contemporary Art* 18 (3): 273–82.

UNESCO. 2008. *World Heritage Information Kit.* Paris: UNESCO World Heritage Center.

Urteaga Castro Pozo, Maritza. 2009. "Juventudes y procesos de hibridación." Paper presented at the conference Voces híbridas, Universidad Autónoma Metropolitana, Mexico City, October 28.

Verón, Eliseo, and Martine Levasseur. 1983. *Ethnographie de l'exposition: L'espace, le corps et le sens.* Paris: Centre Georges Pompidou.

Vila, Pablo. 2009. "Identificaciones múltiples y sociología narrativa: Una propuesta metodológica para complejizar los estudios sobre juventud." Paper presented at the conference Voces híbridas, Universidad Autónoma Metropolitana, Mexico City, October 28.

Villoro, Juan. 2000. "Lección de arena: Pedro Páramo." In *Efectos personales.* Mexico City: Era.

Watson, Cate. 2003. "Unreliable Narrators? 'Inconsistency' (and Some Inconstancy) in Interviews." *Qualitative Research* 6 (3): 367–84.

Wayne, Michael. 2003. "Post-Fordism, Monopoly Capitalism, and Hollywood's Media Industrial Complex." *International Journal of Communication Studies* 6 (1): 82–103.

INDEX

>

Index

www.ingramcontent.com/pod-product-compliance
Lightning Source LLC
Chambersburg PA
CBHW070418290526
45791CB00005B/1737